Guided Math Lessons in First Grade

Guided Math Lessons in First Grade provides detailed lessons to help you bring guided math groups to life. Based on the bestselling *Guided Math in Action*, this practical book offers 16 lessons, taught in a round of 3—concrete, pictorial, and abstract. The lessons are based on the priority standards and cover fluency, word problems, operations and algebraic thinking, and place value. Author Dr. Nicki Newton shows you the content as well as the practices and processes that should be worked on in the lessons, so that students not only learn the content but also how to solve problems, reason, communicate their thinking, model, use tools, use precise language, and see structure and patterns.

Throughout the book, you'll find tools, templates, and blackline masters so that you can instantly adapt the lesson to your specific needs and use it right away. With the easy-to-follow plans in this book, students can work more effectively in small guided math groups—and have loads of fun along the way!

Dr. Nicki Newton has been an educator for over 30 years, working both nationally and internationally with students of all ages. She has worked on developing Math Workshop and Guided Math Institutes around the country; visit her website at www.drnickinewton.com. She is also an avid blogger (www.guidedmath.wordpress.com), tweeter (@drnickimath) and Pinterest pinner (www.pinterest.com/drnicki7).

Also Available from Dr. Nicki Newton
(www.routledge.com/eyeoneducation)

Guided Math Lessons in Second Grade:
Getting Started

Guided Math Lessons in Kindergarten:
Getting Started

Day-by-Day Math Thinking Routines in Kindergarten:
40 Weeks of Quick Prompts and Activities

Day-by-Day Math Thinking Routines in First Grade:
40 Weeks of Quick Prompts and Activities

Day-by-Day Math Thinking Routines in Second Grade:
40 Weeks of Quick Prompts and Activities

Day-by-Day Math Thinking Routines in Third Grade:
40 Weeks of Quick Prompts and Activities

Day-by-Day Math Thinking Routines in Fourth Grade:
40 Weeks of Quick Prompts and Activities

Day-by-Day Math Thinking Routines in Fifth Grade:
40 Weeks of Quick Prompts and Activities

Leveling Math Workstations in Grades K–2:
Strategies for Differentiated Practice

Daily Math Thinking Routines in Action:
Distributed Practices Across the Year

Mathematizing Your School:
Creating a Culture for Math Success
Co-authored by Janet Nuzzie

Math Problem Solving in Action:
Getting Students to Love Word Problems, Grades K–2

Math Problem Solving in Action:
Getting Students to Love Word Problems, Grades 3–5

Guided Math in Action:
Building Each Student's Mathematical Proficiency with Small-Group Instruction

Math Workshop in Action:
Strategies for Grades K–5

Math Running Records in Action:
A Framework for Assessing Basic Fact Fluency in Grades K–5

Math Workstations in Action:
Powerful Possibilities for Engaged Learning in Grades 3–5

Guided Math Lessons in First Grade

Getting Started

Dr. Nicki Newton

Routledge
Taylor & Francis Group

NEW YORK AND LONDON

First published 2022
by Routledge
605 Third Avenue, New York, NY 10158

and by Routledge
2 Park Square, Milton Park, Abingdon, Oxon, OX14 4RN

Routledge is an imprint of the Taylor & Francis Group, an informa business

© 2022 Taylor & Francis

The right of Nicki Newton to be identified as author of this work has been
asserted by her in accordance with sections 77 and 78 of the Copyright, Designs
and Patents Act 1988.

All rights reserved. No part of this book may be reprinted or reproduced or utilised
in any form or by any electronic, mechanical, or other means, now known or hereafter
invented, including photocopying and recording, or in any information storage or
retrieval system, without permission in writing from the publishers.

Trademark notice: Product or corporate names may be trademarks or registered
trademarks, and are used only for identification and explanation without intent to
infringe.

Library of Congress Cataloging-in-Publication Data
Names: Newton, Nicki, author.
Title: Guided math lessons in first grade : getting started / Nicki Newton.
Description: New York, NY : Routledge, 2022.
Identifiers: LCCN 2021001719 (print) | LCCN 2021001720 (ebook) |
  ISBN 9780367901905 (hardback) | ISBN 9780367901899 (paperback) |
  ISBN 9781003022947 (ebook)
Subjects: LCSH: Mathematics—Study and teaching (Elementary) | Group guidance
  in education. | Group work in education.
Classification: LCC QA20.G76 N498 2021 (print) | LCC QA20.G76 (ebook) |
  DDC 372.7/044—dc23
LC record available at https://lccn.loc.gov/2021001719
LC ebook record available at https://lccn.loc.gov/2021001720

ISBN: 978-0-367-90190-5 (hbk)
ISBN: 978-0-367-90189-9 (pbk)
ISBN: 978-1-003-02294-7 (ebk)

Typeset in Palatino
by Apex CoVantage, LLC

This series is dedicated to Lin Goodwin. She has been a magnificent part of my becoming a teacher educator. I worked under her tutelage for several years at Columbia University. She led me, guided me, and taught me a whole bunch of stuff about teaching and learning. She also chaired my dissertation committee. I will ever be grateful to her and I thank God for putting her in my life as one of my guiding angels.

Contents

Acknowledgments

I thank God for life and happiness. I thank my family and friends for all their support. I thank my editor Lauren who is the best in the world! I thank all the reviewers who gave feedback that helped make the series what it is!

I thank the copyediting and production team for all their hard work.

I would also like to thank Math Learning Center (https:/www.mathlearningcenter.org/apps), Braining Camp (https://www.brainingcamp.com/) and Didax (https://www.didax.com/math/virtual-manipulatives.html) for the use of screenshots of their fabulous virtual manipulatives.

Meet the Author

Dr. Nicki Newton has been an educator for over 30 years, working both nationally and internationally, with students of all ages. Having spent the first part of her career as a literacy and social studies specialist, she built on those frameworks to inform her math work. She believes that math is intricately intertwined with reading, writing, listening, and speaking. She has worked on developing Math Workshop and guided math institutes around the country. Most recently, she has been helping districts and schools nationwide to integrate their state standards for mathematics and think deeply about how to teach these within a Math Workshop model. Dr. Nicki works with teachers, coaches, and administrators to make math come alive by considering the powerful impact of building a community of mathematicians who make meaning of real math together. When students do real math, they learn it. They own it, they understand it, and they can do it. Every one of them. Dr. Nicki is also an avid blogger (www.guidedmath. wordpress. com), tweeter (drnickimath) and Pinterest pinner (www.pinterest.com/drnicki7/).

Dr. Nicki Newton, Educational Consultant
Phone: 347-688-4927
Email: drnicki7@gmail.com

Find More Online!

Resources, videos, and conversations with Dr. Nicki can be found in the Guided Math Dropbox Resources: https://bit.ly/2Ja4sMY

1

Introduction

Figure 1.1 Guided Math Example 1

I pull a group of 1st graders who are working on their make 5 facts. This particular group of students is still really shaky on making 5, so we are using the 5 frame and playing a game where they have to build the number and then say how many more to 5. It provides them with a scaffold (which will eventually be phased out). They giggle with a sense of confidence as they pull and show the fact. When we are done, we talk about what we did and students give examples. They also talk about who thinks this is easy and who thinks it is tricky.

Figure 1.2 Guided Math Example 2

I pull a different group of 1st graders and we are working on doubles facts. We are playing a doubles domino game. They have to pull a double domino and calculate the sum. Whoever has the largest sum wins a counter. Whoever gets 10 counters first wins the game. They have a toolbox right there in case they need a number path, rekenrek, or ten frame. Some of them just know it while others are counting on using their fingers.

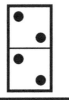

Guided math is a small-group instructional strategy that teaches students in their zone of proximal development around the priority standards. There are so many standards, but every state has priority focus standards. Those are the standards that you teach in a small guided math group. It is a time for hands-on, minds-on learning based on the standards. It is a time for discussing ideas, listening to the thinking of others, reasoning out loud, and becoming a confident, competent mathematician.

Guided math groups are for everyone! Too often, students are rushed through big ideas, understandings, and skills. They are left with ever widening gaps. Guided math groups give teachers the time needed to work with students in a way that they can all learn. Guided math groups can be used to remediate, to teach on grade-level concepts, and to address the needs of students that are working beyond grade level.

Guided math groups can be heterogeneous or homogeneous. It depends on what you are trying to do. If you are teaching a specific skill, counting on, one group could be working with visually leveled flashcards and another group could be working with more abstract number flashcards. You could also pull a group that is still exploring it just concretely on the beaded number line for another session. The groups are flexible, and students work in different groups

Figure 1.3 Visually Leveled Flashcards **Figure 1.4** Marked Number Line

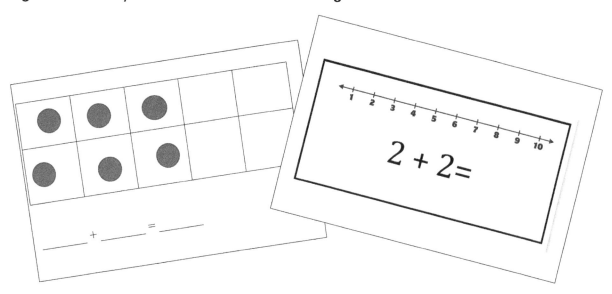

at different times, never attached to any one group for the entire year. Students meet in a particular guided math group for three or four times based on their specific instructional needs and then they move on.

Guided math groups can occur in all types of classrooms. Typically, they are part of a Math Workshop. In a Math Workshop (see Figure 1.5) there are three parts.

Opening

♦ Energizers and Routines
♦ Problem Solving
♦ Mini-Lesson

Student Activity

♦ Math Workstations
♦ Guided Math Groups

Debrief

♦ Discussion
♦ Exit Slip
♦ Mathematician's Chair Share

What Are the Other Kids Doing?

The other students should be engaged in some type of independent practice. They can be working alone, with partners, or in small groups. They could be rotating through stations based on a designated schedule or they could be working from a menu of Must Do's and Can Do's. The point is that students should be practicing fluency, word problems, and place value and working on items in the current unit of study. This work should be organized in a way that students are working in their zone of proximal development (Vygotsky, 1978).

Differentiating workstations helps to purposefully plan for the learning of all students. The fluency workstation games should be divided by strategy, for example students can be working on either make ten facts, doubles, or bridge ten facts, depending on what they need (Baroody, 2006; Van de Walle, 2007; Henry & Brown, 2008). Another example is word problems. There are 15 single-step problems that first graders are exposed to. Knowing the learning trajectory and understanding the structures that go from simple to complex can help organize the teaching and learning of word problems (Carpenter, Fennema, Franke, Levi, & Empson, 1999; Jitendra, Hoff, & Beck, 1999).

Figure 1.5 Math Workshop

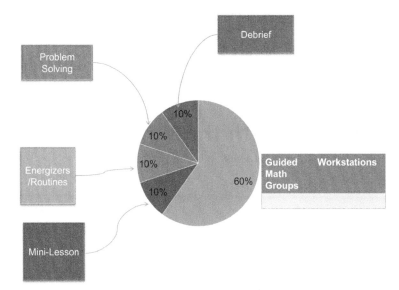

Figure 1.6 Workstations 1

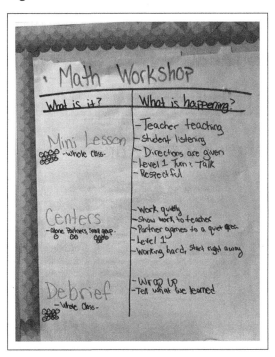

Figure 1.7 Workstations 2

Benefits of Guided Math Groups

♦ See student knowledge in action.
♦ Monitor the concepts and skills that are understood.
♦ Catch and address the misunderstandings.
♦ Ask questions that highlight thinking.
♦ Analyze thinking.
♦ Listen to conversations.

Figure 1.8 Workstation Contract

Workstation Contract

I have the privilege of learning with the Math Workstations.

I will play fair.

I will be a good sport. When I win, I will celebrate appropriately. When I lose, I'll be a good sport.

I will use the math manipulatives the way they are supposed to be used.

I will use the digital resources the way they are supposed to be used.

I will put everything back neatly.

I will work hard every day.

I will keep trying when the going gets tough!

My Signature:_____

- ♦ Assess in the moment.
- ♦ Redirect in the moment.
- ♦ Differentiate as needed.

Key Points

- ♦ Different Reasons: remediate, focus on grade-level topics or working beyond grade level
- ♦ Cycle of Engagement: concrete, pictorial, abstract
- ♦ Heterogeneous and Homogeneous grouping
- ♦ Math Workshop
- ♦ Math Workstations
- ♦ Benefits of Guided Math

Summary

Guided math is a great way to differentiate learning for all your students. Focus on the priority standards. Students approach these standards through a concrete, pictorial, and abstract cycle of engagement. Sometimes the groups are homogeneous groups and other times the groups are heterogeneous. Guided math groups can be done in a variety of ways, either traditional set-ups or a Math Workshop model. The other students should always be doing work that they are familiar with and are practicing in the math workstation. Many times, the work that students are working on in the guided math group is carried over into the math workstation. When the students are in guided math groups, the other students should be meaningfully engaged in math workstations. All of this works together to give all students a chance to learn.

Reflection Questions

1. How are you differentiating instruction around the priority standards right now?
2. Currently, how do you group students? What informs your grouping?
3. Do you have a plan to make sure that everybody fully understands the priority standards?

References

Baroody, A. J. (2006). Why children have difficulties mastering the basic number combinations and how to help them. *Teaching Children Mathematics*, 13, 22–32.

Carpenter, T. P., Fennema, E., Franke, M. L., Levi, L., & Empson, S. B. (1999). *Children's mathematics: Cognitively guided instruction*. Portsmouth, NH: Heinemann.

Henry, V. J., & Brown, R. S. (2008). First-grade basic facts: An investigation into teaching and learning of an accelerated, high-demand memorization standard. *Journal for Research in Mathematics Education*, 153–183.

Jitendra, A. K., Hoff, K., & Beck, M. M. (1999). Teaching middle school students with learning disabilities to solve word problems using a schema based approach. *Remedial and Special Education*, 20, 50–64.

Van de Walle, J. (2007). *Elementary and middle school mathematics: Teaching developmentally*. Boston: Pearson/Allyn and Bacon.

Vygotsky, L. S. (1978). *Mind in society: The development of higher psychological processes*. Cambridge, MA: Harvard University Press.

2

Behind the Scenes

Assessment

Assessment is a crucial element in designing a guided math lesson. Teachers have to know where their students are along the trajectory of learning so that they can plan to teach them purposefully. Teachers need actionable data. Actionable data is data that can be used immediately to develop meaningful lessons. At the beginning of the year, teachers need to get data about the priority standards/major cluster standards from the year before so they can figure out if there are any gaps and make a plan to close them. Richardson (n.d.) notes, "The information gathered from the assessments helps teachers pinpoint what each child knows and still needs to learn. They are not about 'helping children be right,' but about uncovering their instructional needs." Math running records are a great way to check fluency! It's the GPS of fact fluency.

Remember, every summer students lose at least 2.6 months of math (Shafer, 2016). Teachers should assess fluency, word problems, operations and algebraic thinking, and place value in the beginning of the year. At the middle of the year, teachers should assess all the grade-level work done in these areas during the first part of the year. At the end of the year, teachers should assess all the priority standards for the grade. Throughout the year, teachers should rely on entrance and exit slips (Figure 2.2), quizzes, anecdotals, unit assessments, and conferences to get information about students.

Grouping

Guided math groups should have between three and five students. Sometimes they are heterogeneous groups and sometimes they are homogeneous groups. It depends on what you are trying to do. If you are working on big ideas and understanding, you might pull a small group of students and have them work on modeling with different tools. You might pull students together and work on some word problems. However, if you are working on adding basic facts and on a specific strategy, you might pull a group that is working on making 10. You might pull another group that you work with using the doubles facts. Groups should last between 10 and 15 minutes. Remember the attention span rule: age plus a few minutes.

Differentiation

After teachers get the data, they need to use it to differentiate (see Figure 2.1). Some of the work is to close the gaps. Some of the work is to accelerate the learning of the advanced students. Some of the work is to teach in the grade-level zone. A big part of the differentiation aspect of guided math lessons is the concrete, pictorial, and abstract cycle. Sometimes, students know the answer but do not necessarily understand the math. It is crucial to do quick assessments with students to make sure that they understand the math. For example, a student might know that

Figure 2.1 Math Running Records Example

Addition Running Record Recording Sheet

Student: _____ Teacher: _____ Date: _____

Part 1: Initial Observations
Teacher: We are now going to administer Part 1 of the Running Record. I am going to give you a sheet of paper with some problems. I want you to go from the top to the bottom and tell me just the answer. If you get stuck, you can stop and ask for what you need to help you. If you want to pass, you can. We might not do all of the problems. I am going to take notes so I remember what happened. Let's start.

Part 1	Codes: What do you notice?	Initial Observations of Strategies	Data Code Names
0 + 1 a 5s pth	ca fco cah coh wo sc asc dk	0 1 2 3 4M 4	A0----- add 0
2 + 1 a 5s pth	ca fco cah coh wo sc asc dk	0 1 2 3 4M 4	A1----- add 1
3 + 2 a 5s pth	ca fco cah coh wo sc asc dk	0 1 2 3 4M 4	Aw5--- add w/in 5
2 + 6 a 5s pth	ca fco cah coh wo sc asc dk	0 1 2 3 4M 4	Aw10—add w/in 10
4 + 6 a 5s pth	ca fco cah coh wo sc asc dk	0 1 2 3 4M 4	AM10---add making 10
10 + 4 a 5s pth	ca fco cah coh wo sc asc dk	0 1 2 3 4M 4	A10-----add 10 to a #
7 + 7 a 5s pth	ca fco cah coh wo sc asc dk	0 1 2 3 4M 4	AD------add doubles
5 + 6 a 5s pth	ca fco cah coh wo sc asc dk	0 1 2 3 4M 4	AD1-----add dbls +/-1
7 + 5 a 5s pth	ca fco cah coh wo sc asc dk	0 1 2 3 4M 4	AD2----add dbls +/-2
9 + 6 a 5s pth	ca fco cah coh wo sc asc dk	0 1 2 3 4M 4	AHF/C9-add higher facts use compensation w/9
8 + 4 a 5s pth	ca fco cah coh wo sc asc dk	0 1 2 3 4M 4	AHF/C7/8—add higher facts/ use compensation with 7/8
7 + 8 a 5s pth	ca fco cah coh wo sc asc dk	0 1 2 3 4M 4	AHF/C7/8—add higher facts/ use compensation with 7/8
Codes a - automatic 5s - 5 seconds pth - prolonged thinking time	**Types of Strategies** ca - counted all fco – finger counted on cah – counted all in head coh – counted on in head wo - wrong operation sc - self corrected asc - attempted to self-correct dk - didn't know	**Strategy Levels** 0 – doesn't know 1 – counting strategies by ones or skip counting using fingers, drawings or manipulatives 2 - mental math/solving in head 3 - using known facts and strategies 4M - automatic recall from memory 4 – automatic recall and students have number sense	

(Continued)

(Continued)

Part 2: Flexibility/Efficiency

Teacher: We are now going to administer Part 2 of the Running Record. In this part of the Running Record we are going to talk about what strategies you use when you are solving basic addition facts. I am going to tell you a problem and then ask you to tell me how you think about it. I am also going to ask you about some different types of facts. Take your time as you answer and tell me what you are thinking as you see and do the math. I am going to take notes so I can remember everything that happened during this Running Record.

Add 0 0 + 1	Add 1 2 + 1	Add w/in 5 or 10 3 + 2 2 + 6	Add to Make 10 4 + 6
What happens when you add zero to a number?	What strategy do you use when you add 1 to a number?	How do you solve 4 + 0? And 6 + 3?	How do you solve 5 + 5?
___ same # ___ other ___ can't articulate	___ next counting # ___ other ___ can't articulate	___ count on from big # ___ other ___ can't articulate	___ count on from big # ___ other ___ can't articulate
What would be the answer to… 3 + 0 0 + 5 8 + 0	What would be the answer to…. 4 + 1 1 + 7 10 + 1	w/in 5 w/in 10 + 3 5 + 4 + 2 2 + 7	I'm going to give you a number and I want you to give me the number that makes 10 with it. If I give you 7, how many more to make 10? If I give you ___ how many more to 10? 9? 2? 6? 3?
Do they know this strategy? No/Emerging/Yes A0 Level 0 1 2 3 4M 4	Do they know this strategy? No/Emerging/Yes A1 Level 0 1 2 3 4M 4	Do they know this strategy? No/Emerging/Yes A10 Level 0 1 2 3 4M 4	Do they know this strategy? No/Emerging/Yes AM10 Level 0 1 2 3 4M 4
Add 10 10 + 4	Doubles 7 + 7	Doubles +/- 1 5 + 6	Doubles +/- 2 7 + 5
What strategy do you use when you add 10 to a number?	How would you solve 6 + 6?	How would you solve 6 + 7?	If a friend did not know how to solve 7 + 9, what would you tell her to do?
___ teen #s decompose to 10 and 1's ___ other ___ can't articulate	___ doubles ___ other ___ can't articulate	___ doubles +/-1 ___ other ___ can't articulate	___ doubles +/-2 ___ other ___ can't articulate
How would you solve ___? 10 + 2 10 + 6 10 + 8	How would you solve ___? 4 + 4 + 8 + 9	How would you solve ___? + 3 + 4 8 + 9	How would you solve….? 2 + 4 + 6 + 11

Do they know this strategy? No/Emerging/Yes A10 Level 0 1 2 3 4M 4	What kind of facts are these? _____ Do they know this strategy? No/Emerging/Yes AD Level 0 1 2 3 4M 4	Do they know this strategy? No/Emerging/Yes AD1 Level 0 1 2 3 4M 4	Do they know this strategy? No/Emerging/Yes AD2 Level 0 1 2 3 4M 4

Bridge through 10 (9) 9 + 6 If your friend was stuck solving 9 + 5, what would you tell him to do? ___ bridge 10 ___other ___can't articulate How do you solve _____? 9 + 3 9 + 6 Do they know this strategy? No/Emerging/Yes AHF/C9 Level 0 1 2 3 4M 4	**Bridge through 10 (7/8)** 8 + 4 What strategy would you use to solve 8 + 3? ___ bridge 10 ___other ___can't articulate How would you solve ___? 4 + 7? 8 + 5? Do they know this strategy? No/Emerging/Yes AHF/C 7/8 Level 0 1 2 3 4M 4	**Part 3: Mathematical Disposition** Do you like math? What do you find easy? What do you find tricky? What do you do when you get stuck? Question Prompts: That's interesting/fascinating: tell me what you did. That's interesting/fascinating: tell me how you solved it. That's interesting/fascinating: tell me what you were thinking. How did you solve this problem? Can you tell me more about how you solve these types of problems? What do you mean when you say _____? (i.e. ten friends/neighbor numbers etc.)

General Observations (to be filled out after the interview)

Instructional Response:
Fluency Focus areas (circle all that apply): flexibility   efficiency   accuracy   automaticity

What addition strategy should the instruction focus on?

A0 A1 Aw5 Aw10 AM10 A10 AD AD1 AD2 AHF/C9 AHF/C 7/8

For his/her current instructional level, what is the predominant way in which the student is arriving at the answers? 0 1 2 3 4M 4 _____

Overall, what is the way in which the students calculated the answers?: 0 1 2 3 4M 4

Comments/Notes about gestures, behaviors, remarks:

*In most states k fluency is within 5 and 1st grade fluency is within 10 and 2nd grade within 20. However, some states k is within 10 and 1st and 2nd is within 20.

Figure 2.2 Exit Slip Example

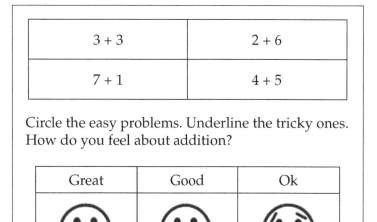

| 3 + 3 | 2 + 6 |
| 7 + 1 | 4 + 5 |

Circle the easy problems. Underline the tricky ones. How do you feel about addition?

Great	Good	Ok
🙂	🙂	🙂

6 + 5 is 11 by counting up. So, they can get an answer but they don't have strategic competence. We want them to have flexibility with numbers, thinking 6 + 5 is 5 plus 5 plus 1 more, or 6 + 6 – 1, or another efficient strategy. We would practice it in a variety of ways with manipulatives, with sketches and with the numbers. We would also have the students verbalize what they are doing and contextualize it by telling stories (NCTM, 2014).

Figure 2.3 Differentiation

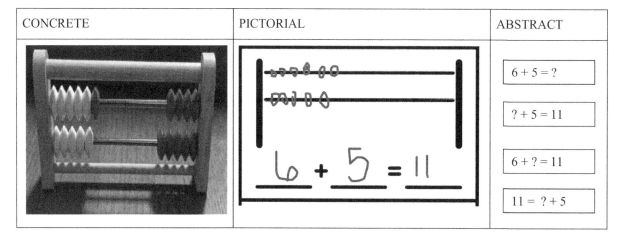

CONCRETE	PICTORIAL	ABSTRACT
	6 + 5 = 11	6 + 5 = ? ? + 5 = 11 6 + ? = 11 11 = ? + 5

Types of Groups

When we are thinking about grouping, it is about meeting the needs of the students where they are and taking them to what they need to learn at that grade level. So students are emerging in their learning along the continuum. It is about creating flexible groups that students can move through as they work on different concepts (see Figure 2.4). These groups should never be "fixed" or track students throughout the year. They are temporary, flexible, focused groups that teach students what they need, when they need it and then students move on to different work.

Figure 2.4 Types of Groups

Group 1: Emergent	Group 2: Early Fluent	Group 3: Fluent	Group 4: Advanced Fluent
These are the students that are working below grade level. They often have many gaps and misunderstandings. It is important to work on closing gaps as well as highly scaffolding (but not overscaffolding) current grade-level material.	These students are approaching grade level. They have some gaps and need some remediation.	These students are right at grade level.	These students are working above grade level. This doesn't mean that the work should be done from the next grade level though; as Kathy Richardson notes, it is important to go deeper with concepts rather than to jump to the next ones.
A student can be an emergent learner in one area and an advanced fluent learner in another. These are not meant to be labels that stick with students all year. As Dr. Kim Reid (personal communication) always said, "Labels are for boxes." Although we need a way to describe how students are doing in particular areas, we must never categorize them with fixed labels. Students move and develop along their own trajectory. With the appropriate scaffolding, we can teach everybody and move them to achieving grade-level standards. Rather than viewing some children as "low" or "behind" or "lacking in skills," kidwatching teachers view all children as creative, capable learners – on their way to "achieving control over the conventions of [math]- always 'in process' always moving forward …" (Flukey, 1997 p.219 cited in Owocki & Goodman, 2002)." Students move and develop along their own trajectory. With the appropriate scaffolding we can teach everybody and move them to achieving grade level standards and beyond.			

Rotations

Teachers can assign students where they are going to go, visiting different stations every day. Another way to do it is to give the student a menu for the week with can do's and must do's. Either way, students should do fluency, word problems, place value, and work from the current unit of study.

Standards-Based

Every guided math lesson should be centered on priority standards. There are so many standards to teach, so we have to focus. We have to get in there, dig deep, and discuss ideas so that students can learn them. When students sit down in the group, the first thing the teacher should talk about is the work they are going to be doing for the day. The "I can" or "I am learning to" statement should be up and the students should discuss what they are going to be learning and what the criteria of success for that learning will look like. There is an ongoing discussion about whether to say "I can" or "I am learning to." "I can" is more of a statement about what students will be able to do in the future. "I am learning to" speaks more to the continuum of learning and allows for students to be at different places along that continuum.

Dixon points out that, sometimes, we shouldn't always tell the students the I can statement at the beginning because then in essence you tell the ending of the story before it begins (2018a).

This is an excellent point; it depends on where you are at in the concept and skill cycle and what the lesson of the day is. If you are trying to get students to explore and wonder about something, then don't upfront it, but discuss it at the end after they have explored the topic. However, if you are working on something that you have been doing for a while, you can say, "Today we are going to continue looking at . . ."

Depth of Knowledge

Guided math lessons are about building depth of knowledge (DOK) with students. They should reach a variety of levels, not just level 1 activities. For example, instead of just telling stories such as "There were 5 ducks and 2 more came. How many ducks are there?" teachers should ask questions such as "The answer is 5 ducks. What is the question?" Instead of just asking what 3 + 2 is, teachers should also say things like "Give me 2 different ways to make 5." We want students to reason about numbers in a variety of ways, using as many scaffolds as they need to become confident and competent.

Scaffolding

Scaffolds are a fundamental part of guided math lessons. There are so many different types of scaffolds. We are going to discuss grouping scaffolds, language scaffolds, and tool scaffolds. Grouping scaffolds help students become proficient by having them work with partners and in small groups, before they practice the skill on their own. This is the social aspect of grappling with the content. Oftentimes, students learn a great deal from each other through discussions and interactions. In the group, you can partner the students up and watch them play the game and take notes and ask different questions to guide them as they work together.

Language is often scaffolded with illustrated pictures of the vocabulary and language stems on sentence strips. Dixon (2018b) discusses how in the beginning of learning about a concept, it can be productive for students to have to explain the topic without the "cover" of the vocabulary. Meaning that sometimes students will use words but not understand the concepts, and their lack of understanding can be hidden by the use of the correct vocabulary. If they don't have that, then they have to explain the math. In later lessons, when students understand the math, then it's ok to upfront the vocabulary.

Scaffolding is so important, yet we have to be really careful not to overscaffold and, as Dixon warns, to also avoid "just in case" scaffolding (2018c). We want to help students as they need it, but we do not want to steal the struggle. Students need the opportunity to engage in the productive struggle, but it should not be an unproductive struggle (Hiebert & Grouws, 2007; Blackburn, 2018). There is a very careful balancing act that teachers conduct when scaffolding in a guided math group.

In the guided math group, teachers should make sure that tools are part of the learning cycle. In planning to unpack the concepts and skills in small groups, teachers should think about the ways in which students can wrestle with topics concretely, pictorially, and abstractly. They should also emphasize verbalization and contextualization (NCTM, 2014). The magic of the manipulatives is the conversation and the activities that are done along with them. Students need to reflect on and explain the concepts and how the manipulatives are being used to model those concepts. In a small group, students should be doing the math and exploring and discussing the ideas as they use the manipulatives (Ball, 1992; Baroody, 1989; Bruner, 1960; Burns, n.d.)

Engagement

Engagement is important. Research links engagement to students' *affect*—their feelings and emotions about learning (McLeod, 1992, cited in Ingram). We find that students' engagement is shaped around the sociocultural environment in which they are learning, how they are constructing knowledge together through discussions, activities, and the norms of learning (Op 't Eynde, 2004; Boaler & Greeno, 2000; Greeno, Collins, & Resnick, 1996). The interactions that students have in small guided math groups are very important. They help to shape students' mathematical identities—who and what they see themselves as in terms of being a mathematician.

We find that students are engaged when they participate in strong lessons in a strong community. A strong lesson has a clear purpose, is relevant, and makes sense to their lives; it is brain-friendly and flows easily, allowing them to quickly get into a "good 'work-flow'" and dive deep into the material (Claflin, 2014). A strong community of learners in essence means that "they've got each other's back!" Everybody is in it to win it with each other. Students are helpful, trusting, risk-taking, and comfortable. In the small group, they should be willing to try things out and be assured that it is not always going to work the first time and they might not get it even the second time around, but that with perseverance they can learn it.

Another really important aspect of working with small children is the wonder of learning. The guided math table is a special experience. I like to have guided math journals and special pencils and toolkits for students to work with at the table. Students look forward to coming to the guided math group. Often, I use dice, dominos, cards, and board games. Since the same structure can be used, the students are ready to work on the content. Meaning, if we play bingo, then students know that structure, so they can immediately focus on the content. I might play a doubles bingo game with one group and a make ten bingo game with another group.

Student Accountability

While the students are working in math workstations, they should be filling out different sheets of the work they are doing (see Figures 2.5, 2.6, and 2.7). They should be recording what they are doing. Some sheets record everything that students are doing. Other games have students record only some of their work.

The most important thing about math workshop is that you organize it well from the beginning. You must do the first 20 days. In the first 20 days you teach the students how to work in the workshop. Here is a resource for that: www.drnickinewton.com/downloads/

Students have to learn how to work independently before you start pulling them into guided math groups. The premise of Math Workshop is to let all students work on their own productively, before you start working with them in small groups.

There are two key elements to a good workstation. The first is a clear goal for the workstation. Students need to know what the math is, how they are going to work on that math, and what it looks like when they are actually learning that math. The second is that they have an accountability system so that they know the teacher will be monitoring their work.

Figure 2.5 Student Recording Sheet Example 1

Comparing Numbers		
Roll the dice. Record your roll. Compare with the symbols. Whoever has the highest number wins a point. Whoever gets 5 points first wins the round. Whoever wins 3 rounds wins the game.		
Partner 1	**< = >**	**Partner 2**

Figure 2.6 Student Recording Sheet Example 2

Recording Sheet: Top It
I had 7 + 8 which made 15. My partner had 4 + 5 which made 9. I had more because 15 is greater than 9.
1 2 3 4 5 6 7 8 9 10 11 12 13 14 15 16 17 18 19 20
_____ is greater than _____.
_____ is less than _____.
_____ is the same as _____.

Figure 2.7 Student Recording Sheet Example 3

Recording Sheet: Board Game
When I went around the board, I solved several half facts problems. I can use my doubles to help me.
I solved:
$14 - 7 = 7$ $12 - 6 = 6$ $10 - 5 = 5$

Key Points

♦ Assessment
♦ Grouping
♦ Differentiation
♦ Rotations
♦ Standards-Based
♦ Depth of Knowledge
♦ Scaffolding
♦ Engagement
♦ Student Accountability

Summary

The key to great guided math groups is assessment. When you have great assessments, you can group appropriately for differentiation that matters. Lessons should be standards-based. Teachers must always plan for the level of rigor in the lesson. Lessons should be scaffolded with language supports, tools, templates, and student grouping. All the other students must be accountable for the work they are doing in the workstations. Engagement is necessary.

Reflection Questions

1. What specific assessments do you have around the priority standards?
2. In what ways are you evaluating your lessons for rigor?
3. In what ways are you scaffolding lessons?
4. How do you know that the other students are on task and learning in the math workstation?

References

Ball, D. L. (1992). Magical hopes: Manipulatives and the reform of math education. *American Educator: The Professional Journal of the American Federation of Teachers, 16*(2), 14–18, 46–47.

Baroody, A. J. (1989). Manipulatives don't come with guarantees. *Arithmetic Teacher, 37*(2), 4–5.

Baroody, A. J. (2006). Why children have difficulties mastering the basic number combinations and how to help them. *Teaching Children Mathematics, 13*, 22–32.

Blackburn, B. (2018). *Productive struggle is a learners' sweet spot.* Retrieved January 5, 2020 from www.ascd.org/ascd-express/vol14/num11/productive-struggle-is-a-learners-sweet-spot.aspx

Boaler, J., & Greeno, J. G. (2000). Identity, agency, and knowing in mathematical worlds. In J. Boaler (Ed.), *Multiple perspectives on mathematics teaching and learning* (pp. 171–200). Westport, CT: Ablex Publishing.

Bruner, J. S. (1960). On learning mathematics. *The Mathematics Teacher, 53*(8), 610–619.

Burns, M. (n.d.). *How to make the most of manipulatives.* Retrieved August 28, 2016 from http://teacher.scholastic.com/lessonrepro/lessonplans/instructor/burns.htm?nt_id=4&url=http://store.scholastic.com/Books/Hardcovers/Harry-Potter-and-the-Chamber-of-SecretsThe-Illustrated-Edition-Book-2?eml=SSO/aff/20160429/21181/banner/EE/affiliate/////2-247765/&affiliate_id=21181&click_id=1707726852

Carpenter, T. P., Fennema, E., Franke, M. L., Levi, L., & Empson, S. B. (2015). *Children's mathematics: Cognitively guided instruction.* Portsmouth, NH: Heinemann.

Claflin, P. (2014). *A student engagement checklist.* Retrieved January 20, 2020 from www.theanswerisyes.org/2014/12/08/student-engagement-checklist/

Clarke, S. (2008). *Active learning through formative assessment.* London: Hodder Education.

Dixon. (2018a). *Five ways we undermine efforts to increase student achievement and what to do about it.* Retrieved January 4, 2020 from www.dnamath.com/blog-post/five-ways-we-undermine-efforts-to-increase-student-achievement-and-what-to-do-about-it/

Dixon. (2018b). *Five ways we undermine efforts to increase student achievement and what to do about it.* Retrieved January 4, 2020 from www.dnamath.com/blog-post/five-ways-we-undermine-efforts-to-increase-student-achievement-and-what-to-do-about-it-part-4-of-5/

Dixon. (2018c). *Five ways we undermine efforts to increase student achievement and what to do about it.* Retrieved January 4, 2020 from www.dnamath.com/blog-post/five-ways-we-undermine-efforts-to-increase-student-achievement-and-what-to-do-about-it-part-3-of-5/

Greeno, J. G., Collins, A. M., & Resnick, L. B. (1996). Cognition and learning. In D. C. Berliner & R. C. Calfee (Eds.), *Handbook of educational psychology* (pp. 15–46). London: Prentice Hall International.

Henry, V., & Brown, R. (2008, March). First-grade basics: An investigation into teaching and learning of an accelerated, high-demand memorization standard. *Journal for Research in Mathematics Education, 39*(2), 153–183.

Hiebert, J., & Grouws, D. A. (2007). The effects of classroom mathematics teaching on students' learning. In F. K. Lester Jr. (Ed.), *Second handbook of research on mathematics teaching and learning* (pp. 371–404). Charlotte, NC: Information Age.

Jitendra, A. K., Hoff, K., & Beck, M. M. (1999). Teaching middle school students with learning disabilities to solve word problems using a schema-based approach. *Remedial and Special Education, 20*(1), 50–64. https://doi.org/10.1177/074193259902000108

McLeod, D. B. (1992). Research on affect in mathematics education: A reconceptualization. In D. Grouws (Ed.), *Handbook of research on mathematics teaching and learning* (pp. 575–596). New York: NCTM and Macmillan.

National Council of Teachers of Mathematics. (2014). *Principles to actions: Ensuring mathematical success for all.* Reston, VA: NCTM.

Op 't Eynde, P. (2004). A socio-constructivist perspective on the study of affect in mathematics education. In M. J. Hoines & A. B. Fuglestad (Eds.), *28th Conference of the International Group for the Psychology of Mathematics Education* (Vol. 1, pp. 118–122). Bergen, Norway: Bergen University College.

Owocki, G., & Goodman, Y. M. (2002). *Kidwatching: Documenting children's literacy development.* Portsmouth, NH: Heinemann.

Richardson, K. *Assessing math concepts.* Retrieved January 17, 2020 from http://assessingmathconcepts.com/

Shafer, L. (2016). *Summer math loss: Why kids lose math knowledge, and how families can work to counteract it.* Retrieved January 15, 2019 from www.gse.harvard.edu/news/uk/16/06/summer-math-loss

Van de Walle, J. A., & Lovin, L. A. H. (2006). *Teaching student-centered mathematics: Grades 3–5.* Boston: Pearson.

Vygotsky, L. S. (1978). *Mind in society: The development of higher psychological processes.* Cambridge, MA: Harvard University Press.

3

Architecture of a Small-Group Lesson

Guided math groups can appear as many different things. Sometimes they are more of an exploration of a concept with manipulatives like ten frames and counters, other times they are skill practice in the form of a dice game. The elements of the guided math lesson are the same, but the sequencing can be different. For example, you might start with an energizer and then review a skill and play a game to practice that skill. On the other hand, you might be exploring decompositions of a number with Cuisenaire™ rods first and then afterwards discuss what the math you were exploring was about.

Every small-group lesson should begin with an introduction to the lesson. In this introduction, students will often go over the agenda. The teacher should usually write it up as an agenda so students know what the general outline of the lesson is and what they will be doing. At some point in the lesson, depending on the type of lesson, the teacher would then go over the "I am learning to" statement as well as what it looks like when students can actually do that skill or understand that concept.

After that is discussed, everyone should talk about the math vocabulary and phrases that are associated with the current topic, if they are already familiar with the words. This is very important because everyone will use this vocabulary throughout the lesson. However, sometimes the vocabulary is discussed at the end of the lesson (see Dixon, 2018b). In this case, the students talk about what they were doing and name it with math words.

Then, the lesson begins with either a discussion, an exploration, or an activity. The teacher might model it or might just jump into the topic. Oftentimes, the teacher will ask the students to give their input about the topic before they begin. After a time of exploration, the students will begin to further explore the topic, either on their own, with a partner, or with the whole small group.

At the end, the teacher will lead the debrief. This is where the students will discuss what the math was for the day, as well as how they practiced that math. They should also talk about how they feel they are doing with that math. This is the part of the lesson where students are reflecting and monitoring their progress. They talk about the parts of the topic that are "easy-peasy" and the parts that are "tricky." Language is important, so instead of saying difficult or hard, I tend to say "tricky, fuzzy, or climbing." Using a mountain metaphor can help students explain their journey. I explain to students that they could be just looking at the mountain from the base, climbing but not at the top yet, almost at the top, or at the top (whereby they can say, "it's sunny on the summit").

Planning

Planning is key (see Figures 3.1 through 3.6 for templates). As you are planning for the guided math lesson, it is important to think about the differences between the content, the context, and the activity. The content could be to teach students how to compose ten. The context could be a story about finding ways to make ten. The activity could be to play a card game where they have to make tens. This comes up when mapping math content. There is a difference between an activity and a skill. An activity is to actually do something, like play a doubles board game. The skill is the verb—to be able to double a number. The teacher should be planning success criteria for both the product and the process. An example of the content criteria:

I am going to *play a make 5 game.*
So that I can *practice make 5 facts.*
I will know that I can do it *when I can make 5 from any number from 0 to 5 using mental math.*

An example of process criteria is to think about what practices you want students to be able to do:

♦ I can *explain* how to make 5 with any number.
♦ I can *model* a make 5 fact.

Clarke (2008) states that when we define process success criteria for students, it helps them do these six things:

1. Ensure appropriate focus
2. Provide opportunity to clarify their understanding
3. Identify success for themselves
4. Begin to identify where the difficulties lie
5. Discuss how they will improve
6. Monitor their own progress

(cited in Dyer, n.d.)

In the guided math group, everyone should know what the criteria are and should discuss them. Dyer notes,

> When students are allowed to answer the question "How will we know?" and when they understand the learning behind the learning target, they are developing their own success criteria. This enables students to better understand what teachers expect them to know, understand, or be able to do, as well as what constitutes a proficient performance. This allows students to support each other and take responsibility for their own learning by helping them accurately and appropriately evaluate learning against shared expectations and make any necessary adjustments to the learning. Students become activated as learners.
>
> (n.d.)

Think about this in terms of your guided math lessons. Do the students understand the success criteria? Do they know what they are expected to know, understand, and be able to do? What are you looking for in the products or performances to know that the students were successful? How will you judge if it was successful? What will you use to judge the effectiveness of the product or performance? What counts as successful?

If the objective is for students to learn different efficient, flexible strategies for adding, then the success criteria might be:

♦ Students' explanations include the names of the strategies.
♦ Students can discuss different ways to think about the same problem.

- In the explanations, students include a clear description of what they did (they can verbalize the strategy).
- Students can model their thinking.

You could also have this discussion at the end of the lesson, after students have explored many different strategies. You could then talk about what it means to be flexible and efficient. You could have a checklist or rubric that has the criteria on it.

In the guided math group, the goal is for both teacher and students to be questioning. The expected answers should require thinking, not just a quick yes or no. Students should be thinking and explaining the work. Guided math should not be show and tell. It should be teachers spring boarding students into mathematical thinking. The guided math group is a space for the "having of very good ideas" by all. In the guided math group, the students should by taking the responsibility for learning and reflecting on their learning, as well as evaluating themselves and others. They should not be passive listeners or just "yes men and women." They should be active participants in the construction of rich mathematical ideas. To make this happen, there must be a great deal of planning.

More Planning

In the guided math group, there can be an agenda. Whether or not you make it public, the teacher should have an idea of the structure of the lesson. I usually make it public.

Introduction

Agenda

- I am learning to/I can
- Vocabulary/Language Frames
- Launch by Teacher
- Student Activity (alone/pairs/group)
- Wrap-Up/Reflection
- Next Steps

Planning and Preparation

Figure 3.1 Quick Plan

Week	Assessments	Workstations
Big Idea:	Entrance Slips:	Group 1
Enduring Understanding:	Exit Slips:	Group 2
Essential Question		Group 3
I am learning to. . . .		Group 4

Figure 3.2 Guided Math Planning Template 1

Unit of Study: Big Idea: Enduring Understanding: Standard:			Essential Question: Vocabulary: Language Frame: I Can Statement:		
	Group 1:	**Group 2:**	**Group 3:**	**Group 4:**	
Monday	Lesson: Materials: DOK Level: Concrete/Pictorial/ Abstract	Lesson: Materials: DOK Level: Concrete/Pictorial/ Abstract	Lesson: Materials: DOK Level: Concrete/Pictorial/ Abstract	Lesson: Materials: DOK Level: Concrete/Pictorial/ Abstract	
Tuesday	Lesson: Materials: DOK Level: Concrete/Pictorial/ Abstract	Lesson: Materials: DOK Level: Concrete/Pictorial/ Abstract	Lesson: Materials: DOK Level: Concrete/Pictorial/ Abstract	Lesson: Materials: DOK Level: Concrete/Pictorial/ Abstract	
Wednesday	Lesson: Materials: DOK Level: Concrete/Pictorial/ Abstract	Lesson: Materials: DOK Level: Concrete/Pictorial/ Abstract	Lesson: Materials: DOK Level: Concrete/Pictorial/ Abstract	Lesson: Materials: DOK Level: Concrete/Pictorial/ Abstract	
Thursday	Lesson: Materials: DOK Level: Concrete/Pictorial/ Abstract	Lesson: Materials: DOK Level: Concrete/Pictorial/ Abstract	Lesson: Materials: DOK Level: Concrete/Pictorial/ Abstract	Lesson: Materials: DOK Level: Concrete/Pictorial/ Abstract	
Friday	Lesson: Materials: DOK Level: Concrete/Pictorial/ Abstract	Lesson: Materials: DOK Level: Concrete/Pictorial/ Abstract	Lesson: Materials: DOK Level: Concrete/Pictorial/ Abstract	Lesson: Materials: DOK Level: Concrete/Pictorial/ Abstract	

Figure 3.3 Guided Math Planning Template 2

Guided Math Groups	
Big Ideas: Enduring Understandings: Essential Questions: Vocabulary: Language Frames:	Cycle of Engagement: Concrete, Pictorial, Abstract Depth of Knowledge Level: 1 2 3 4 Standard/I can statement:
Group 1:	Group 2:
Group 3:	Group 4:

Figure 3.4 Guided Math Planning Template 3

Guided Math Lesson Plan: Group:		
Week: Big Idea: Enduring Understanding:	Standard: I can/I am learning to statement:	Vocabulary: Language Frame: Materials:

Lesson:

Intro:

Guided Practice:

Individual Practice:

Sharing:

Debrief:

Comments/Notes:

Next Steps:

Figure 3.5 Guided Math Planning Template 4

Guided Math Lesson		
Big Ideas: Enduring Understandings: Essential Questions:	Vocabulary: Language Frame:	Standard: I can/I am learning to. . . . Concrete/Pictorial/Abstract
DOK Level: 1 2 3 4	Goal: ♦ Remediate ♦ Teach ♦ Dive Deeper	Materials/Tools <table><tr><td>dice</td><td>board games</td><td>cubes/bears/tiles</td></tr><tr><td>dominos</td><td>counters</td><td>base ten blocks</td></tr><tr><td>deck of cards</td><td>calculators</td><td>pattern blocks</td></tr><tr><td>white boards/ markers</td><td>guided math journals</td><td>geoboards</td></tr></table>
Beginning of the Lesson	Guided Practice	Independent Practice
Assessment/Exit Slip	Discussion	Questions
Comments/Notes: Ahas: Wow: Rethink: Next Moves:		

Figure 3.6 Guided Math Planning Template 5

Guided Math		
Group: **Week:**		
Big Idea: Enduring Understandings: Essential Questions:	Vocabulary: Language Frame: DOK Level: 1 2 3 4	Lessons: 1st 2nd 3rd
Content Questions:		
Name	What I Noticed	Next Steps

Figure 3.7 Guided Math Planning Template 6

Tens and Ones	
Big Idea: **Enduring Understanding:** **Essential Question:** **I can statement:**	Materials
Cycle of Engagement **Concrete:** **Pictorial:** **Abstract:**	**Vocabulary & Language Frames** Vocabulary: Talk Frame:
	Other Notes:

Figure 3.8 Guided Math Planning Template 7

Three Differentiated Lessons		
Emerging	On Grade Level	Above Grade Level

WATCH OUT Misunderstandings and Misconceptions

Figure 3.9 Guided Math Planning Template 8

Guided Math Planning Sheet	
Launch	
Model	
Checking for Understanding	
Guided Practice/ Checking for Understanding	
Set Up for Independent Practice	

Key Points

♦ Architecture of the Lesson

  ○ I am learning to/I can
  ○ Vocabulary/Language Frames
  ○ Launch by Teacher
  ○ Student Activity (alone/pairs/group)
  ○ Wrap-Up
  ○ Next Steps

♦ Planning Template
♦ Discussion Throughout

Summary

There is a suggested architecture for small guided math groups. Teachers must plan for the learning goal, the vocabulary supports, the tools, the launch of the lesson, the students practicing the math and the wrap up, the reflection, and the next steps. All of these elements are an important part of the lesson. They all contribute to the success of the guided math group. Using planning templates, with these elements on them, helps teachers plan for each of the elements.

Reflection Questions

1. Do your guided math lessons have all of the elements in them?
2. What types of templates are you currently using for guided math groups?
3. What is an element that you need to focus on in the architecture?

References

Dixon, J. Small Group Instruction {from the (Un)Productive Practices Series}. Five Ways we Undermine Efforts to Increase Student Achievement (and what to do about it)
  Blog Post 4: http://www.dnamath.com/blog-post/five-ways-we-undermine-efforts-to-increase-student-achievement-and-what-to-do-about-it-part-4-of-5/
Dyer, K. *What you need to know when establishing success criteria in the classroom.* Retrieved January 20, 2020 from www.nwea.org/blog/2018/what-you-need-to-know-when-establishing-success-criteria-in-the-classroom/

4

Guided Math Talk

One of the most important things that happens in the guided math group is the discussion. We have to teach students to be active participants and engaged listeners. We want them to respect each other deeply and seek to truly understand each other without judgement. They have to learn to develop and defend their thinking, justify their answers, and respectfully disagree with each other. The National Council of Teachers of Mathematics (NCTM) defines math talk as "the ways of representing, thinking, talking, and agreeing and disagreeing that teachers and students use to engage in [mathematical] tasks" (NCTM, 1991).

Questions

It is so important to ask good questions. The questions should reach beyond the answer. As Phil Daro notes, we have to go "beyond answer-getting." The questions in the guided math group should be designed to get students to understand more fundamentally the mathematics of the grade level. Good questions don't just happen—they are planned for. The teacher should know ahead of time the types of questions that she will ask and why she will ask them. In the plan for the lesson, the teacher should brainstorm some possible questions that push student thinking. These are not yes or no questions, but rather ones that require students to explain themselves, show what they know, and defend and justify their thinking (see Figure 4.1).

When students are sitting in that group, they should be having an engaging experience that builds mathematical knowledge and skills. At the table, students should be encouraged to actively participate. They should be thinking out loud, sharing their thoughts, respectively analyzing and critiquing the thoughts and actions of others, and taking risks throughout the explorations. We should always be thinking about the levels of rigor of the conversation that the students are engaged in (see Figure 4.2).

It is very important to include open questions as part of your repertoire at the guided math table. Here is an example: "The answer is 12 elephants. What is the question?"

Although you will ask some questions that require students to remember a fact or show you that they can do a skill, your questions must extend beyond this level. You should be focusing on questions that have more than one answer or way of solving the problem.

Questions That Pique Curiosity

Your questions should pique curiosity. They should lead students into further explorations. They don't have to be answered immediately. Students should have a sense of wonder. There should be some "Aha" moments, some "Wow" moments, and some "I don't get it" moments.

For example, "What if we didn't have addition?" "Tell me three situations in which you would use subtraction." "Why is addition important in real life?"

Figure 4.1 Planning for Great Questions

Before the Lesson	During the Lesson	After the Lesson
Plan what you want to get your students to think about. The tasks that we choose will determine the thinking that occurs.	**Observe, monitor, and note what is happening in the group. Checklists, post-its, and anecdotal note structures work well here.**	**Reflect, assess, and decide what's next.**
How will you go about that? What questions will you ask them?	What is your data collection system during the lesson?	What did you see?
		What did you hear?
How will you set them up to actively listen and productively participate?	How will you scaffold student questioning?	What did the students do?
How will you get them to engage with the ideas of others?	How will you scaffold student-to-student interactions?	What do you need to do next?
		What instructional moves will you make?
How will you get them to offer detailed explanations of their own thinking using numbers, words, and models?		What pedagogical moves will you make?
Plan for misconceptions. How will you address them and redirect students?		

Figure 4.2 Depth of Knowledge

DOK 1	DOK 2	DOK 3
	At this level, students explain their thinking.	At this level, students have to justify, defend, and prove their thinking with objects, drawings, and diagrams.
What is the answer to . . . ? Can you model the problem? Can you identify the answer that matches this equation?	How do you know that the equation is correct? Can you pick the correct answer and explain why it is correct? How can you model that problem in more than one way? What is another way to model that problem? Can you model that on the . . . ? Give me an example of a . . . type of problem. . . . Which answer is incorrect? Explain your thinking.	Can you prove that your answer is correct? Prove that . . . Explain why that is the answer. . . . Defend your thinking Show me how to solve that and explain what you are doing. Why did you do that?

Note: In terms of rigor, there are four levels of questions. Level 4 is more strategic project-based thinking.

Student-to-Student Conversations

It is crucial that the teacher sets up a discussion where students ask each other questions. They could have question rings, bookmarks, mini-anchor charts, or other scaffolds to help them ask each other questions (see Figures 4.3–4.5). In these conversations, one of the things that students are doing is listening to each other and comparing what they did.

Probing Questions

Teacher questions as well as student-to-student questions should provide insight into student thinking. During the guided math lesson and after it, teachers should jot down what they have learned about student thinking, student knowledge, and how students are making sense of the math they are learning.

Figure 4.3 Question Bookmark

Question Bookmark
Questions we could ask each other: How do you know?   Are you sure about that?   What is another way to do that?   Why did you use that model?   Can you explain your thinking?

Figure 4.4 Talk Cards/Talk Ring

I agree because...	I disagree because..	I need some time to think.	Why is that true?

Are you sure?	Do you agree or disagree?	Can you think of another way?	I'm confused still..

Yes I'm sure because

No, I'm not sure. I'm thinking about it.

or

Way 1
Way 2

Figure 4.5 5 Talk Moves Poster

5 Talk Moves				
Revoice	Restate	Reason	Wait Time	Group Participation
I heard you say...	*Who can say what she said in your own words?*	*Are you sure? Can you prove it?*	*Give me a few seconds.*	*Who wants to add to that?*

Scaffolding Questions for ELLs

Students should understand the questions being asked. The language should be accessible, and everyone should have a way to enter into the conversation. When thinking about instruction with English language learners (ELLs), we must consider the type of language support they will need (https://mathsolutions.com/math-talk/; http://fspsscience.pbworks.com/w/file/fetch/80214878/Leveled_20Questions_20for_20ELLs; www.aworldoflanguagelearners.com/asking-answering-questions-with-ells/). Oftentimes, they will need help with syntax and sentence structure, so it is important to scaffold these into the conversation. Give students an opportunity to refer to language stems, use language bookmarks, and write down and/or draw the answer (see Figure 4.6).

Figure 4.6 Scaffolding for ELLs

Low Levels of Support (advanced language learners) (levels 3 & 4)	Moderate Levels of Support (developing language learners) (level 2)	High Levels of Support (emerging language learners) (level 1)
Use a word bank (illustrated)	Use a sentence frame	Allow students to draw/ write the answer.
Explain how s/he did that.	I got the answer by _____.	Point to the . . .
Explain your thinking.	How can you use _____ to help you solve _____?	Show me your answer. . . .
Explain your model/ strategy.	How can you model that?	Which is the best answer?
What are two ways you could model your thinking?	What is the name of that strategy? (mini-anchor chart)	What is the name of that strategy? Do you see it here? (mini-anchor chart of strategies)
Can you describe your thinking?	How did you do that?	Give students a model sentence and a sentence frame.
Can you show us what you did?	Why did you use that model/strategy?	How did you get the answer?
Can you describe how you did it?	How did s/he do that?	How did you _____?
Can you explain what s/he did?	Is it this or that?	Do you agree? Yes or no
Why is that true?	Which strategy did you use? (visual support)	Show me the _____.
Why is that not true?		Circle the _____.
Explain how you did it.		Can you point to the strategy you used?
Decide if s/he is correct.		

Source: Adapted from http://fspsscience.pbworks.com/w/file/fetch/80214878/Leveled_20Questions_20for_20ELLs www.aworldoflanguagelearners.com/asking-answering-questions-with-ells/

Although these are structures for ELLs, they are great question types to consider with the various students you are working with. They are also great ways to think about scaffolding questions for special education students.

Five Talk Moves and More

The idea of having a framework for how students engage with each other is very important. Chapin, O'Connor, and Anderson (2009) theorized this framework around five talk moves: revoicing, restating, wait time, group participation, and reasoning. There are also other really helpful frameworks (Kazemi & Hintz, 2014; O'Connell & O'Connor, 2007). In the following section, we will explore how some of these can help us structure the discussions in guided math groups. Oftentimes, these structures are used together, for example a teacher might ask someone to restate what someone said and then encourage the group to add on (see Figures 4.7 to 4.15).

Figure 4.7 Revoicing

What It Is	What It Does	What It Sounds Like
The teacher restates in the words of the student what they just said.	This allows the student to hear back what they said, the other students to hear and process what has been said, and everyone to think about it and make sure they understand it. This teaches students the power of hearing what they have said and trying to make sense of it.	*So you said . . . Is that correct?* *Let me make sure I understand, you are saying . . .* *So first you . . . and then you . . .* *So you used this model?* *So you used this strategy?*

Figure 4.8 Restating

What It Is	What It Does	What It Sounds Like
The teacher or other students restate in their own words what has been said. Then, they verify that restating with the original student.	This allows the student to hear back what they said, the other students to hear and process what has been said, and everyone to think about it and make sure they understand it. This requires that students listen and pay attention to each other so they can restate what has been said. This teaches students how to listen to each other and make sense of what their peers are saying.	*Who can restate what Susie just said?* *Who can tell in their own words what Jamal just said?* *Who can explain what Carol meant when she said . . . ?*

Figure 4.9 Reasoning

What It Is	What It Does	What It Sounds Like
Teachers and students are asking each other for evidence and proof to defend and justify what they are saying.	This requires students to engage with each other's thinking. They must compare, contrast, justify, and defend their thinking with the other group members. This teaches students the power of defending and justifying their thinking with evidence and proof.	*Why did you do that?* *Is that true?* *Why did you use that strategy?* *Can you prove it?* *Are you sure?* *How do you know?* *Why did you use that model?* *Does that make sense?* *Do you agree or disagree, and why or why not?* *How is your thinking like Tom's?* *Is there another way?*

Figure 4.10 Group Participation

What It Is	What It Does	What It Sounds Like
Students write down or model their thinking and then share it with the whole group.	This allows students to focus on their own strategies and models, jot them down, and then share them. This teaches students the power of justifying and defending their thinking.	*Use a model to show . . .* *Illustrate your strategy.* *On your white boards, show us . . .* *In your guided math journal, show your thinking with numbers, words, or pictures . . . be ready to share it with the group. . . .*

Figure 4.11 Wait Time

What It Is	What It Does	What It Sounds Like
Teachers and students give each other 20–30 seconds of uninterrupted time to think, write, or draw about what they are doing. This is done after the question is asked and then also when the answer is given. Students should be given the time to think about the answer and then respond to it.	This allows students the time to gather their thoughts, to clarify their thinking for themselves, and just to think. It gives students more time to process what is happening. It teaches them the power of stopping to think instead of rushing into a conversation.	*Ok, now I am going to ask some questions, but I want you to take some think time before you answer.* *Terri just gave an answer. Let's think about what she just said before we respond.* *Show me with a silent hand signal when you are ready.* *Let's give everyone some time to think about this. . . .* *Is everybody ready to share or do you need more time . . . ? Show me with a hand signal. . . .*

Figure 4.12 Making Connections

What It Is	What It Does	What It Sounds Like
Teachers and students are asking each other to make connections with what has been said at the table.	It requires students to listen to each other and think about how what they did connects to what someone else did. This teaches students the power of making connections with each other's thinking.	*How is that the same as what Marta did?* *How is that different from what Joe did?* *This is like what Trini did . . .* *How are these models the same and how are they different?* *How are these strategies the same and how are they different?*

Figure 4.13 Partner Talk

What It Is	What It Does	What It Sounds Like
Students talk with their math partners about the math before they share out with the group. They might even draw or write something to share out.	This allows students to think out the math with each other, try to make sense of it, and then be able to explain it to the whole group. This teaches students the power of working together to make sense of the math.	*Turn and talk to your partner.* *Tell your partner what you think and why you think that.* *Show and explain to your partner what you did.* *Defend your thinking to your partner.*

Figure 4.14 Prompting for Student Participation

What It Is	What It Does	What It Sounds Like
The teacher or the students encourage each other to participate in the conversation.	This allows students to participate with each other in the discussion. It openly asks for participation that builds on what has just been said. This teaches students the power of participating in a discussion.	*Who would like to add to that?* *Who wants to say more?* *How did you do it that is the same or different from the way Hong did it?* *Is there another model?* *Is there another strategy?* *Is there another way?*

Figure 4.15 Clarifying One's Own Thinking

What It Is	What It Does	What It Sounds Like
Teachers and students take the time to clarify their thinking.	It allows students to expand on their original thoughts. It requires them to give more examples, show more models, and explain at a deeper level.	*Can you explain that further?* *Can you tell us more?* *What does that mean?* *Can you show us a model and explain it?* *Can you illustrate your strategy and explain it?*

Figure 4.16 Reflecting/Revising/Probing

What It Is	What It Does	What It Sounds Like
The teacher and the students take time to reflect on what has been said and possibly revise their thinking.	This gives students an opportunity to rethink about what they have just done. They get permission to change their minds. It teaches them the power of reflecting and revising their work.	*Did anybody change their mind?* *Did anybody revise their thinking?* *Now that you see this model, what do you think?* *Now that you see this strategy, what do you think now?* *Thinking about what Jamal just said, how does that help us with our thinking?*

It is very important to use different talk moves with students during guided math group in order to scaffold the discussions. The previous structures can definitely get you started doing this. It is important to plan for what you want to work on so that it isn't just random conversations. You should be explicit with students when teaching these structures. For example, you might say, "Today we are working on wait time. I want you to think about giving each other the time to think as we talk. Remember, just because you are ready doesn't mean your neighbor is yet."

Key Points

♦ Questions Matter
♦ Plan for Great Questions
♦ DOK Questions
♦ Questions That Pique Curiosity
♦ Student-to-Student Conversations
♦ Scaffolding Questions for ELLs
♦ Five Talk Moves and More

Summary

We must plan for good conversations. Planning matters. We must think about the ways in which we want our students to engage with each other and then actively do that in our groups. Think about the level of rigor of our questions. Think about what kinds of questions that curiosity and how we get students to engage with each other respectfully, confidently, and competently. We must stay conscious of scaffolding our questions for ELLs so that everyone has a way to enter into the conversations. We need to consider the different types of talk moves that allow us to have rigorous, engaging, and productive conversations.

Reflection Questions

1. What stands out for you in this chapter?
2. What will you enact right away?
3. What questions do you still have?

References

A World of Language Learners. *Asking and answering questions for ELLs*. Retrieved November 24, 2020 from www.aworldoflanguagelearners.com/asking-answering-questions-with-ells/

Chapin, S., O'Connor, C., & Anderson, N. (2009). *Classroom discussions: Using math talk to help students learn, grades K-6*, 2nd ed. Sausalito, CA: Math Solutions Publications.

Daro, P. *Against "answer-getting"*. Retrieved February 5, 2021 from https://vimeo.com/79916037

Kazemi, E., & Hintz, A. (2014). *Intentional talk: How to structure and lead productive mathematical discussions*. Portsmouth, NH: Stenhouse.

Leveled 20 questions. Retrieved November 24, 2020 from http://fspsscience.pbworks.com/w/file/fetch/80214878/Leveled_20Questions_20for_20ELLs

Math Solutions. *Math talk*. Retrieved November 24, 2020 from https://mathsolutions.com/math-talk/

Michaels, S., & O'Connor, C. (2012). *Talk science primer, TERC 2012 (Supported by the National Science Foundation, grant #0918435A)*.

NCTM. (1991). *Professional standards for teaching mathematics*. Reston, VA: NCTM.

O'Connell, S., & O'Connor, K. (2007). *Introduction to communication, grades 3–5*. Portsmouth, NH: Heinemann.

5

Small-Group Fluency Lessons

Basic fact fluency is a major part of first grade. Research says that we should devote at least 10 minutes a day to fluency practice (NCEE, 2009). It should be done as energizers and routines, in workstations, and sometimes as guided math lessons. Teachers should integrate fluency work throughout the year because students learn their basic facts at different times.

Fluency is a multidimensional concept. We like to think of it as a four-legged stool: accuracy, flexibility, efficiency, and instant recall. Although we eventually want students to have instant recall, we need them to understand what they are doing with the numbers first. The emphasis in the guided math group is to do a variety of engaging, interactive, rigorous, student-friendly activities that build a fundamental understanding of how numbers are in relationship with each other. The research resoundingly states that computational fluency is multidimensional (speed and accuracy, flexibility, and efficiency) (Brownell, 1935, 1987; Kilpatrick, Swafford, & Findell, 2001; NCTM, 2000).

As you explore the facts with the students, be sure to do concrete, pictorial, and abstract activities with them. There should be several ways for students to practice that are fun and challenging. Students should keep track of how they are doing as well. In this chapter we will explore:

♦ Count on Facts
♦ Make 10 Facts
♦ Doubles
♦ Subtraction

Overview

Figure 5.1 Overview

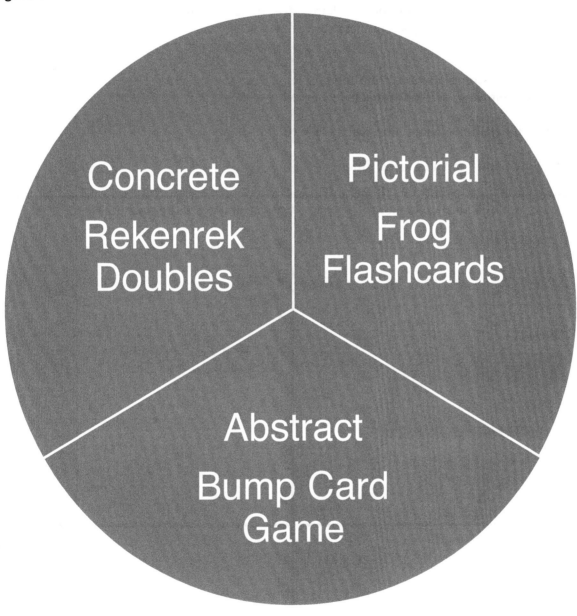

Figure 5.2 Planning Sheet

Planning Template

Big Idea: Addition is joining together. **Enduring Understanding:** We can use different strategies to solve addition problems. Counting on from the largest number is an addition strategy. **Essential Question:** How can counting on strategies help us to be more efficient? **Content Question:** What is counting on? **I can statement:** I can add using different strategies.	**Materials** ♦ Tools: Rekenrek ♦ Rekenrek Paper ♦ Templates: Ten Frame ♦ Cards ♦ Crayons
Cycle of Engagement **Concrete:** Rekenrek **Pictorial:** 7 + 2 = **Abstract:** Play Largest Sum | 2 + 5 | | 3 + 5 |	**Vocabulary & Language Frames** ♦ Count on ♦ Addends ♦ Sum ♦ Total ♦ Strategy ♦ Model Start with _____ and count on. The sum of ___ and ____ is _____
Levels of Understanding ♦ Novice ♦ Apprentice ♦ Practitioner ♦ Expert	

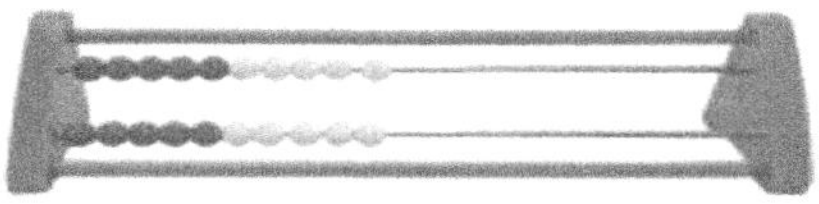

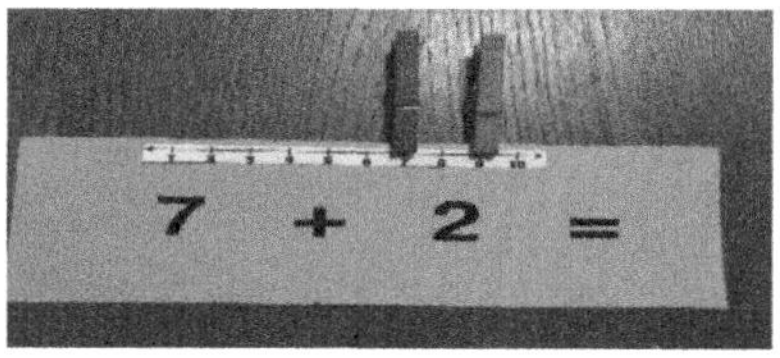

Figure 5.3 Differentiation

Three Differentiated Lessons		
In this series of lessons, students are working on the concept of *counting on with different models*. They are developing this concept through concrete activities, pictorial activities, and abstract activities. Here are some things to think about as you do these lessons.		
Emerging	**On Grade Level**	**Above Grade Level**
Review counting to add. Use number paths so students can see the big number and count on.	Use color-coded flashcards to scaffold students' work with count on facts. Eventually phase out the cards and use traditional flashcards.	Expand the number range for count on facts.

 Looking for Misunderstandings and Common Errors

When students are first learning addition, they will *count on* inconsistently. Oftentimes, they will start with whichever addend comes first. Some expressions, such as 2 + 6, are especially tricky for students. Even students who know how to count on get confused when they see this problem. Some researchers think that it has to do with the order of the addends. For example, if you give the students 6 + 2, they don't have trouble with the problem. So, scaffolding the idea of counting on with number paths and number lines helps students to remember to start with the larger number. After students have had plenty of opportunities doing it this way, you can move onto color coding the numbers as a scaffold of which number to begin with. Finally, you can use regular flashcards. Remember to play tons of games where students have to count on, such as war, bingo, bump, and tic tac toe.

Figure 5.4 Anchor Chart

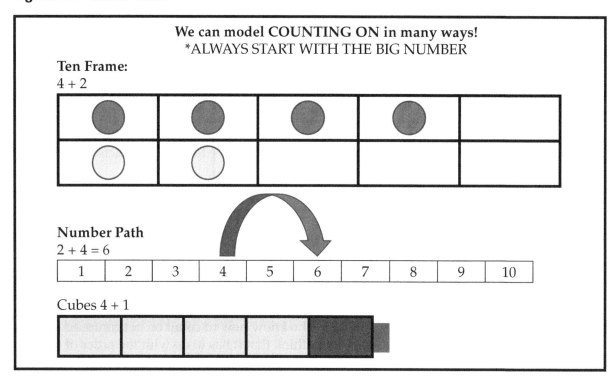

Concrete Lesson

Figure 5.5 Concrete Introduction

	Introduction
Launch	**Teacher:** Today we are going to work on COUNTING ON with different models. **Vocabulary:** count on, big number, small number, strategy, model, addend, sum, total **Math Talk:** _____ and ____ make _____. _____ + _____ = _____ **Teacher:** Today we are going to work on count on facts. Who knows what it means to count on?
Model	**Jamal:** They are when you add and you ALWAYS start with the big number. **Teacher:** Yes. Why? **Tami:** Because like say you had 8 + 1 . . . you don't want to have to hop all the way from 1 . . . so you start at 8 and hop 1 . . . **Teacher:** Excellent example. Who has another one? **Kelli:** It's like when we were using the hop on bunny. We have put the bunny on the big number and then hop. **Teacher:** Ok, who has an example of where the hop on bunny would start. **Mark:** Like if you had 5 + 3, you would start at 5. $$\begin{array}{\|c\|c\|c\|c\|c\|c\|c\|c\|c\|c\|} \hline 1 & 2 & 3 & 4 & 5 & 6 & 7 & 8 & 9 & 10 \\ \hline \end{array}$$
Checking for Understanding	**Teacher:** Ok, smarty pants. . . . I am going to hand out the count on bunny and the number line. You guys will each get one. Take your cards and solve the problems. I am going to watch you and ask questions. Be ready to share your thinking with the group.

Figure 5.6 Student Activity

	Student Activity
Guided Practice/ Checking for Understanding	The teacher passes out the count on bunny and the number path. | 1	2	3	4	5	6	7	8	9	10 | **Todd:** I had 2 + 4. That makes 6. I started on the 4 and hopped 2. | 1	2	3	4	5	6	7	8	9	10 | **Melissa:** I had 2 + 5. I started on 5 and hopped 2. That makes 7.
Set Up for Independent Practice	*Everyone starts practicing. The teacher asks the students questions individually. Then, the teacher goes around the circle and has each student share one of their problems and explain what they did.*

Figure 5.7 Lesson Close

Close
♦ What did we do today? ♦ What was the math we were practicing? ♦ What were we doing with the count on strategy? ♦ Was this easy or tricky? ♦ Turn to a partner and state one thing you learned today.

Figure 5.8 Cards

2 + 3	5 + 1
4 + 1	5 + 2
3 + 5	1 + 8
6 + 2	2 + 7
1 + 9	2 + 4
3 + 1	4 + 2

Pictorial Lesson

Figure 5.9 Pictorial Introduction

	Introduction
Launch	**Teacher:** Today we are going to continue to work on counting on facts. I am going to give you a set of cards to work with a partner. You are going to show your partner how you would solve the problem. I am going to listen in to your conversations and ask questions. Later on, we are going to share out to the whole group. What can you tell me about these flashcards? **Vocabulary:** count on, big number, small number, strategy, model, addend, sum, total **Math Talk:** _____ and ____ make _____. _____ + _____ = _____
Model	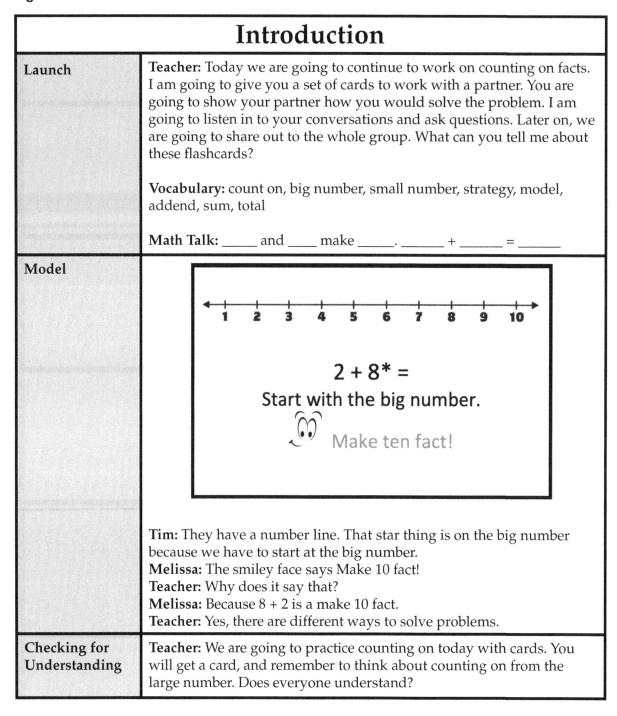 **Tim:** They have a number line. That star thing is on the big number because we have to start at the big number. **Melissa:** The smiley face says Make 10 fact! **Teacher:** Why does it say that? **Melissa:** Because 8 + 2 is a make 10 fact. **Teacher:** Yes, there are different ways to solve problems.
Checking for Understanding	**Teacher:** We are going to practice counting on today with cards. You will get a card, and remember to think about counting on from the large number. Does everyone understand?

Figure 5.10 Student Activity

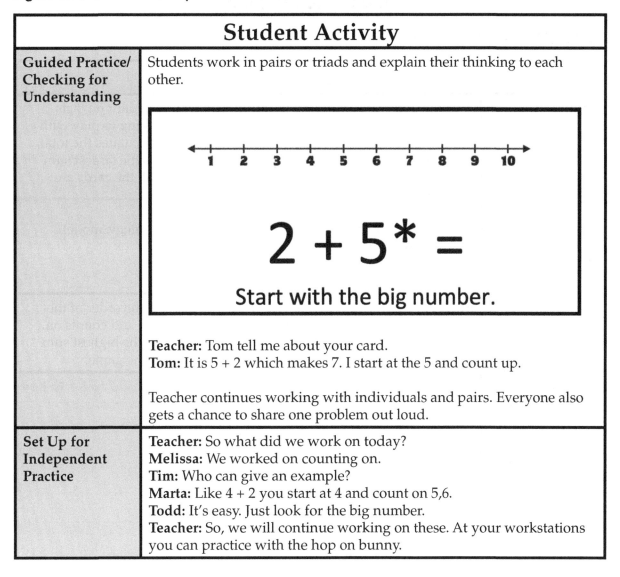

	Student Activity
Guided Practice/ Checking for Understanding	Students work in pairs or triads and explain their thinking to each other. **Teacher:** Tom tell me about your card. **Tom:** It is 5 + 2 which makes 7. I start at the 5 and count up. Teacher continues working with individuals and pairs. Everyone also gets a chance to share one problem out loud.
Set Up for Independent Practice	**Teacher:** So what did we work on today? **Melissa:** We worked on counting on. **Tim:** Who can give an example? **Marta:** Like 4 + 2 you start at 4 and count on 5,6. **Todd:** It's easy. Just look for the big number. **Teacher:** So, we will continue working on these. At your workstations you can practice with the hop on bunny.

Figure 5.11 Lesson Close

Close
◆ What did we do today? ◆ What was the math we were practicing? ◆ What were we doing with our flashcards? ◆ Was this easy or tricky? ◆ Turn to a partner and state one thing you learned today.

Abstract Lesson

Figure 5.12 Abstract Introduction

	Introduction
Launch	**Teacher:** Today we are going to continue to work on count on facts. Today's game is called "Biggest Number." You are going to play with a partner or in a triad. Each person picks a card and calculates the total, and then everyone compares the sums. Whoever has the largest sum wins the cards. Whoever has the most cards, when all the cards are done, wins the game. **Vocabulary:** count on, big number, small number, strategy, model, addend, sum, total **Math Talk:** _____ and ____ make _____. _____ + _____ = _____
Model	**Student Activity:** Remember to that no matter what the order of the addends, the frog always starts at the biggest number and counts on. Use your number paths if you need to. Whoever has the highest sum wins both cards. Whoever wins the most pairs wins the game.
Checking for Understanding	 **Teacher:** Does everybody understand what we are going to do? **George:** Yes, we are going to take a card and count on. Whoever gets the highest sum wins the pair. | 1	2	3	4	5	6	7	8	9	10	

The cards show:

1 + 2	1 + 3	1 + 4	7 + 1
2 + 1	3 + 1	1 + 8	1 + 7

Figure 5.13 Frog Cards

Guided Practice/ Checking for Understanding	Teacher listens in and asks questions. She asks Yessenia, "What are you thinking when you see your card?"
	Yesenia: I have 7 + 1 . . . it's just 1 more. 8.
	Tami: I have 3 + 1 which is 4. It's 1 more.
	Yesinia: My sum is greater. I keep the pair.
	 | 1 + 2	1 + 3	1 + 4	7 + 1
2 + 1	3 + 1	1 + 8	1 + 7	
Set Up for Independent Practice	**Teacher:** What math did we study today? **George:** We worked on count on facts. **Tami:** That's when you start at the big number and count on. **Teacher:** Any tricky parts? **Tom:** No. **Melissa:** We can play this in workstations!

Figure 5.14 Lesson Close

Close
◆ What did we do today? ◆ What was the math we were practicing? ◆ Was this easy or tricky? ◆ Turn to a partner and state one thing you learned today.

Figure 5.15 Number Path

1	2	3	4	5	6	7	8	9	10

Figure 5.16 Cards

4 + 2	2 + 6	3 + 4
3 + 9	7 + 1	2 + 8
7 + 2	3 + 6	2 + 4
1 + 9	7 + 3	1 + 8

Make 10 Facts

Overview

Figure 5.17 Overview

Make Ten Guided Math Lessons		
Concrete: Build and Break Ten Wand	**Pictorial:** Color Ten Wand	**Abstract:** Ten Friend Card Game

Figure 5.18 Planning Template

Combinations of 10

Big Idea: There are certain number combinations that make 10. **Enduring Understanding:** Students will understand and be able to recall the number combinations to 10. **Essential Question:** What are the ways to make 10? **I can statement:** I can make 10 in different ways.	**Cycle of Engagement** **Concrete:** Ten Wand (ten frame: first five cells shaded) **Pictorial:** Ten Wand Diagram (ten frame, blank) **Abstract:** Match Addends and the Sum $2 + 8$ 10
Materials ♦ Tools: Cubes ♦ Templates: Ten Frame ♦ Cards ♦ Crayons	
Vocabulary & Language Frames ♦ Make 10 ♦ Addends ♦ Sum ___ and ___ make _____ The sum of ___ and ____ is _____	**Levels of Understanding** ♦ Novice ♦ Apprentice ♦ Practitioner ♦ Expert

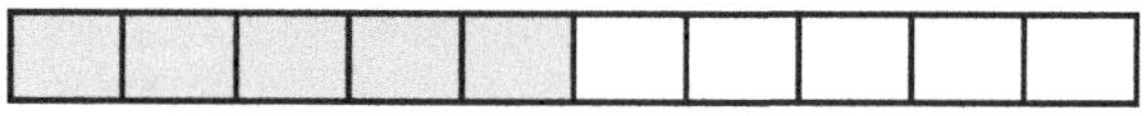

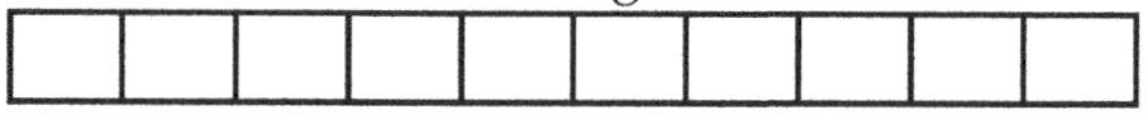

Figure 5.19 Differentiation

Three Differentiated Lessons		
In this series of lessons, students are working on the concept of *counting on with different models*. They are developing this concept through concrete activities, pictorial activities, and abstract activities. Here are some things to think about as you do these lessons.		
Emerging	**On Grade Level**	**Above Grade Level**
Review adding within 10. Be sure to work on lower doubles. Use different manipulatives to show how to make ten, including the rekenrek, the ten frame and Cuisenaire™ rods.	Students should work with the ten frame. They should play many games and do missing addend problems.	Expand the number range.

 Looking for Misunderstandings and Common Errors

Make ten facts are foundational. Spend as much time as students need, to make sure that everyone learns these combinations. They should do a great deal of work with looking at the combinations and then a great deal of work to see it visually with the ten frame.

Figure 5.20 Anchor Chart

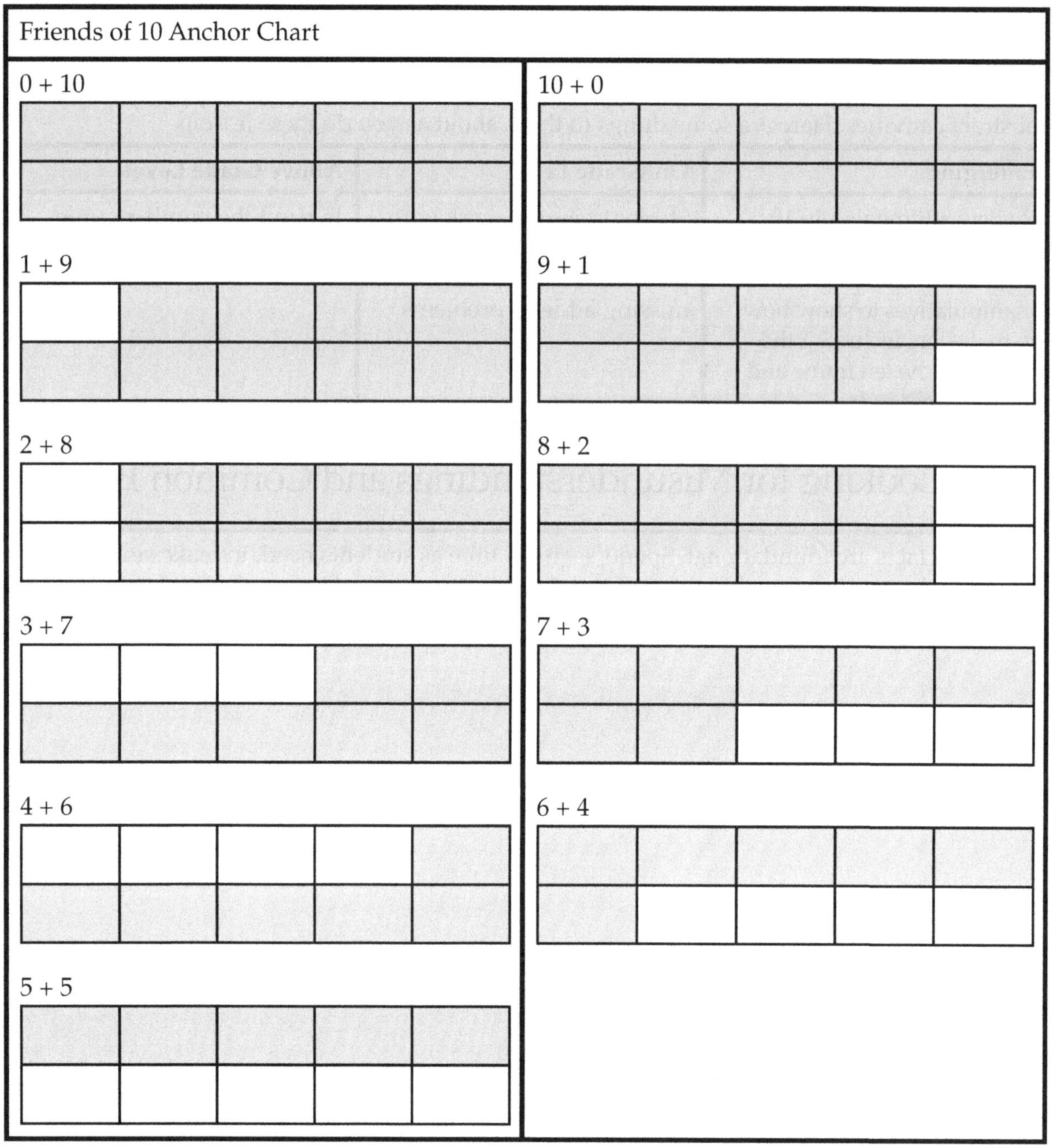

Friends of 10 Anchor Chart	
0 + 10	10 + 0
1 + 9	9 + 1
2 + 8	8 + 2
3 + 7	7 + 3
4 + 6	6 + 4
5 + 5	

Concrete Lesson

Figure 5.21 Concrete Introduction

	Introduction
Launch	**Teacher:** Today we are going to work on combinations of ten with our ten wands. Our goal is to learn different "combinations" to ten. Sometimes we call these "ten friends." **Vocabulary:** combinations, ten, ten friends, decompose, compose **Math Talk:** My ten friend is . . . _____ and _____ make 10. We have an anchor chart here to help us think about ten friends. The chart is the one we made in whole group.
Model	*Teacher passes out ten wands to every child.* **Teacher:** Let's look at them. What do you notice? *Students should talk about how there are 5 of one color and 5 of another color.* **Teacher:** What if we broke it apart. We have 9 in one hand, what would be in the other hand? Students answer. **Teacher:** What if we broke it apart? We have 5 in one hand, what would be in the other hand? (Student's answer)
Checking for Understanding	**Teacher:** Now you all are going to each break apart the ten wands. We will go around the table and each of you will tell us how you broke it apart. Remember how we talk about it._____ and _____make _____

Figure 5.22 Student Activity

Student Activity	
Guided Practice/ Checking for Understanding	Students go around the table and each of them tells how they broke apart the number wand. You could also scaffold this by giving each student a number and they have to break off that many of their number bond and say what their number sentence is. For example: **Version A:** Student gets the card and breaks the wand into that number and the other part. 2 and ☐ make 10.  A more complex version is using the addition sign in an equation. **Version B:** Student gets a card: 3 + ☐ = 10 
Set Up for Independent Practice	**Teacher:** What is the math that we were practicing today? **Hong:** Working on ten friends? **Kelly:** What is a ten friend? **Yoli:** A ten friend is 2 numbers that make 10. **Teacher:** Ok, we are going to keep working on this because making 10 is super important for doing other math.

Figure 5.23 Lesson Close

Close
♦ What did we do today?
♦ What was the math we were practicing?
♦ What were we doing with our number wands?
♦ Was this easy or tricky?
♦ Turn to a partner and state one thing you learned today.

Figure 5.24 Cards

1 and [ ] make 10.	2 and [ ] make 10.
3 and [ ] make 10.	4 and [ ] make 10.
5 and [ ] make 10.	6 and [ ] make 10.
7 and [ ] make 10.	8 and [ ] make 10.
9 and [ ] make 10.	0 and [ ] make 10.
10 and [ ] make 10.	__ and [ ] make 10.

1 + ☐ = 10.	2 + ☐ = 10.
3 + ☐ = 10.	4 + ☐ = 10.
5 + ☐ = 10.	6 + ☐ = 10.
7 + ☐ = 10.	8 + ☐ = 10.
9 + ☐ = 10.	10 + ☐ = 10.
0 + ☐ = 10.	___ + ☐ = 10.

Pictorial Lesson

Figure 5.25 Pictorial Introduction

	Introduction
Launch	**Teacher:** Today we are going to work on combinations of ten with our ten wands. Our goal is to learn different "combinations" to ten. Sometimes we call these "ten friends." **Vocabulary:** combinations, ten, ten friends, decompose, compose **Math Talk:** My ten friend is . . . _____ and _____ make 10. We have an anchor chart here to help us think about ten friends. The chart is the one we made in whole group.
Model	**Teacher:** Today we are going to continue to work on making 10 with our ten wands. *Teacher passes out ten wands to every child.* What do you remember about them? *Students should talk about what they did last time.* **Teacher:** Today we are going to break apart our wands and then record our work. **Step 1:** Watch what I do. Here is my ten wand. I am going to break it into 2 different parts. **Step 2:** I broke it into 3 and 7. 3 and 7 make 10. **Step 3:** Now I am going to record my work on the cube template.
Checking for Under-standing	**Teacher:** What are we going to do today? **Yoli:** We are going to break apart the ten wand and draw a picture. **Teacher:** Ok, let's get started.

Figure 5.26 Student Activity

Student Activity	
Guided Practice/ Checking for Understanding	**Teacher:** Let's do one together. Everybody get your number wand ready. Let's break it into 5 and ? (Students answer "5.")Ok, now let's color that on our template. Who can explain what we did?(Student explains.)Ok, now each of you gets to break apart your ten frame and then color the template and explain what you did to us. The students go around and break their ten frame, record their work and explain it to the group. **Lilly:** I am going to break it into 2 different parts. **Step 2:** I broke it into 4 and 6. 4 and 6 make 10. **Step 3:** Now I am going to record my work on the cube template.
Set Up for Independent Practice	**Teacher:** What was the math that we were studying today? **Aiko:** We worked on ten friends. **Tami:** Ten friends are when 2 numbers make 10. **Teacher:** Ok, we are going to continue working on this in workstations. Any questions?

Figure 5.27 Lesson Close

Close
♦ What did we do today? ♦ What was the math we were practicing? ♦ What were we doing with our number wands? ♦ Was this easy or tricky? ♦ Turn to a partner and state one thing you learned today.

Figure 5.28 Recording Sheet

Number Wand Recording Sheet

_____ + _____ = 10

_____ + _____ = 10

_____ + _____ = 10

Abstract Lesson

Figure 5.29 Abstract Introduction

	Introduction
Launch	**Teacher:** Today we are going to continue to work on making 10. We are going to play a card game today though. Let's look at our make 10 anchor chart so we can talk about what we have been working on. What does this chart help us to see? **Vocabulary:** combinations, ten, ten friends, decompose, compose **Math Talk:** My ten friend is . . . _____ and ____ make 10. We have an anchor chart here to help us think about ten friends. The chart is the one we made in whole group.
Model	**Student:** We can see the different ways to make 10. Like 4 and 6. **Teacher:** Who can tell me another way to make 10? **Student:** 5 and 5. **Teacher:** Ok, today we are going to see how well you all know your make ten friends. We are going to play a match game like before but we are matching ten friends. You can use your tools if you need help.
Checking for Understanding	**Teacher:** Any questions?

Figure 5.30 Student Activity

Student Activity	
Guided Practice/ Checking for Understanding	Today we are going to play a card game. It is a match game. We have 20 cards and they are all turned face down. We will take turns trying to find all the matches of ways to make 10. If you get stuck, you can look at our anchor chart. To start, we are going to each roll the dice. Whoever has the largest number starts the game. Then we take turns. The person on your left goes after you and we continue going in that direction. 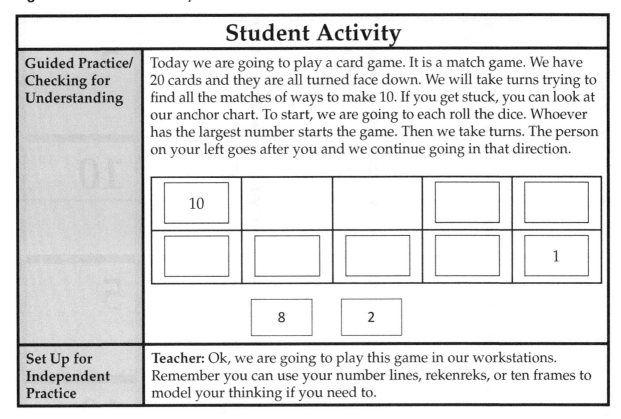
Set Up for Independent Practice	**Teacher:** Ok, we are going to play this game in our workstations. Remember you can use your number lines, rekenreks, or ten frames to model your thinking if you need to.

Figure 5.31 Lesson Close

Close
◆ What did we do today? ◆ What was the math we were practicing? ◆ Was this easy or tricky? ◆ Turn to a partner and state one thing you learned today.

Figure 5.32 Cards

1	2	3	4	5
6	7	8	9	10
1	2	3	4	5
6	7	8	9	10

Section Summary

Making 10 is one of the most important ideas that students learn in math in first grade. They will use this throughout the rest of their learning. They will use it most immediately when they are learning how to bridge through ten to add and subtract. There should be many opportunities for students to make 10 with the rekenrek, the ten frame, the ten wand, and other manipulatives. Also, using ten frame flashcards is key because students can work on visualizing the facts. After students do a great deal of work on the ten frames, they should work with a variety of games where they have to recall the facts.

Overview

Figure 5.33 Overview

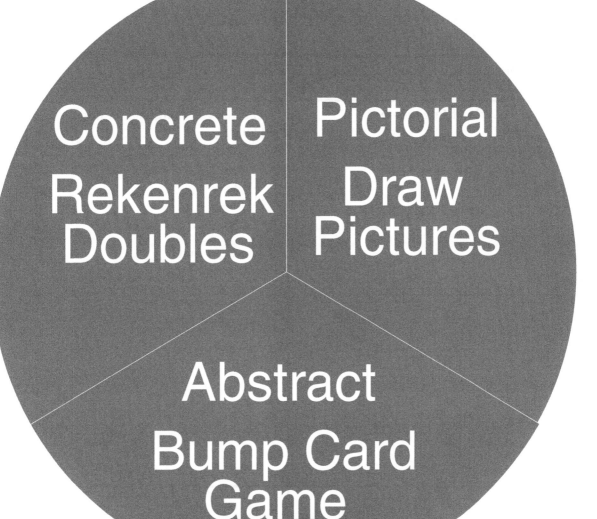

Figure 5.34 Planning Template

Addition Doubles	
Big Idea: Addition is joining together. **Enduring Understanding:** We can use different strategies to solve addition problems. Doubles is an addition strategy. **Essential Question:** What are different addition strategies? **I can statement:** I can add using different strategies.	**Materials** ♦ Tools: Rekenrek ♦ Rekenrek Paper ♦ Templates: Ten Frame ♦ Cards ♦ Crayons
Cycle of Engagement **Concrete:** Rekenrek **Pictorial:** **Abstract:** Match Addends and the Sum $\boxed{3 + 3}$ $\boxed{5 + 5}$	**Vocabulary & Language Frames** ♦ Doubles ♦ Addends ♦ Sum ♦ Total ♦ Strategyc ♦ Model ___ and ___ make _____ The sum of ___ and ____ is _____
Levels of Understanding ♦ Novice ♦ Apprentice ♦ Practitioner ♦ Expert	

Figure 5.35 Differentiation

Three Differentiated Lessons		
In this series of lessons, students are working on the concept of *making doubles with different models*. They are developing this concept through concrete activities, pictorial activities, and abstract activities. Here are some things to think about as you do these lessons.		
Emerging	**On Grade Level**	**Above Grade Level**
Review adding doubles. Practice making them with tools including the rekenrek, the ten frame, and Cuisenaire™ rods.	Students should work with the ten frame. They should play many games and do missing addend problems.	Expand the number range.

 Looking for Misunderstandings and Common Errors

When you teach doubles, teach the doubles within ten first and then the larger doubles. In first grade, the emphasis should be the doubles within ten.

Figure 5.36 Anchor Chart

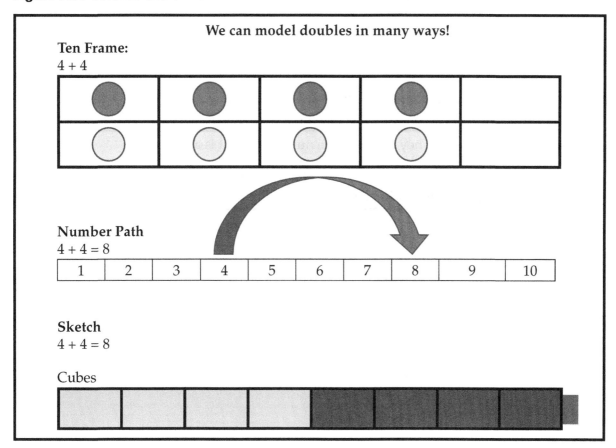

Concrete Lesson

Figure 5.37 Concrete Introduction

Introduction	
Launch	**Teacher:** Today we are going to work on adding doubles with different models. Let's look at them. What do you notice? **Vocabulary:** doubles, strategy, model, addend, sum, total **Math Talk:** _____ and ____ make _____. _____ + _____ = _____
Model	**Teacher:** Today we are going to work on exploring doubles. Who knows what doubles are? **Jamal:** They are when you add. **Teacher:** Yes. Add what? **Jamal:** Like 1 + 1 is doubles. **Teacher:** Does anyone else know any doubles? **Kelli:** Yes. 2 + 2. **Mark:** 3 + 3. **Teacher:** How are all these facts alike? Let's look at them. (Teacher writes down the facts on the white board).
Checking for Understanding	**Mark:** They are the same number. Like it is a double. **Missy:** Like a twin. **Teacher:** Yes, like a twin. They are actually called doubles facts. We are going to work on modeling these on the rekenrek today.

Figure 5.38 Student Activity

	<div align="center">**Student Activity**</div>
Guided Practice/ Checking for Understanding	The teacher passes out addition doubles facts. Students pull a card and act out their problems. The students each get a chance to share their problem and explain how they solved it. Students pull up a virtual rekenrek on their iPads or laptops and then show their work. **Maria:** I had 3 + 3. That makes 6. See. 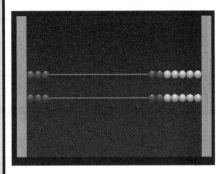 **Todd:** I had 4 + 4. That makes 8. See. 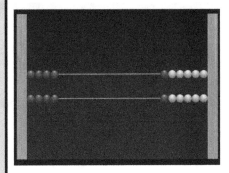 **Teacher:** Who thinks they could solve their doubles fact and then draw it on the rekenrek paper? All the children raise their hand. **Todd:** I had 4 + 4. That makes 8. See. 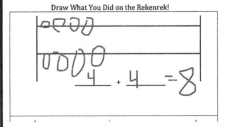 **Tina:** I know how. See if I pull 2 + 2. I model it. Then I draw that. Just like we do on the rug. **Teacher:** Yes, let's do that. (*Teacher passes out the rekenrek paper.*) Everyone models their problem and shares their thinking with a neighbor.
Set Up for Independent Practice	*Everyone goes around and shares their thinking. This is a practitioner level group and so the teacher introduces the rekenrek paper in the same lesson.*

Figure 5.39 Lesson Close

Close
♦ What did we do today?
♦ What was the math we were practicing?
♦ What were we doing with our rekenreks?
♦ Was this easy or tricky?
♦ Turn to a partner and state one thing you learned today.

Figure 5.40 Cards

$0 + 0$	$5 + 5$
$1 + 1$	$2 + 2$
$3 + 3$	$4 + 4$
$0 + 0$	$5 + 5$
$1 + 1$	$2 + 2$
$3 + 3$	$4 + 4$

Pictorial Lesson

Figure 5.41 Pictorial Introduction

Introduction	
Launch	**Teacher:** Today we are going to continue to work on doubles. We are going to play a concentration game. You all know how to play concentration. You and your partner will get a deck of cards. You will turn them face down and then take turns trying to find the matches. We are matching doubles models and their equations. **Vocabulary:** doubles, strategy, model, addend, sum, total **Math Talk:** _____ and _____ make _____. _____ + _____ = _____
Model	**Teacher:** You are going to be looking for pairs of double facts, the model, and the expression. For example: 4 + 4
Checking for Understanding	**Teacher:** Does everybody understand? Who can explain it? **Teddy:** We are playing doubles concentration. It's easy! **Sara:** We get it! Let's start.

Figure 5.42 Student Activity

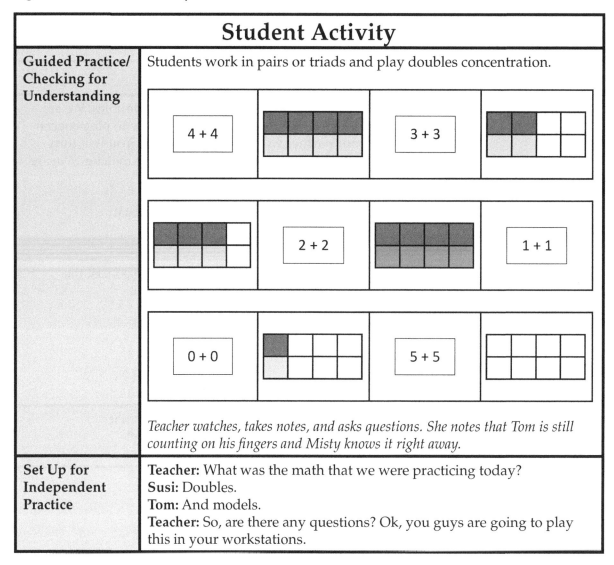

Student Activity

Guided Practice/ Checking for Understanding	Students work in pairs or triads and play doubles concentration. *Teacher watches, takes notes, and asks questions. She notes that Tom is still counting on his fingers and Misty knows it right away.*
Set Up for Independent Practice	**Teacher:** What was the math that we were practicing today? **Susi:** Doubles. **Tom:** And models. **Teacher:** So, are there any questions? Ok, you guys are going to play this in your workstations.

Figure 5.43 Lesson Close

Close

♦ What did we do today?
♦ What was the math we were practicing?
♦ What was the math we were studying?
♦ Was this easy or tricky?
♦ Turn to a partner and state one thing you learned today.

Figure 5.44 Model Cards

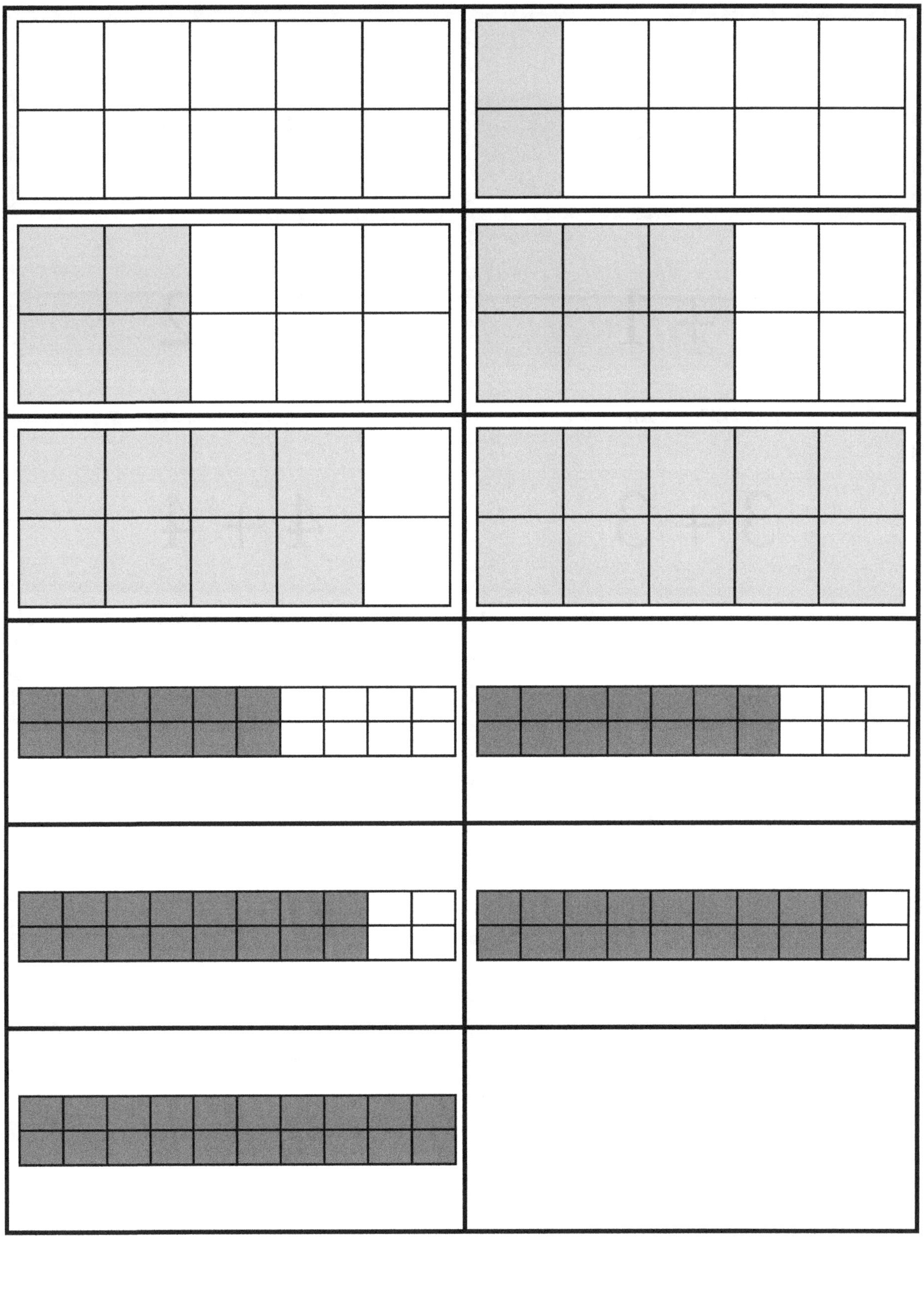

Figure 5.45 Expression Cards

$0 + 0$	$5 + 5$
$1 + 1$	$2 + 2$
$3 + 3$	$4 + 4$
$0 + 0$	$5 + 5$
$1 + 1$	$2 + 2$
$3 + 3$	$4 + 4$

Abstract Lesson

Figure 5.46 Abstract Introduction

	Introduction
Launch	**Teacher:** Today we are going to continue to work on doubles. We will be playing a board game today. How many of you like board games? In this game, you will get a doubles fact. You add it up and cover the sum. Whoever gets four in a row, wins. **Vocabulary:** doubles, strategy, model, addend, sum, total **Math Talk:** _____ and _____ make _____. _____ + _____ = _____
Model	Here is the game board. Use 9 sided dice or number cards. **Connect Four** **Addition Doubles** (even 2-20) (2) (12) (16) (6) (4) (14) (18) (2) (18) (10) (10) (6) (12) (14) (20) (2) (8) (20) (4) (10) (18) (16) (4) (8) (6)
Checking for Understanding	**Teacher:** Who can explain the game? **Kofi:** It's a Connect 4 but with doubles. You have to roll the dice and double the number. You are trying to get 4 in a row. **Teacher:** Any questions? Ok, let's start.

Figure 5.47 Student Activity

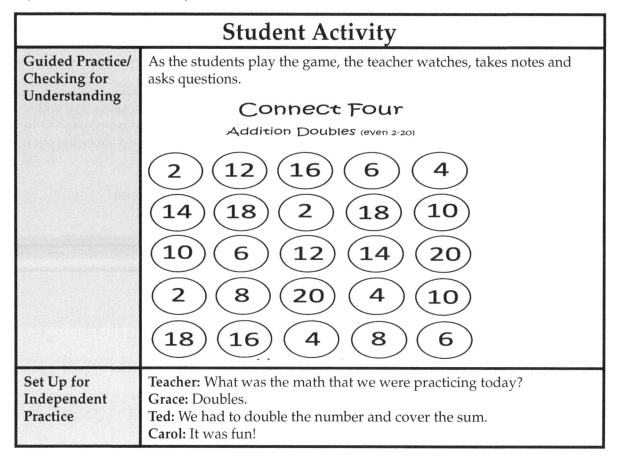

Student Activity	
Guided Practice/ Checking for Understanding	As the students play the game, the teacher watches, takes notes and asks questions. **Connect Four** **Addition Doubles** (even 2-20) 2 12 16 6 4 14 18 2 18 10 10 6 12 14 20 2 8 20 4 10 18 16 4 8 6
Set Up for Independent Practice	**Teacher:** What was the math that we were practicing today? **Grace:** Doubles. **Ted:** We had to double the number and cover the sum. **Carol:** It was fun!

Figure 5.48 Lesson Close

Close
♦ What did we do today? ♦ What was the math we were practicing? ♦ Was this easy or tricky? ♦ Turn to a partner and state one thing you learned today.

Figure 5.49 Doubles Cards

$0 + 0$	$5 + 5$
$1 + 1$	$2 + 2$
$3 + 3$	$4 + 4$
$6 + 6$	$7 + 7$
$8 + 8$	$9 + 9$
$10 + 10$	$4 + 4$

Note: These can be used for the Connect 4 game instead of dice.

Section Summary

Teaching doubles is important. Be sure to scaffold doubles by doing the lower double facts first and then the higher doubles. Give students various opportunities to build it, draw it, and then write the equation. For example, they might pull a card, build the fact on a twenty frame, shade it in on a template, and then write the equation. Students should also play individual, partner, and group games, like tic tac toe, bump, and bingo.

Overview

Figure 5.50 Overview Circle of Subtraction

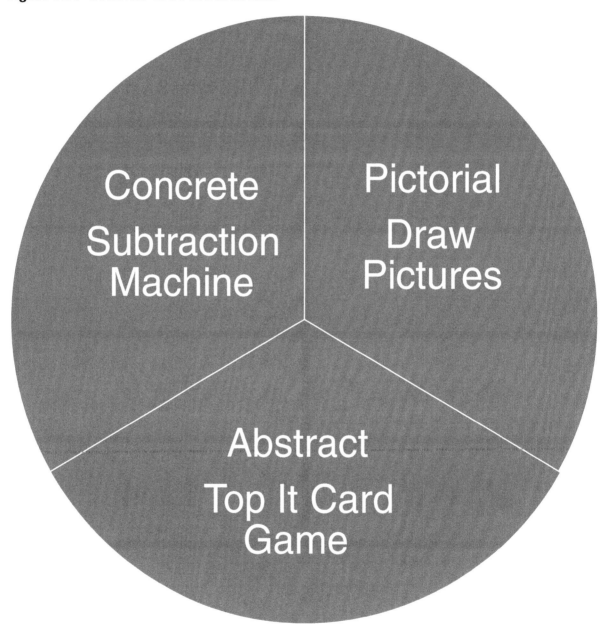

Figure 5.51 Planning Template

Subtraction	
Big Idea: Subtraction is about taking away a number from another number. **Enduring Understanding:** We can model subtraction in many ways. **Essential Question:** What are the ways to model subtraction? **I can statement:** I can model subtraction in many ways.	**Materials** ♦ Tools: Cubes ♦ Templates: Ten Frame ♦ Cards ♦ Crayons
Cycle of Engagement **Concrete:** Subtraction Machine **Pictorial:** Drawing **Abstract:** Match Addends and the Sum | 3		7 – 4		**Vocabulary & Language Frames** ♦ Subtract ♦ Take Away ♦ Difference ____take away ____ is ____
Levels of Understanding ♦ Novice ♦ Apprentice ♦ Practitioner ♦ Expert	

Figure 5.52 Differentiation

Three Differentiated Lessons
In this series of lessons, students are working on the concept of *taking away numbers to find a difference*. They are developing this concept through concrete activities, pictorial activities, and abstract activities. Here are some things to think about as you do these lessons.

Emerging	On Grade Level	Above Grade Level
A substantial number of first graders come into first grade not having a firm handle on beginning subtraction. In the beginning, make sure that students can subtract within 5. Make sure they have a firm understanding of taking away 1, counting back, and taking away zero. Use different manipulatives to show how to subtract including the rekenrek, the ten frame, and Cuisenaire™ rods.	Once students can subtract within 5, then move on to subtraction within 10. Once they get that, practice subtracting from 10. Students should work with the ten frame. They should play many games and do missing number problems.	Expand the number range.

 Looking for Misunderstandings and Common Errors

Spend time on subtraction. In schools, we tend to spend more time on addition than on subtraction. We need to make sure that there is an equal amount of time spent on both operations. Once students understand addition within 5, make sure that they understand subtraction within 5. After they master this, then go on and do it within 10.

Figure 5.53 Anchor Chart

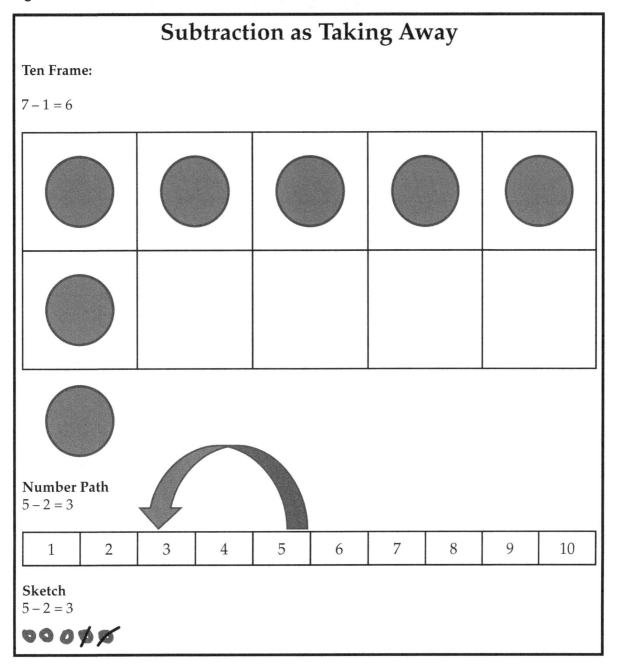

Subtraction as Taking Away

Ten Frame:

$7 - 1 = 6$

Number Path
$5 - 2 = 3$

| 1 | 2 | 3 | 4 | 5 | 6 | 7 | 8 | 9 | 10 |

Sketch
$5 - 2 = 3$

Concrete Lesson

Figure 5.54 Concrete Introduction

<table>
<tr><td colspan="2" align="center"><h2>Introduction</h2></td></tr>
<tr>
<td>Launch</td>
<td>

Teacher: Today we are going to work on subtracting with different models. Let's look at them. What do you notice?

Vocabulary: subtract, take away, minus, difference, big number, small number

Math Talk: I had _____. I took away _____. I have _____ left.

</td>
</tr>
<tr>
<td>Model</td>
<td>

Teacher: Here we have a subtraction machine. Here we have 7 counters in the big box. We are going to take away 5. They will go in our cup. We have 2 left. That will go in the small box. That is called the difference. It is the difference between what we had in the beginning and what we took away.

</td>
</tr>
<tr>
<td>Checking for Understanding</td>
<td>

Teacher: Let's try another one. Let's say I had 8. I took away 4. I put them in the cup. I have 4 left and those slide down to the little box. That is the difference between what we had and what we took away.

Teacher: Now you all are each going to have your own subtraction machine.

</td>
</tr>
</table>

Figure 5.55 Student Activity

	Student Activity
Guided Practice/ Checking for Understanding	The teacher passes out subtraction cards. Students pull a card and act out their problems. The students each get a chance to share their problem and explain how they solved it. **Maria:** I had 5. I took away 1. I have 4 left. ┌──┐ │ **Math Talk:** I had _____. I took away _____. I have _____ left. │ └──┘ 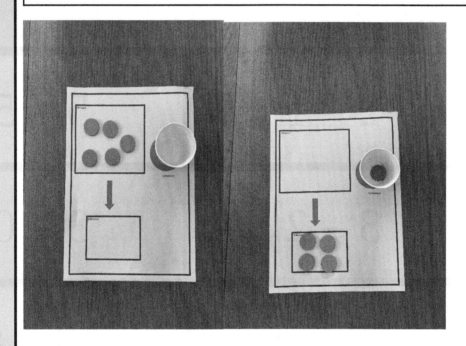 **Teacher:** If we wanted to double-check the answer, what could we do? **Todd:** We could count on our fingers. **Teacher:** Yes, we could see if we get the same answer. Let's do that. **Marta:** We could use the number path.
Set Up for Independent Practice	**Teacher:** Yes, let's do that. You know what. There is also another way to check. We could count our difference and the part we took away to see if we had the same amount that we had at the beginning. Watch. I could count 2 in the cup and 3 in the difference box and that makes 5. So I know that 5 take away 2 is 3. We are going to be talking more about that in the upcoming days. Are there any questions? What was interesting today? What was tricky?

Figure 5.56 Lesson Close

Close
♦ What did we do today?
♦ What was the math we were practicing?
♦ Was this easy or tricky?
♦ Turn to a partner and state one thing you learned today.

Figure 5.57 Expression Cards

2 – 1	5 – 5
3 – 2	3 – 0
10 – 9	10 – 8
7 – 5	6 – 3
9 – 7	8 – 1

Figure 5.58 Subtraction Mat

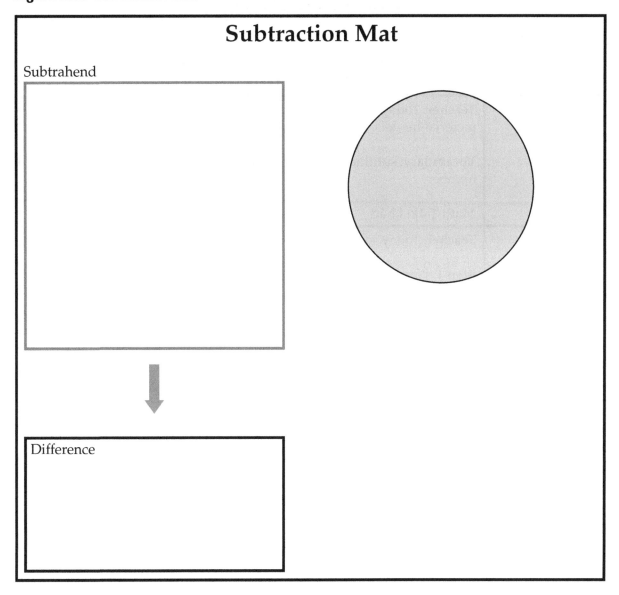

Subtraction Mat

Subtrahend

Difference

Pictorial Lesson

Figure 5.59 Pictorial Introduction

Introduction	
Launch	**Teacher:** Today we are going to continue to work on subtracting using pictorial models. (*Students should talk about what they did last time.*) **Vocabulary:** subtract, take away, minus, difference, big number, small number **Math Talk:** I had _____. I took away _____. I have _____ left.
Model	**Teacher:** Today we are going to record our thinking with sketches. **Step 1:** Watch what I do. Here is my problem: 5 – 4 = 1
Checking for Understanding	**Teacher:** Now, what do you notice? **Lucy:** You drew 5 and crossed out 1. **Teacher:** How do we know it is correct? **Lucy:** We can double-check. **Teacher:** We need to count to make sure. Let's check it. It's always good to double-check. **Tom:** 1 is left. **Teacher:** Interesting . . . so they are the same. What is another way to think about this? The crossing out is the model. What strategy could I use when taking away 1 from a number? **Lucy:** You could just go back 1. It's the number before. **Teacher:** Yes. Did you notice how I drew a picture to model my thinking? We can do it by drawing. Our thinking strategy is just to think about the number that comes before the number we are taking something away from. Ok, now you all are going to try it. I am going to pass around a problem to each person and you will model it and then share your thinking.

Figure 5.60 Student Activity

	Student Activity
Guided Practice/ Checking for Understanding	**Kate:** I used the number path. I started on 7 and I hopped back 2. I got 5.

I can model subtraction many ways.
7 – 2

1	2	3	4	5	6	7	9	9	10

Model Bank: drawing, ten frame, number path, counters

Set Up for Independent Practice	*Students go around and everyone shows their work and shares their thinking.*

Figure 5.61 Lesson Close

Close

♦ What did we do today?
♦ What was the math we were practicing?
♦ Was this easy or tricky?
♦ Turn to a partner and state one thing you learned today.

Abstract Lesson

Figure 5.62 Abstract Introduction

<table>
<tr><td colspan="2" align="center">Introduction</td></tr>
<tr>
<td>Launch</td>
<td>

Teacher: Today we are going to continue to work on subtracting with models. Let's review our vocabulary and our anchor chart.

Vocabulary: subtract, take away, minus, difference

Who wants to talk about our vocabulary?

Sara: Difference is the answer.

David: Subtract means to take away.

Mike: We use the minus sign in the number sentence to subtract.
</td>
</tr>
<tr>
<td>Model</td>
<td>

Teacher: We are going to play a subtraction game. You have to pull a card, move that many spaces, and then tell the strategy you used to find the difference. Here is the game board.

$10 - ? = 10$	$10 - ? = 5$
$10 - ? = 9$	$10 - ? = 4$
$10 - ? = 8$	$10 - ? = 3$
$10 - ? = 7$	$10 - ? = 2$
$10 - ? = 6$	$10 - ? = 1$
$10 - ? = 5$	$10 - ? = 0$
$10 - ? = 4$	$10 - ? = 8$
$10 - ? = 3$	$10 - ? = 9$
$10 - ? = 2$	$10 - ? = 10$
</td>
</tr>
<tr>
<td>Checking for Understanding</td>
<td>You have to pull a card and do what it says, either move forward, move back, or move that many spaces. Any questions? Look at the anchor chart if you need ideas for a model.</td>
</tr>
</table>

Figure 5.63 Anchor Chart

We can subtract with our fingers. 	We can subtract with our ten frame. 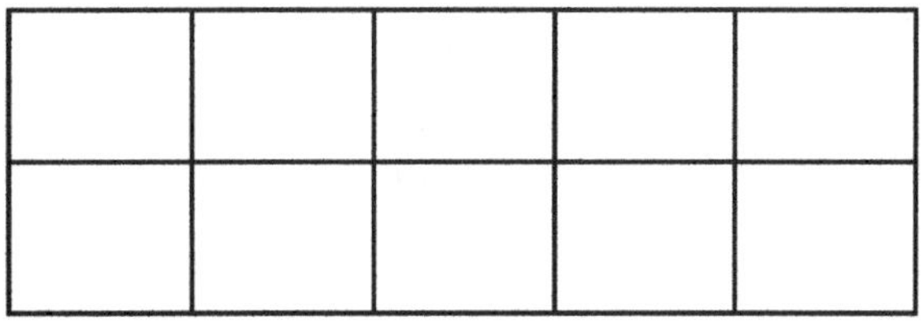
We can subtract with a rekenrek. 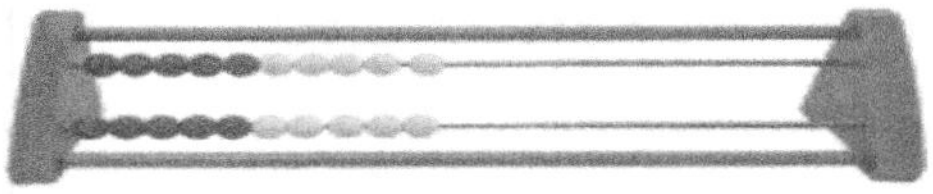	We can subtract with a drawing. 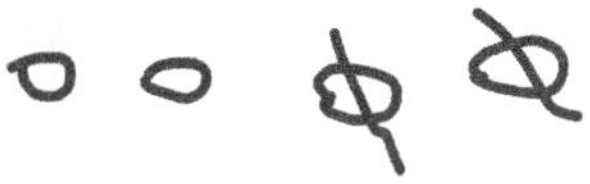
We can subtract on a number path. | 1 | 2 | 3 | 4 | 5 | 6 | 7 | 8 | 9 | 10 |	We can subtract with counters. 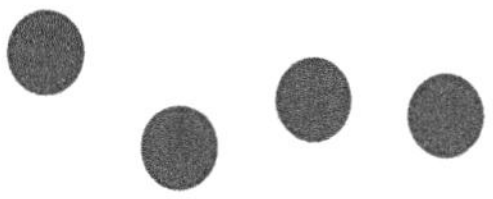

Figure 5.64 Student Activity

Student Activity	
Teacher: Ok, we are going to play the game. We will play rock, paper, scissors to see who goes first. We then take turns going.	
Guided Practice/ Checking for Understanding	Teacher watches game and asks questions.

10 − ? = 10	10 − ? = 5
10 − ? = 9	10 − ? = 4
10 − ? = 8	10 − ? = 3
10 − ? = 7	10 − ? = 2
10 − ? = 6	10 − ? = 1
10 − ? = 5	10 − ? = 0
10 − ? = 4	10 − ? = 8
10 − ? = 3	10 − ? = 9
10 − ? = 2	10 − ? = 10

Claire: I got move ahead 3. I landed on 10 − ? = 4. I got 6 because I know that 4 and 6 make 10. I used a ten friend fact.

Harry: I got move ahead 2. I landed on 10 − ? = 2. I got 8 because I know that 8 + 2 is 10. It's a ten friend too.

Set Up for Independent Practice	**Teacher:** What was the math that we practiced today? **Kimi:** We worked on subtracting 10. **Tom:** We used ten friends to help. **Kimi:** We could also look at the chart for help. **Teacher:** I am moving this game to workstations.

Figure 5.65 Lesson Close

Close
♦ What did we do today? ♦ What was the math we were practicing? ♦ Was this easy or tricky? ♦ Turn to a partner and state one thing you learned today.

Section Summary

Teaching subtraction is foundational. Students need to actually do many subtraction problems on different models, including the ten frame, rekenrek, and number lines. There should be an equal amount of time spent on subtraction as on addition, and the connections between the two should be constantly being made. The research says that subtraction is much more difficult for children than addition (Kamii, Kirkland, & Lewis, 2001, p. 33). It is important for students to master addition so that they can use that knowledge to help them with subtraction (Kamii et al., 2001). Make sure to build a strong foundation with concrete materials and drawings before rushing students to solve just abstract problems.

Depth of Knowledge

Depth of Knowledge is a framework that encourages us to ask questions that require that students to think, reason, explain, defend, and justify their thinking (Webb, 2002). Here is a snapshot of what that can look like in terms of fluency work. It is important to continually reflect on what the level of the lesson is. In working in small groups on fluency, be sure to ask open questions so that students can think and reason out loud with others.

Figure 5.66 DOK Chart

	What are different strategies and models that we can use to explore the *count on* strategy?	What are different strategies and models to explore make 10 combinations?	What are different strategies and models that we can use to explore doubles facts?	What are different strategies and models that we can use to explore subtraction?
DOK Level 1 (These are questions where students are required to simply recall/reproduce an answer/do a procedure.)	2 + 5	Name 3 facts that make 10.	8 + 8	8 – 4
DOK Level 2 (These are questions where students have to use information, think about concepts, and reason.) This is considered a more challenging problem than a level 1 problem.	What does it mean to count on? Why should we start at the larger number when we add?	8 + ? = 10 ___ + 4 = 10 Explain what make 10 facts are? What is your strategy for solving a make 10 fact?	Fill in the doubles facts. 16 = __ + ___ 14 = __ + ___ Explain what doubles facts means.	5 – ___ = 4
DOK Level 3 (These are questions where students have to reason, plan, explain, justify, and defend their thinking.)	Give me an example of a count on fact. Model it in two different ways. Explain how you know your answer is correct.	Give me an example of a make 10 fact. Model it in two different ways. Explain how you know your answer is correct.	Is 5 + 2 a doubles fact? Why or why not? Explain your thinking and defend your answer.	Tell me a subtraction problem. Model and solve it. Explain how you know your answer is correct.

Figure 5.67 Asking Rigorous Questions

DOK 1 At this level, students recall, reproduce an answer, or do a procedure.	DOK 2 At this level, students explain their thinking.	DOK 3 At this level, students have to justify, defend, and prove their thinking with objects, drawings, and diagrams.
What is the answer to . . . ? Can you model the problem? Can you identify the answer that matches this equation?	How do you know that the equation is correct? Can you pick the correct answer and explain why it is correct? How can you model that problem in more than one way? What is another way to model that problem? Can you model that on the . . . ? Give me an example of a . . . type of problem. . . . Which answer is incorrect? Explain your thinking.	Can you prove that your answer is correct? Prove that . . . Explain why that is the answer. . . . Show me how to solve that and explain what you are doing. Defend your thinking . . .

Resources

A great resource for asking open questions is Marion Small's *Good Questions: Great Ways to Differentiate Mathematics Instruction in the Standards-Based Classroom* (2017).

Also, Robert Kaplinsky has done a great job in pushing our thinking forward with the Depth of Knowledge Matrices he created (https://robertkaplinsky.com/depth-knowledge-matrix-elementary-math/). Kentucky Math Department (2007) has these great math matrices as well.

Key Points

- Count on Facts
- Make 10
- Doubles
- Subtraction

Summary

It is essential that we work on basic fact fluency with students in small guided math groups. We have to take them through the cycle of concrete, pictorial, and abstract activities. We need to make sure that students understand, can explain, and appropriately use the various strategies. Just because the book teaches a specific strategy in no way implies that the students are actually ready to be working on that strategy. Therefore, it is essential that we pull groups and work with students in their zone of proximal development. We then follow this work up with workstations and homework that correlates with the concepts they are working on. Fluency is a continuum and all the students are working toward the grade-level fluency, but they are not all starting at the same point.

Reflection Questions

1. How are you currently teaching basic math fact fluency?
2. Are you making sure that you do concrete, pictorial, and abstract activities?
3. What do your students struggle with the most and what ideas are you taking away from this chapter that might inform your work around those struggles?

References

Brownell, W. A. (1935). Psychological considerations in the learning and the teaching of arithmetic. In W. D. Reeve (Ed.), *The teaching of arithmetic* (Tenth Yearbook of the National Council of Teachers of Mathematics, pp. 1–31). New York: Columbia University, Teachers College, Bureau of Publications.

Brownell, W. A. (1987). AT classic: Meaning and skill—Maintaining the balance. *Arithmetic Teacher*, 34(8), 18–25. (Original work published 1956).

Kamii, C., Kirkland, L., & Lewis, B. (2001). Fluency in subtraction compared with addition. *Journal of Mathematical Behavior*, 20, 33–42.

Kentucky Department of Education (2007). Support Materials for Core Content for Assessment Version 4.1 Mathematics. Retrieved from the internet on January 15th, 2017.

Kilpatrick, J., Swafford, J., & Findell, B. (2001). *Adding it up: Helping children learn mathematics.* Washington, DC: National Academy Press.

National Center for Education Evaluation and Regional Assistance. (2009). *Assisting students struggling with mathematics: Response to Intervention (RtI) for elementary and middle schools. 2009–4060.* Retrieved from IES website http://ies.ed.gov/ncee and http://ies.ed.gov/ncee/wwc/publications/practiceguides/

NCTM. (2000). *Principles and standards for school mathematics.* Reston, VA: NCTM.

Small, M. (2017). *Good questions: Great ways to differentiate mathematics instruction in the standards-based classroom.* 3rd ed. New York: Teachers College Press.

Stacey, K., & MacGregor, M. (1999). Learning the algebraic method of solving problems. *The Journal of Mathematical Behavior*, 18(2), 149–167. https://doi.org/10.1016/S0732-3123(99)00026-7

Webb, N. L. (2002). *Depth-of-knowledge levels for four content areas.* Madison, WI: Wisconsin Center for Education Research. Retrieved from http://facstaff.wcer.wisc.edu/normw/All%20content%20areas%20%20DOK%20levels%2032802.doc.

6

Small-Group Lessons for Algebraic Thinking and Operations

Algebraic thinking is one of the linchpins of developing mathematical proficiency. First grade is where several algebraic concepts are introduced. In first grade, students are introduced to the commutative and associative property of addition. They need many opportunities to explore these ideas concretely, pictorially, and abstractly. Even in the upper elementary grades, students still struggle with these properties, especially associative. These concepts should not only be taught during their unit of study, but also explored throughout the year in daily energizers and routines as well as practiced in math workstations.

First graders also are supposed to come away with a strong understanding of the equal sign as meaning "is the same as." Missing number problems are often challenging for students. They tend to just look at the equal sign as the answer and then just compute accordingly. They also just combine numbers, for example they will interpret $2 + \_\_\_ = 10$ as 12. They just work with the numbers that they see. They need a lot of time to explore how to get the answer concretely by building it. Meaning specifically putting 2 cubes on one side and then asking the students how many more to make 10. They see that they have to add 8. Doing this with scales is also really important for the visual.

Didax has a great virtual manipulative to help with this (see Figure 6.1). Students also begin exploring how $2 + 5 = 7 - 0$. This is often hard for students because they will say "Well it's not the same sign so it's different." Without even calculating, they will say this. Again, not focusing on concept of the equal sign as "is the same as."

Figure 6.1 Didax Scale

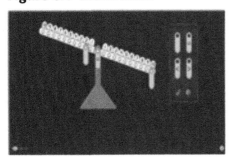

Source: www.didax.com/apps/math-balance/index.html

Research Note 🔍

◆ Developing early algebraic thinking can be done and it matters (CCSSI, 2010; NCTM, 2000; Greenes, 2004).

◆ "Elementary school really is the critical place for fixing America's algebra problem," said James Kaput, a professor of mathematics at the University of Massachusetts Dartmouth (cited in Hoff, 2001).

◆ Greenes posits three big ideas for developing algebraic thinking:

1. Variables

   ○ Representing Unknowns
   ○ Representing Quantities That Vary

2. Patterns and Functions

   ○ Generalizing Properties

3. Proportions and Proportional Thinking (upper elementary)

In this chapter we will look at:

◆ Commuatative Poperty
◆ Associative Property
◆ Missing Numbers
◆ Equal Sign

Overview

Figure 6.2 Overview

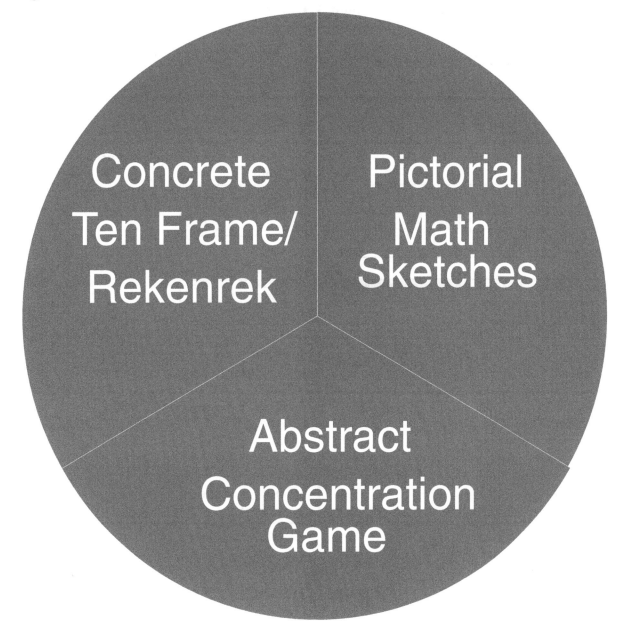

Figure 6.3 Planning Template

Commutative Property

Big Idea: The order of the addends doesn't matter. **Enduring Understanding:** We can add numbers in any order. **Essential Question:** How do we model math problems? **I can statement:** I can prove that 5 + 2 is the same as 2 + 5.	**Materials** ♦ Tools: Cubes ♦ Templates: Ten Frame ♦ Cards ♦ Crayons
Turn Around Facts 2 + 3 3 + 2 4 + 5 5 + 4	**Cycle of Engagement** **Concrete** **Pictorial** **Abstract** 2 + 3 = 3 + 2
Questions ♦ What is a turn around fact? ♦ Why is that true? ♦ How do you know? ♦ Are you sure? ♦ Can you prove it?	**Vocabulary & Language Frames** ♦ Addends ♦ Sum ♦ Turn around fact ___ and ___ make _____ The sum of ___ and ____ is _____

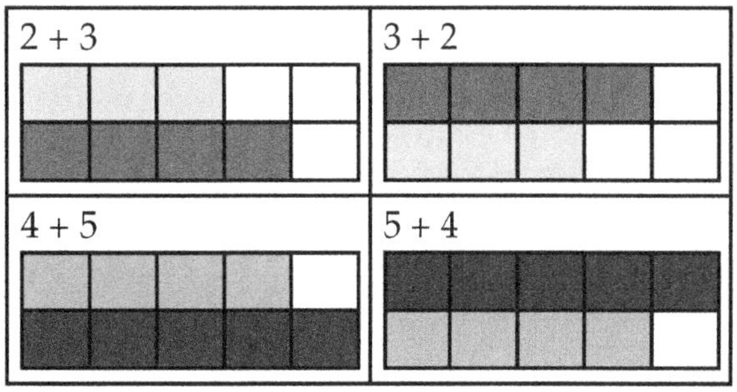

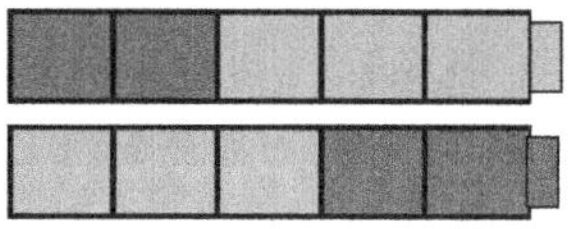

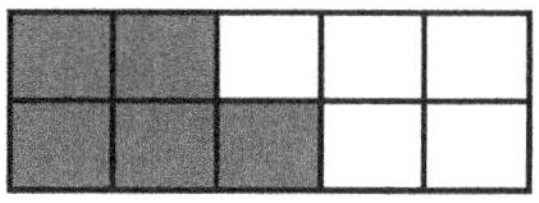

Figure 6.4 Differentiated Lessons

Three Differentiated Lessons

In this series of lessons, students are working on the concept of *turn around facts*. They are developing this concept through concrete activities, pictorial activities, and abstract activities. Everybody should do the cycle. Some students progress through it more quickly than others. Here are some things to think about as you do these lessons.

Emerging	On Grade Level	Above Grade Level
Review adding. As you introduce this to students, do a lot of work with cubes and counters so students can see the idea.	The grade-level standard is that students can model it and explain it. So do lots of this work where students are modeling it and explaining it. Also show and talk about exemplars and non-exemplars of this concept.	Once they have the concept, play lots of abstract games, including card games, board games, and dice games.

 Looking for Misunderstandings and Common Errors

This concept tends to be easy for most students. It is still really important that they can explain what they are doing and can prove that the equation is true with concrete manipulatives and math sketches. Given the equation $3 + 2 = 2 + 3$, students should be able to defend their thinking with models.

Concrete Lesson

Figure 6.5 Concrete Introduction

Introduction

Launch	

Teacher: Today we are going to talk about "turn around facts." This means that when we are adding, it doesn't matter which number that we add first because the answer will be the same. (*Teacher passes out counters to every child.*) Let's look at this idea.

Vocabulary: addends, "turn around fact", sum, total, equals, same as

Math Talk:

My turn around fact is _____ and _____.

This is a turn around fact because _____ and _____.

Is 2 + 3 the same as 3 + 2?

Model

Teacher: How might we figure that out? Think about how we can prove things. Here is our anchor chart of ways we prove things.

I can prove my thinking with:

Counters

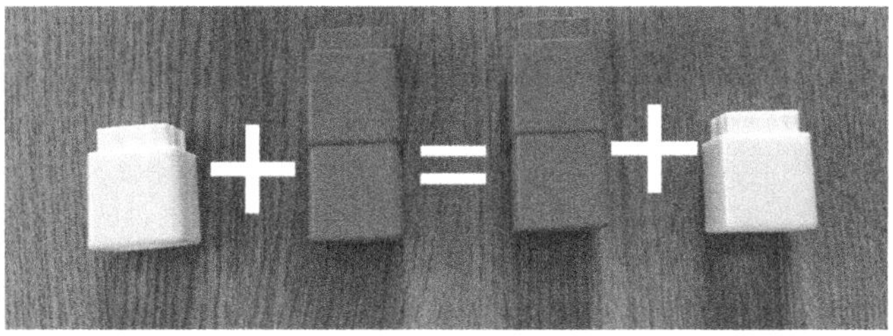

Number Path

1	2	3	4	5	6	7	8	9	10

Ten Frame

Picture

Sean: We could use counters.

Checking for Understanding	Teacher: Ok. How would that look? Let's use counters on the ten frame.

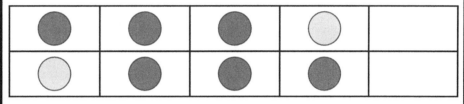

Teacher: What do you notice? Is it the same amount?

Tracie: It's 5.

Teacher: Yes. It is 5. So we could say that 2 + 3 is the same as 3 + 2. Let's look at another one.

Is 3 + 1 the same as 1 + 3?

Maria: Let's do it on the ten frame again.

Teacher: Ok, you show us.

Teacher: What do you see?

Carl: It makes 4.

Teacher: Ok. So we can say that 3 + 1 is the same as 1 + 3. Let's pull another one. This time, let's try to model it another way.

Is 4 + 2 the same as 2 + 4?

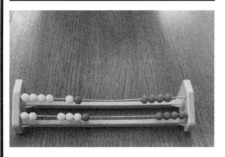

Let's do it on the rekenrek.

Teacher: What do you notice?

Tracie: It's the same again.

Teacher: Ok, now I am going to give each one of you a card and I want you to model your fact and then talk about it.(*Teacher passes out the problems.*)

Figure 6.6 Student Activity

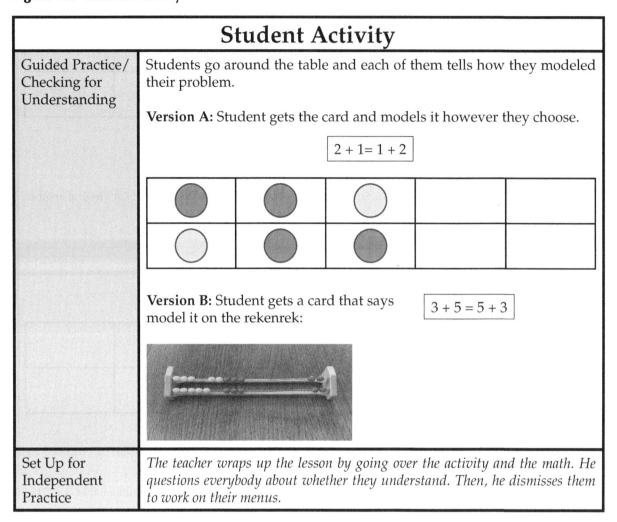

Student Activity	
Guided Practice/ Checking for Understanding	Students go around the table and each of them tells how they modeled their problem. **Version A:** Student gets the card and models it however they choose. $2 + 1 = 1 + 2$ **Version B:** Student gets a card that says model it on the rekenrek: $\quad 3 + 5 = 5 + 3$
Set Up for Independent Practice	*The teacher wraps up the lesson by going over the activity and the math. He questions everybody about whether they understand. Then, he dismisses them to work on their menus.*

Figure 6.7 Lesson Close

Close
◆ What did we do today? ◆ What was the math we were practicing? ◆ What are ways we were modeling our thinking? ◆ Was this easy or tricky? ◆ Turn to a partner and state one thing you learned today.

Pictorial Lesson

Figure 6.8 Pictorial Introduction

	Introduction
Launch	**Teacher:** Today we are going to talk about "turn around facts." This means that when we are adding, it doesn't matter which number that we add first because the answer will be the same. (*Teacher passes out counters to every child.*) Let's look at this idea. **Vocabulary:** addends, "turn around fact", sum, total, equals, same as **Math Talk:** My turn around fact is _____ and _____. This is a turn around fact because _____ and _____.
Model	**Teacher:** Today we are going to continue to work on proving that the order of the addends doesn't matter. What did welook at last time? *Students should talk about what they did last time.* **Teacher:** Today we are going to record our thinking with sketches. **Step 1:** Watch what I do. Here is my problem: 5 + 4 = 4 + 5 **Teacher:** Now, what do you notice? **Lucy:** They are the same amount.
Checking for Understanding	**Teacher:** How do we know? **Lucy:** Because it's the same. **Teacher:** We need to count to make sure. Let's add: 5 + 4 is what? **Tom:** 9 **Teacher:** How do you know? **Kate:** Because 4 + 4 is 8 and 1 more is 9.

Figure 6.9 Student Activity

	Student Activity
Guided Practice/ Checking for Understanding	**Kate:** I had 3 + 4 and I proved that it is the same as 4 + 3. It is 7 circles on both sides. 3 + 4 = 4 + 3 Are they the same amount? Is 3 + 4 the same as 4 + 3? Yes or No **Teacher:** Yes. This is a great. I have one more question. What is a strategy for adding 3 + 4? **Maria:** That's easy. 3 + 3 is 6 and so 1 more is 7. **Teacher:** This is brilliant thinking! Who's next?
Set Up for Independent Practice	*Students go around and everyone shows their work and shares their thinking. At the end, the teacher debriefs and goes over the math activity. The teacher also checks in to see how students are feeling about the math they are doing. Then, he dismisses everyone to work on their menus.*

Figure 6.10 Lesson Close

Close
◆ What did we do today? ◆ What was the math we were practicing? ◆ Was this easy or tricky? ◆ Turn to a partner and state one thing you learned today.

Figure 6.11 Prove It

Prove that: $$2 + 3 = 3 + 2$$ Are they the same amount? Yes or No	Prove that: $$2 + 4 = 4 + 2$$ Are they the same amount? Yes or No
Prove that: $$2 + 5 = 5 + 2$$ Are they the same amount? Yes or No	Prove that: $$2 + 6 = 6 + 2$$ Are they the same amount? Yes or No
Prove that: $$2 + 7 = 7 + 2$$ Are they the same amount? Yes or No	Prove that: $$2 + 8 = 8 + 2$$ Are they the same amount? Yes or No
Prove that: $$5 + 3 = 3 + 5$$ Are they the same amount? Yes or No	Prove that: $$3 + 4 = 4 + 3$$ Are they the same amount? Yes or No
Prove that: $$4 + 1 = 1 + 4$$ Are they the same amount? Yes or No	Prove that: $$4 + 6 = 6 + 4$$ Are they the same amount? Yes or No
Prove that: $$1 + 7 = 7 + 1$$ Are they the same amount? Yes or No	Prove that: $$1 + 8 = 8 + 1$$ Are they the same amount? Yes or No

Abstract Lesson

Figure 6.12 Abstract Introduction

	Introduction
Launch	**Teacher:** Today we are going to talk about "turn around facts." This means that when we are adding, it doesn't matter which number that we add first because the answer will be the same. Let's look at this idea. **Vocabulary:** addends, "turn around fact", sum, total, equals, same as **Math Talk:** My turn around fact is _____ and _____. This is a turn around fact because _____ and _____.
Model	**Teacher:** Today we are going to continue to work on turn around facts. We are going to play a card game. Let's review our vocabulary and our anchor chart. **Vocabulary:** turn around fact, addend, sum, total **Teacher:** Who wants to talk about our vocabulary? **Sara:** Turn around fact is like 2 + 3 equals 3 + 2. **David:** Sum and total are the answer. **Mike:** Addend is one of the numbers you are adding.
Checking for Understanding	**Teacher:** It is a concentration game. You have to find the turn around facts. When you match a pair you can keep it. Whoever has the most cards at the end wins.

Figure 6.13 Student Activity

	Student Activity

Guided Practice/ Checking for Understanding	**Teacher:** Ok and here in our anchor chart we can see some examples. Today we are going to play a concentration game. You are going to work in a group of two or three and you are going to lay your cards in an array and then look for the matches that are the turn around facts. So, you if you turn over 1 + 5 then you will be looking for 5 + 1. Any questions? The winner is the person with the most matches when all the cards are gone. Ok, let's start. *Teacher passes out card decks to each group and students start to play.*
	
	  | 2 + 7 | 8 + 2 | 2 + 8 | | |
	  | | | | | 7 + 2 |

Set Up for Independent Practice	*The teacher watches the game and asks students questions. She asks them to prove their thinking and explain how they know it is true. The teacher eventually wraps up the lesson by asking the students to discuss the math they were practicing and how they were practicing it. Students also check in about how well they are understanding the math. Students are dismissed to go and work on their menus.*

Figure 6.14 Lesson Close

Close
♦ What did we do today? ♦ What was the math we were practicing? ♦ Was this easy or tricky? ♦ Turn to a partner and state one thing you learned today.

Figure 6.15 Cards

1 + 2	2 + 1	3 + 2	2 + 3
4 + 5	5 + 4	6 + 3	3 + 6
3 + 5	5 + 3	4 + 6	6 + 4
5 + 2	2 + 5	1 + 9	9 + 1
2 + 4	4 + 2	3 + 4	4 + 3
3 + 1	1 + 3	2 + 6	6 + 2
5 + 0	0 + 5	5 + 1	1 + 5

Section Summary

Teaching the commutative property should be done from the beginning and done throughout the year. Be sure to let students explore it with cubes, the rekenrek, one-inch tiles, bears, sketches, and plenty of games. Be sure to also use dominos because they are so visual. Students can even count the pips. They record their work. Scales are important as well because they help students to see and play around with the idea. There should be a focus on students explaining what they are doing and proving that it is true. This idea is a bedrock for developing algebraic thinking.

Associative Property

Overview

Figure 6.16 Overview

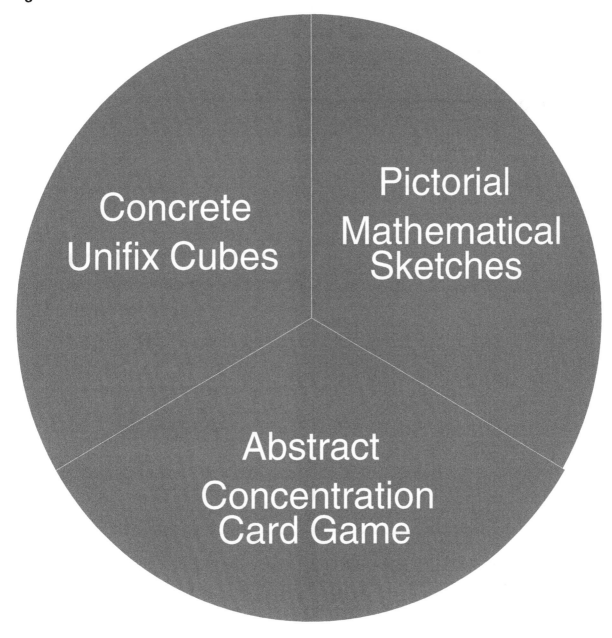

Concrete
Unifix Cubes

Pictorial
Mathematical
Sketches

Abstract
Concentration
Card Game

Figure 6.17 Planning Template

Associative Property

Big Idea: When adding, grouping numbers together in different ways does not change the answer.

Enduring Understanding: We can group addends together in different ways to make problems easier.

Essential Question: How do we group addends together to make problems easier?

I can statement: I can prove that 4 + 2 + 2 is the same as 4 + 4.

Materials
- ◆ Tools: Cubes
- ◆ Templates: Ten Frame
- ◆ Cards
- ◆ Crayons

Group it!

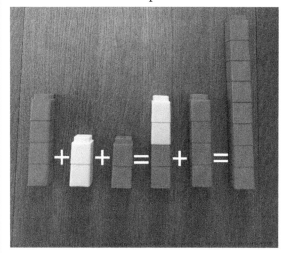

Cycle of Engagement

Concrete: Tile Build

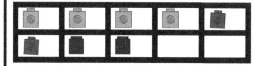

Pictorial: Tile Color
Draw it to Prove it!

Abstract:: Match Turn Around Facts

| 4 + 2 + 2 | 4 + 4 |

Questions:
- ◆ Does this work?
- ◆ Is this true?
- ◆ How do you know?
- ◆ Can you prove it?
- ◆ Can you explain your thinking?

Vocabulary & Language Frames
- ◆ Group
- ◆ Addends
- ◆ Sum

___ and ___ and ____make _____
The sum of ___ and ____ and is _____.

Figure 6.18 Differentiation

Three Differentiated Lessons		
In this series of lessons, students are working on the concept of the *associative property*. They are developing this concept through concrete activities, pictorial activities, and abstract activities. Everybody should go through the cycle. All students need to explore it concretely, so they can draw it with understanding and discuss their work. They need to connect that to the abstract as they are doing it. Here are some things to think about as you do these lessons.		
Emerging	**On Grade Level**	**Above Grade Level**
Review adding and combining numbers. When you get to teaching this, students should know and be good at seeing and making tens and lower doubles. What this means is that, given the problem 4 + 6 + 2, you want students to already be really comfortable with the idea that 4 plus 6 makes 10 so they can combine those numbers.	The grade-level standard is that students understand this concept and can model and explain it.	Expand the number range.

 ## Looking for Misunderstandings and Common Errors

Students struggle with combining numbers that are different across the equal sign. So, many times they will say things like 2 + 7 + 3 is not the same as 10 + 3 because the numbers are not the same on both sides. You should do a lot of work with proving it with physical manipulatives first.

Concrete Lesson

Figure 6.19 Concrete Introduction

Introduction

Launch	**Teacher:** Today we are going to talk about "adding numbers in any order." This means that when we are adding, it doesn't matter which number that we add first because the answer will be the same. (*Teacher passes out ten wands to every child.*) Let's look at this idea. **Vocabulary:** addends, grouping numbers, sum, total, equals, same as **Math Talk:** I added _____ and _____. I grouped _____ and _____ together first and then I got _____. **Teacher:** How might we figure that out? Think about how we can prove things. Here is our anchor chart of Is 2 + 3 + 2 the same as 3 + 4?
Model	**Teacher:** How might we figure that out? Think about how we can prove things. Here is our anchor chart of ways we prove things. I can prove my thinking with: Counters Number Path

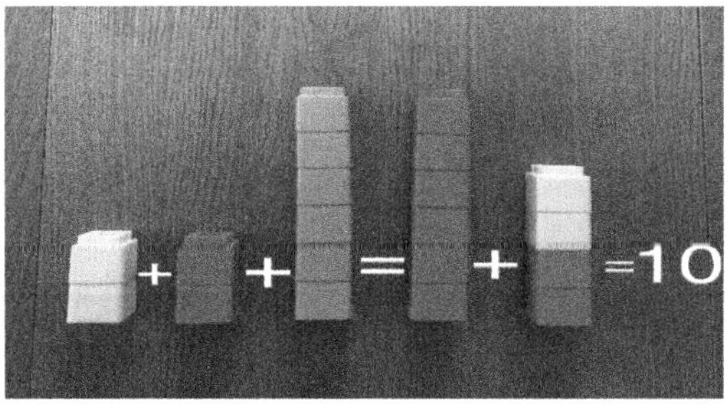

1	2	3	4	5	6	7	8	9	10

Ten Frame

Picture

Checking for Understanding	**Teacher:** Ok. How would that look? $4 + 2 + 3 = 4 + 5$ 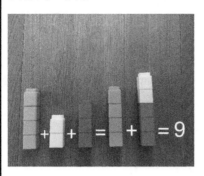 **Teacher:** What do you notice? Is it the same amount? **Tracie:** It's 9. **Sean:** We could use counters. **Teacher:** Yes. It is 9. So we could say that $4 + 2 + 3$ is the same as $4 + 5$. Let's look at another one. Is $6 + 4 + 2$ the same as $6 + 6$? **Teacher:** Ok Let's build it with the cubes again? 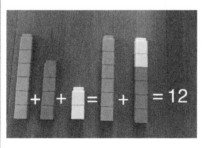 **Teacher:** What do you see? What could we group together to make an easier problem? **Carl:** $4 + 2$ makes 6. 6 and 6 make 12. **Teacher:** Ok. **Teacher:** What do you notice? **Tim:** It's the same again. **Teacher:** Ok, now I am going to give each one of you a card and I want you to model your fact and then talk about it. (*Teachers passes out the problems.*)

Figure 6.20 Student Activity

Student Activity

Guided Practice/ Checking for Understanding	Students go around the table and each of them tells how they modeled their problem.

Student A: Student gets the card and models it however they choose.

2 + 1 + 1 = 2 + 2

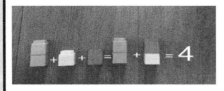

Student B: Student gets a card:

3 + 5 + 2 = 5 + 5

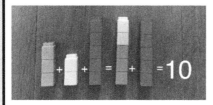

Students do lots of explorations of the problems using cubes. The teacher asks several questions about combining the numbers and why they are doing that.
Teacher: Juan why did you combine the 1 and the 1?
Juan: Because it makes 2 and then 2 and 2 make 4.
Teacher: Melissa, why did you combine the 3 and 2?
Melissa: Because instead of having all those numbers, I made two numbers. 3 and 2 make 5 and 5 and 5 make 10. So it's easier.

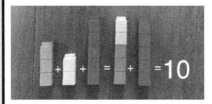 |
| **Set Up for Independent Practice** | *After several problems, the teacher wraps up the lesson and asks the students to explain the math they have been working on and why it is important. Also, she asks if it is easy or tricky. Finally, she dismisses them to work on their menus.* |

Figure 6.21 Lesson Close

Close
◆ What did we do today? ◆ What was the math we were practicing? ◆ What are ways we were modeling our thinking? ◆ Was this easy or tricky? ◆ Turn to a partner and state one thing you learned today.

Pictorial Lesson

Figure 6.22 Pictorial Introduction

<table>
<tr>
<td colspan="2" align="center"><h2>Introduction</h2></td>
</tr>
<tr>
<td>Launch</td>
<td>

Teacher: Today we are going to continue to work on proving that the order of the addends doesn't matter. What did you look at last time?

Students should talk about what they did last time.

Vocabulary: addends, grouping numbers, sum, total, equals, same as

Math Talk:

I added _____ and _____.
I grouped _____ and _____ together first and then I got _____.

</td>
</tr>
<tr>
<td>Model</td>
<td>

Teacher: Today we are going to record our thinking with sketches.

Step 1: Watch what I do. Here is my problem: 5 + 4 + 1 = 5 + 5

Teacher: Now, what do you notice?

Lucy: They are the same amount.

Teacher: How do we know?

Lucy: Because it's the same.

Teacher: We need to count to make sure. Let's add: 5 + 4 + 1 is what?

Tom: 10.

Teacher: Ok, what is 5 + 5?

Kate: 10.

Teacher: Interesting . . . so they are the same. Which numbers did you add together and why?

Tom: You add 4 and 1 and that makes 5 and then you add 5 and 5 and that makes 10.

</td>
</tr>
<tr>
<td>Checking for Understanding</td>
<td>

Teacher: Yes. Did you notice how I drew a picture to model my thinking? We can do it by drawing. Ok, now you all are going to try it. I am going to pass around a problem to each person and you will model it and then share your thinking.

</td>
</tr>
</table>

Figure 6.23 Student Activity

	Student Activity
Guided Practice/ Checking for Understanding	**Kate:** I had 3 + 4 + 1 and I proved that it is the same as 4 + 4. It is 8 circles on both sides. **3 + 4 + 1 = 4 + 4** Are they the same amount? Is 3 + 4 + 1 the same as 4 + 4? Yes or No **Teacher:** Yes. This is a great. I have one more question. What is a strategy for adding 3 + 4 + 1? **Maria:** That's easy. 3 + 1 is 4 and then 4 and 4 is 8. So you are doing a plus 1 fact and then doubles. **Teacher:** This is brilliant thinking! Who's next?
Set Up for Independent Practice	*Students go around and everyone shows their work and shares their thinking. Then the teacher facilitates a recap of what was done, discusses how students are experiencing the math, and then releases them to workstations.*

Figure 6.24 Lesson Close

Close

♦ What did we do today?
♦ What was the math we were practicing?
♦ Was this easy or tricky?
♦ Turn to a partner and state one thing you learned today.

Figure 6.25 Cards

Prove that: $$2 + 3 + 1 = 3 + 3$$ Are they the same amount? Yes or No	Prove that: $$2 + 4 + 2 = 4 + 4$$ Are they the same amount? Yes or No
Prove that: $$2 + 5 + 3 = 5 + 5$$ Are they the same amount? Yes or No	Prove that: $$2 + 2 + 6 = 6 + 4$$ Are they the same amount? Yes or No
Prove that: $$2 + 7 + 1 = 7 + 3$$ Are they the same amount? Yes or No	Prove that: $$1 + 1 + 8 = 8 + 2$$ Are they the same amount? Yes or No
Prove that: $$1 + 6 + 3 = 1 + 9$$ Are they the same amount? Yes or No	Prove that: $$1 + 4 + 4 = 8 + 1$$ Are they the same amount? Yes or No
Prove that: $$1 + 1 + 3 = 2 + 3$$ Are they the same amount? Yes or No	Prove that: $$3 + 3 + 6 = 6 + 6$$ Are they the same amount? Yes or No
Prove that: $$6 + 1 + 7 = 7 + 7$$ Are they the same amount? Yes or No	Prove that: $$1 + 9 + 2 = 10 + 2$$ Are they the same amount? Yes or No

Abstract Lesson

Figure 6.26 Abstract Introduction

	Introduction
Launch	**Teacher:** Today we are going to continue to work on grouping facts. We are going to play a card game. Let's review our vocabulary and our anchor chart. **Vocabulary:** grouping, addend, sum, total Anchor Chart Grouping Facts <table><tr><td>$2 + 3 + 2$</td><td>$6 + 2 + 2$</td></tr><tr><td>$4 + 3$</td><td>$6 + 4$</td></tr><tr><td>7</td><td>10</td></tr></table> Who wants to talk about our vocabulary? **Sara:** Grouping is like $2 + 3 + 2$ when you put 2 and 2 to make 4 and then add 3. **David:** Sum and total are the answer. **Mike:** Addend is one of the numbers you are adding.
Model	**Teacher:** Ok and here in our anchor chart we can see some examples. Today we are going to play a concentration game. You are going to work in a group of two or three and you are going to lay your cards in an array and then look for the matches that are the "grouping" facts. So, you if you turn over $1 + 5 + 2$ then you will be looking for $5 + 3$. Any questions? The winner is the person with the most matches when all the cards are gone. Ok, let's start. (*Teacher passes out card decks to each group and students start to play.*) <table><tr><td>$2 + 7 + 1$</td><td></td><td></td><td></td><td></td></tr><tr><td></td><td></td><td></td><td></td><td>$7 + 3$</td></tr></table> <table><tr><td>$1 + 8 + 1$</td><td>$2 + 8$</td></tr></table>
Checking for Under-standing	**Teacher:** Does everybody understand how to play? Give me a thumbs up if yes, a thumbs down if no, and a thumb sideways if you are not sure.

Figure 6.27 Student Activity

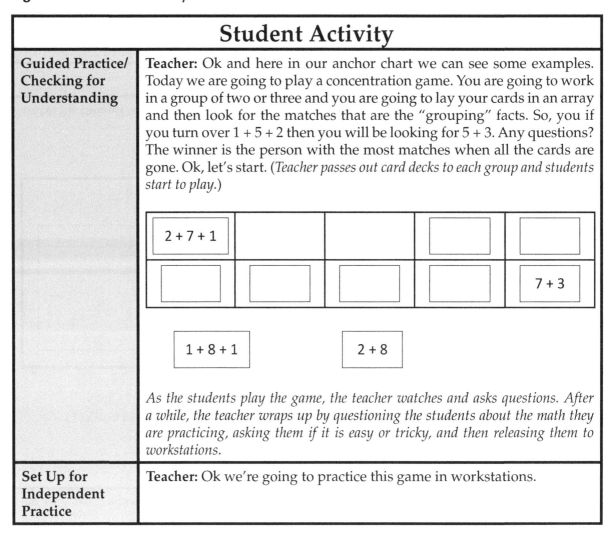

Guided Practice/ Checking for Understanding	**Teacher:** Ok and here in our anchor chart we can see some examples. Today we are going to play a concentration game. You are going to work in a group of two or three and you are going to lay your cards in an array and then look for the matches that are the "grouping" facts. So, you if you turn over 1 + 5 + 2 then you will be looking for 5 + 3. Any questions? The winner is the person with the most matches when all the cards are gone. Ok, let's start. *(Teacher passes out card decks to each group and students start to play.)*
	2 + 7 + 1 ▢ ▢ ▢ ▢ ▢ ▢ ▢ ▢ 7 + 3 1 + 8 + 1 ▢ 2 + 8
	As the students play the game, the teacher watches and asks questions. After a while, the teacher wraps up by questioning the students about the math they are practicing, asking them if it is easy or tricky, and then releasing them to workstations.
Set Up for Independent Practice	**Teacher:** Ok we're going to practice this game in workstations.

Figure 6.28 Lesson Close

Close

♦ What did we do today?
♦ What was the math we were practicing?
♦ Was this easy or tricky?
♦ Turn to a partner and state one thing you learned today.

Figure 6.29 Cards

1 + 2 + 1	2 + 2	3 + 2 + 2	3 + 4
4 + 5 + 5	10 + 4	6 + 3 + 1	6 + 4
3 + 5 + 2	5 + 5	2 + 6 + 2	6 + 4
5 + 2 + 1	2 + 5 + 5	1 + 9 + 5	3 + 3 + 4
5 + 3	10 + 2	10 + 5	6 + 4
4 + 3 + 4	8 + 3	2 + 2 + 4	4 + 4
5 + 5 + 1	10 + 1	2 + 3 + 1	3 + 3

Section Summary

Associative property is one of the other building blocks of fluency. It is part of teaching students to be flexible and efficient. We want students to be on friendly terms with numbers and to be comfortable with moving them around to make easier problems. This lays the crucial foundation for working with multidigit numbers and doing mental math. If students understand that 4 + 3 + 6 makes 10 + 3 then when they have 24 + 36 they can pull a 10 and add 20 + 30 + 10. So, teach this concept throughout the year, with energizers and routines as well as ongoing work in the math workstations.

Missing Number

Overview

Figure 6.30 Overview

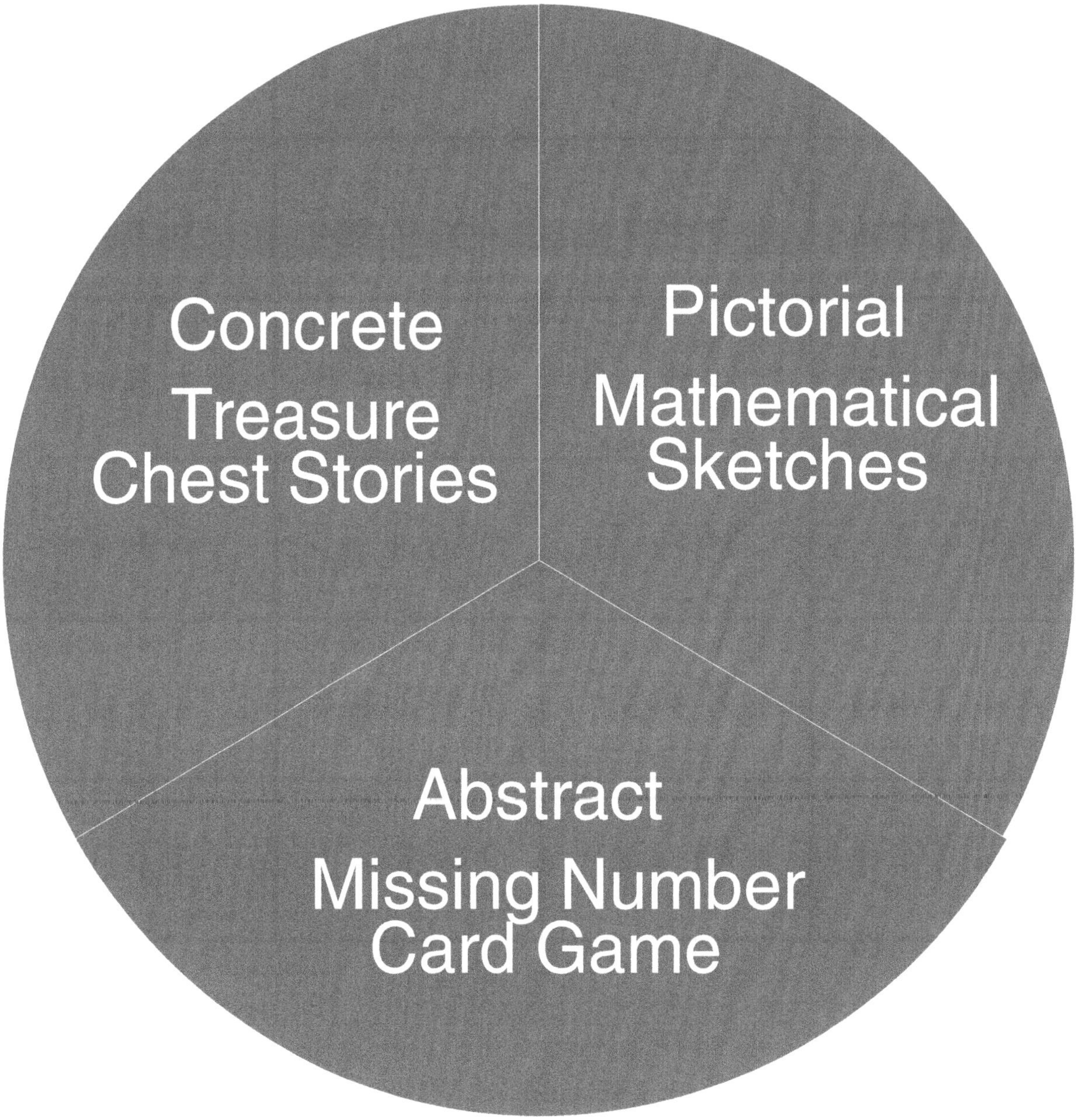

Figure 6.31 Planning Template

Missing Numbers

Big Idea: There are problems where you know some of the parts but not the others.

Enduring Understanding: We can find the missing parts in different ways.

Essential Question: How do we find the missing numbers?

I can statement: I can find missing numbers in equations.

Materials
- Tools: Cubes
- Templates: Ten Frame
- Cards
- Crayons

Missing number problems are notoriously difficult for students. You should start by working with counters and then do drawings and stickers, and then have them use number lines and eventually their mental number line.

Cycle of Engagement

Concrete:

$$4 + ? = 7$$

Pictorial:

Draw It to Prove It!

Abstract:

$$4 + ? = 7$$

Count up from 4 or Count back from 7

Questions
- Why would we combine numbers?
- Does this always work?
- Can you prove your thinking?
- Are you sure about your answer?
- Is it true?
- Can you defend it?

Vocabulary & Language Frames
- Group
- Addends
- Sum
- Missing Numbers

___ and ___ and ___ make _____

The sum of ___ and ____ and ____ is _____.

Figure 6.32 Differentiation

Three Differentiated Lessons		
In this series of lessons, students are working on missing number problems. They are developing this concept through concrete activities, pictorial activities, and abstract activities. Everybody should do the cycle. Some students progress through it more quickly than others. Here are some things to think about as you do these lessons.		
Emerging	**On Grade Level**	**Above Grade Level**
Review adding. As you introduce this to students, do a lot of acting the problems out with actual students, and also work with manipulatives so students can see the idea. Have the students then draw what they act out and connect it to the abstract problems.	The grade-level standard is that students can model it and explain it. So do lots of this work where students are modeling it and explaining it. Also show and talk about error patterns.	Once they have the concept, play lots of abstract games, including card games, board games, and dice games.

 Looking for Misunderstandings and Common Errors

Students have trouble understanding the missing number concept. For example: $4 + 2 = 5 + ?$ Many students will say 6. They see the missing number as the answer to the first part of the equation. So, students should start by building this out concretely with manipulatives and explaining the equal sign as meaning *the same as*.

Concrete Lesson

Figure 6.33 Concrete Introduction

	Introduction
Launch	**Teacher:** Today we are going to talk about "missing numbers." **Vocabulary:** addends, missing numbers, sum, total, equals, same as **Math Talk:** The missing number is _____ and _____ is the same as _____.
Model	**Teacher:** How might we find missing numbers in a number sentence (equation)? Think about how we can prove things. Here is our anchor chart of ways we prove things. I can prove my thinking with: Counters ⬤ ⬤ ⬤ Number Path | 1 | 2 | 3 | 4 | 5 | 6 | 7 | 8 | 9 | 10 | Ten Frame Picture **Teacher:** Let's look at this problem. The mermaid had 5 jewels. An octopus swam by and took some. Now there are only 3 left. How many did the octopus take? ⬤ ⬤ ⬤

	Tracie: 2. ⚫ ⚫
	Teacher: How do you know?
	Tracie: Because 3 plus 2 is 5.
	Teacher: Ok let's see. If we have 5 jewels and we take away 2 we have 3. Ok, here is another problem . . . The mermaid had 10 jewels and the octopus swam by and took some. Now she only has 2 left. How many did the octopus take?
	Carl: 8 because 8 and 2 make 10.
Checking for Understanding	**Teacher:** Ok. I like the way that you all are using your number sense. You are thinking about the numbers. Let's see. The mermaid had 8 jewels, the octopus swam by and took some. Now there are only 4 left. How many did the octopus take?
	Terri: 4 because 4 and 4 make 8.
	Teacher: Ok, now I am going to give each of you some jewels so that you can tell a story.

Figure 6.34 Student Activity

Student Activity	
Guided Practice/ Checking for Understanding	Students go around the table and each of them tells and models a word problem with a missing addend. **Verna:** There was a mermaid. She had 4 jewels. The whale came and took some. Now she only has 1 left. How many did he take? **Teacher:** Verna, what does the number sentence look like for your story? What does the 4 represent? What does the question mark tell us? How many were left? What was your strategy for solving that problem? **Verna:** $4 - ? = 1$. He took 3 away. So I have 4 and then what he took away, and the 1 is what is left. **Teacher:** Who wants to tell another story? **Todd:** There was a pirate that had 5 jewels. The octopus came by and took 5. Now he has none left. How many did the octopus take? **Teacher:** Todd what does the number sentence look like for your story? What does the 5 represent? What does the question mark tell us? How many were left? What was your strategy for solving that problem? **Todd:** $5 - 5 = 0$. There were 5 and all 5 went away. So, there are 0 left. 5 take away 5 is zero.
Set Up for Independent Practice	*Everybody gets a chance to solve word problems and explain their thinking. At the end, the teacher wraps up by asking the students what math they have been learning today and if they think it was easy or tricky. Then, the teacher dismisses everyone to their workstation activities.*

Figure 6.35 Lesson Close

Close
♦ What did we do today? ♦ What was the math we were practicing? ♦ What are ways we were modeling our thinking? ♦ Was this easy or tricky? ♦ Turn to a partner and state one thing you learned today.

Pictorial Lesson

Figure 6.36 Pictorial Introduction

	Introduction
Launch	**Teacher:** Today we are going to continue to work on finding the missing number. *Students should talk about what they did last time.* **Vocabulary:** addends, missing numbers, sum, total, equals, same as **Math Talk:** The missing number is ____ and _____ is the same as _____.
Model	**Teacher:** Today we are going to record our thinking with sketches. $$5 - ? = 4$$ **Teacher:** How could we solve this problem with math sketches? **Lucy:** I know the answer, it is 1! **Teacher:** How do we know? **Lucy:** Because if you have 5 and you take away 1 you get 4. **Teacher:** Ok, I want you all to prove it with a picture. What would that look like? **Tom:** I could draw 5 and then cross out until there are 4 left. Like this: ○ ○ ○ ○ ⊘ **Teacher: Interesting . . . so can someone explain what Tom just did?** **Sylvia:** He drew 5 circles and crossed out 1 because there are 4 left.
Checking for Understanding	**Teacher:** Yes. Did you notice how he drew a picture to model his thinking? We can do it by drawing. Ok, now you all are going to try it. I am going to pass around a problem to each person and you will model it and then share your thinking.

Figure 6.37 Student Activity

Student Activity	
Introduction	
Guided Practice/ Checking for Understanding	**Kate:** I had 8 − ? = 5. $$8 - ? = 5$$ O O O o o ∅ ∅ ∅ How many did you draw? How many did you cross out? What is the missing addend? **Teacher:** Yes. This is a great. I have one more question. What is a strategy for solving this problem? **Maria:** You could count back. **Teacher:** This is brilliant thinking! How does that sound? Show us. **Maria:** 8 − 7, 6, 5 so the answer is 3 you have to count back 3.
Set Up for Independent Practice	*Students go around and everyone shows their work and shares their thinking. At the end, the teacher wraps up by asking the students what math they have been learning today and if they think it was easy or tricky. Then, the teacher dismisses everyone to their workstation activities.*

Figure 6.38 Lesson Close

Close
♦ What did we do today? ♦ What was the math we were practicing? ♦ Was this easy or tricky? ♦ Turn to a partner and state one thing you learned today.

Figure 6.39 Cards

Find the Missing Number $$7 - ? = 2$$ How many did you draw? How many did you cross out? What is the missing addend?	Missing Number $$8 - ? = 4$$ How many did you draw? How many did you cross out? What is the missing addend?
Find the Missing Number $$10 - ? = 5$$ How many did you draw? How many did you cross out? What is the missing addend?	Find the Missing Number $$4 - ? = 1$$ How many did you draw? How many did you cross out? What is the missing addend?
Find the Missing Number $$5 - ? = 1$$ How many did you draw? How many did you cross out? What is the missing addend?	Find the Missing Number $$6 - ? = 3$$ How many did you draw? How many did you cross out? What is the missing addend?

Abstract Lesson

Figure 6.40 Abstract Introduction

	Introduction
Launch	**Teacher:** Today we are going to continue to work on missing numbers. It is Missing Number Kaboom! It is like regular Kaboom/Kabang, but with missing numbers. On each card is a missing number problem. We have a cup that has a variety of missing number problems. You and your partner take turns pulling a card. You get to keep the card if you get the answer correct. If you pull Kaboom, you have to put all your cards back in the cup. Mix them up. But, if you get a Kabang, you get to choose 3 cards and solve them. After each person has had 10 turns, the game is over. Whoever has the most cards wins! **Vocabulary:** missing number, addend, sum, total **Math Talk:** The missing number is _____ and _____ is the same as _____.
Model	**Teacher:** Here are examples of the Kaboom/Kabang cards. $7 - ? = 2$ Kaboom! Kabang!
Checking for Understanding	Is everybody ready? Any questions?

Figure 6.41 Student Activity

	Student Activity
Guided Practice/ Checking for Understanding	Students play the game with a partner. The teacher watches, comments, and asks questions. **Teacher:** Katie what did you pick? **Katie:** I have 8 – ? = 3. I know that I can count back or up. I counted up from 3 to 8. The answer is 5. **Teacher:** Herb, how did you solve that? **Herb:** I counted back. I went 8 – 7, 6, 5, 4, 3. The answer is 5.
Set Up for Independent Practice	**Teacher:** What did we do today? Give me an example. **Mike:** We worked on finding missing numbers. **Teacher:** So the math was finding missing numbers and the activity was Kaboom/Kabang! Tell me more about finding missing numbers. Is that easy, tricky, or somewhere in between? **Kate:** I think sometimes it's easy but sometimes it's tricky. **Don:** Counting up is easier. **Gerard:** Counting back is kinda tricky. **Teacher:** Okay, we are going to keep working on this more in our workstations and talking about it in whole group as well. You all can go and keep working on your menus. *At the end, the teacher wraps up by asking the students what math they have been learning today and if they think it was easy or tricky. Then, the teacher dismisses everyone to their workstation activities.*

Figure 6.42 Lesson Close

Close
◆ What did we do today? ◆ What was the math we were practicing? ◆ Was this easy or tricky? ◆ Turn to a partner and state one thing you learned today.

Figure 6.43 Cards

$7 - ? = 3$	$7 - ? = 2$	$3 - ? = 2$	$3 - ? = 1$
$8 - ? = 4$	$8 - ? = 5$	$2 - ? = 2$	$1 - ? = 0$
$9 - ? = 8$	$9 - ? = 5$	$10 - ? = 2$	$10 - ? = 7$
$5 - ? = 3$	$5 - ? = 0$	$5 - ? = 5$	$6 - ? = 5$
$6 - ? = 3$	$6 - ? = 2$	$4 - ? = 4$	$4 - ? = 2$

Section Summary

This is such a tricky concept for students. You have to spend a lot of time having students act it out and explain their thinking. Even when they are working with the number path and number line, have them explain what they are doing and why. Of course, eventually you want students to be able to look at it and compute it mentally.

Overview

Figure 6.44 Overview

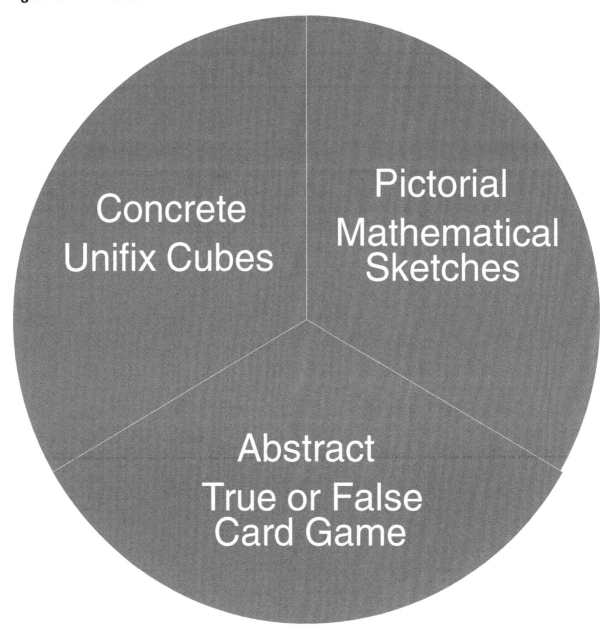

Figure 6.45 Overview

Equal Sign	
Big Idea: The equal sign means "the same as." **Enduring Understanding:** Students will understand that both sides of the equal sign should be the same amount. **Essential Question:** How do we determine if equations are true or false? **I can statement:** I can determine if equations are true or false.	**Materials** ♦ Tools: Cubes ♦ Templates: Ten Frame ♦ Cards ♦ Crayons
Vocabulary & Language Frames 1. Group 2. Addends 3. Sum 4. True 5. False 6. Same _____ is the same as _____. These are equal. These are not equal.	**Cycle of Engagement** **Concrete** **3 + 1** **1 + 3** is the same as **Pictorial** Draw it to Prove it! $4 + 4 = 5 + ?$ **Abstract** <table><tr><th>True</th><th>False</th></tr><tr><td>$2 + 1 = 3 + 0$</td><td>$5 + 2 = 4 + 5$</td></tr></table>

Figure 6.46 Differentiation

Three Differentiated Lessons

In this series of lessons, students are working on the concept of the equal sign as meaning *is the same as*. They are developing this concept through concrete activities, pictorial activities, and abstract activities. Everybody should do the cycle. Some students progress through it more quickly than others. Here are some things to think about as you do these lessons.

Emerging	On Grade Level	Above Grade Level
Review adding. As you introduce this to students, do a lot of work by acting it out and then doing it with manipulatives. Be sure to have students draw what they acted out and connect it to number models.	The grade-level standard is that students can model it and explain it. So do lots of this work where students are modeling it and explaining it. Also show and talk about errors.	Once they have the concept, play lots of abstract games, including card games, board games, and dice games.

 Looking for Misunderstandings and Common Errors

It is important to do many different explorations with the equal sign. You want students to be able to reason about numbers and not just give instant answers from what they visually see. They should always be asked to explain their thinking, defend their answer with numbers, words, and pictures, and prove their thinking. Students have so much trouble with the equal sign. They often just think it means to put the answer. In this series of lessons, the focus is on students unpacking the equations to prove that they are equal or not equal.

Concrete Lesson

Figure 6.47 Concrete Introduction

	Introduction
Launch	**Teacher:** Today we are going to talk about the equal sign and how equations (number sentences) can be true or false. **Vocabulary:** addends, sum, true, false, same as _____ is the same as _____. **Teacher:** How might we figure that out? Think about how we can prove things. Here is our anchor chart of some ways we can prove things. I can prove my thinking with: Counters Number Path $\begin{array}{\|c\|c\|c\|c\|c\|c\|c\|c\|c\|c\|} \hline 1 & 2 & 3 & 4 & 5 & 6 & 7 & 8 & 9 & 10 \\ \hline \end{array}$ Ten Frame Picture $2 + 2 = 3 + 1$

Model	**Teacher:** Let's look at this problem. Is it true or false? How can I figure it out?
	Tracie: We could use counters.
	Teacher: Show me how.
	Tracie: . . . so 2 and 2 make 4 and 3 and 1 make 4 so it is true.
	● ● ● ● ● ● ● ●
	Teacher: Who agrees? Why? Can you prove it another way?
	Mike: I can use the rekenrek.
	Teacher: Ok, so we all agree that one is true. Let's look at another one. Who wants to prove it?
	$3 + 2 = 4 + 1$
	Dan: I can prove it on my fingers. See 3 and 2 make 5 and 4 and 1 make 5. So, it is true.
	Kelly: I can prove it on my ten frame. See, 3 and 2 make 5 and 4 and 1 make 5. It's true.
Checking for Understanding	**Teacher:** Ok, now I am going to give each of you some problems so that you can solve them.

Figure 6.48 Student Activity

	Student Activity
Guided Practice/ Checking for Understanding	Students go around the table and each of them models their equation and has to prove if it is true or false. They get to choose which tool they will use to justify their thinking. **Verna:** I have $\boxed{5 + 2 = 3 + 4}$ I used the rekenrek. It is true. **Todd:** I have $\boxed{4 + 3 = 7 + 1}$ I did it with the double ten frame. I used the yellow counters on the top and the red counters on the bottom. It is not true.
Set Up for Independent Practice	**Teacher:** We have been looking at how we find out if an equation is true or false. We have practiced how you can prove it with tools and templates. *At the end, the teacher wraps up by asking the students what math they have been learning today and if they think it was easy or tricky. Then, the teacher dismisses everyone to their workstation activities*

Figure 6.49 Lesson Close

Close
◆ What did we do today? ◆ What was the math we were practicing? ◆ What are ways we were modeling our thinking? ◆ Was this easy or tricky? ◆ Turn to a partner and state one thing you learned today.

Pictorial Lesson

Figure 6.50 Pictorial Introduction

Introduction	
Launch	**Teacher:** Today we are going to continue to work with the equal sign and finding out if an equation is true or false.(*Students should talk about what they did last time.*)
Model	**Teacher:** Today we are going to record our thinking with sketches. $$5 + 2 = 3 + 4$$ **Teacher:** How could we solve this problem with math sketches? **Lucy:** I know the answer, we can draw. It is true! **Teacher:** How do we know? **Lucy:** Because they both make 7 **Teacher:** I have a question. How could you determine the sum on both sides? What was your strategy? Like what could you do with the numbers, besides having to count them all? **Sylvia:** I could count up from 5, 6, 7 and then 4–5, 6, 7.
Checking for Understanding	**Teacher:** Yes. So, you used a count up strategy. Did you notice how we can draw a picture to model our thinking? We can do it by drawing. But then, we can use our strategies to think about the numbers. I am going to pass around a problem to each person and you will model it with a sketch and then share your thinking.

Figure 6.51 Student Activity

Student Activity	
Introduction	
Guided Practice/ Checking for Understanding	**Kate:** I had $7 + 2 = 9 - 0$. How many did you draw? Did you get the same amount in both drawings? Is the equation true or false? **Teacher:** What is your strategy for solving the problems? **Maria:** You could count up from $7 - 8$ and 9. Then $9 - 0$ is 9, so it is true. **Teacher:** This is brilliant thinking! How does that sound to everyone?
Set Up for Independent Practice	*Students go around and everyone shows their work and shares their thinking.* *At the end, the teacher wraps up by asking the students what math they have been learning today and if they think it was easy or tricky. Then, the teacher dismisses everyone to their workstation activities.*

Figure 6.52 Lesson Close

Close
◆ What did we do today?   ◆ What was the math we were practicing?   ◆ Was this easy or tricky?   ◆ Turn to a partner and state one thing you learned today.

Figure 6.53 True/False Cards

True or False? $8 + 2 = 3 + 7$ How many did you draw on the left side? How many did you draw on the right side? Is it the same amount? Is this equation true or false?	True or False? $7 + 1 = 8 + 0$ How many did you draw on the left side? How many did you draw on the right side? Is it the same amount? Is this equation true or false?
True or False? $2 + 1 = 4 - 0$ How many did you draw on the left side? How many did you draw on the right side? Is it the same amount? Is this equation true or false?	True or False? $4 - 3 = 1 + 0$ How many did you draw on the left side? How many did you draw on the right side? Is it the same amount? Is this equation true or false?
True or False? $4 + 4 = 10 - 2$ How many did you draw on the left side? How many did you draw on the right side? Is it the same amount? Is this equation true or false?	True or False? $6 + 3 = 9 - 1$ How many did you draw on the left side? How many did you draw on the right side? Is it the same amount? Is this equation true or false?

Abstract Lesson

Figure 6.54 Abstract Introduction

	Introduction
Launch	**Teacher:** Today we are going to work on equations and sorting them. We have worked with tools to prove our thinking. We have worked with drawings. Now, we are going to focus on using our strategies to think about the equations. **Vocabulary:** addends, sum, true, false, same as, difference **Math Talk:** _____ is the same as _____.
Model	Here is a true/false mat. You and your partner are going to get a baggie with equations. You are going to sort your problems on the mat between true or false. You have to think and talk with your partner about which ones are true and which ones are false. Can I just say, "Oh, I think this one is true . . . without finding the number on both sides? **Taylor:** No. You have to find the number on both sides first and then you can say if it is true or false. | True	False
4 + 5 = 7 + 2	7 + 3 = 7 + 1 + 1	
Checking for Understanding	*Students play the game with a partner. The teacher watches, comments, and asks questions.*

Figure 6.55 Student Activity

	Student Activity
Guided Practice/ Checking for Understanding	**Teacher:** Ok Marissa, tell me why you said the statement you are holding is true. **Marissa:** 2 + 1 = 1 + 2 because it is a turn around fact. If you turn them around, they are the same numbers. **Teacher:** Mike, tell me how you know your card is false? **Mike:** Because 4 + 1 = 1 + 5 isn't the same. 4 + 1 is 5 and 5 + 1 is 6.
Set Up for Independent Practice	*At the end, the teacher wraps up by asking the students what math they have been learning today and if they think it was easy or tricky. Then, the teacher dismisses everyone to their workstation activities.*

Figure 6.56 Lesson Close

Close
◆ What did we do today?
◆ What was the math we were practicing?
◆ Was this easy or tricky?
◆ Turn to a partner and state one thing you learned today.

Figure 6.57 True/False Cards

$7 + 1 = 8 + 0$	$7 + 1 = 8 + 0$	$7 + 1 = 8 + 0$	$7 + 1 = 8 + 0$
$8 + 1 = 7 + 0$	$4 + 1 = 5 + 0$	$10 + 0 = 5 + 5$	$7 + 1 = 8 + 0$
$9 + 1 = 8 + 2$	$9 - 5 = 8 - 4$	$4 + 1 = 6 - 1$	$3 + 1 = 4 - 0$
$5 + 1 = 6 - 0$	$6 + 2 = 2 + 6$	$2 + 1 = 3 + 2$	$1 + 9 = 10 + 0$
$6 + 1 = 1 + 6$	$5 + 2 = 8 + 0$	$3 + 1 = 8 + 0$	$5 + 1 = 8 - 2$
$5 + 3 = 6 - 0$	$6 - 3 = 3 + 6$	$2 + 2 = 8 - 4$	$9 - 9 = 0 + 0$
$6 + 3 = 7 - 2$	$5 + 3 = 8 + 0$	$8 - 4 = 2 + 2$	$1 + 1 = 8 - 6$

Figure 6.58 True/False Mat

True	False

Section Summary

Working with the equal sign is always tricky. It has to be done with hands-on activities. Students need to actually build the facts so that they can see what the math is. They should absolutely act out the problems. By this I mean students getting up and acting out 2 + 3 on one side of the equation and then 4 + 1 on the other side of the equation, and they can then see that it is the same amount of kids on each side. Once they can see it, discuss it, and explain it and then model it, draw it, and talk about the equal sign meaning *the same as*, then we know they are beginning to get it. Spend all year working on exploring this concept through energizers, routines, and workstations.

Depth of Knowledge

Depth of Knowledge (see Figure 6.59) is a framework that encourages us to ask questions that require that students think, reason, explain, defend, and justify their thinking (Webb, 2002). Here is snapshot of what that can look like in terms of place value work.

Figure 6.59 DOK Activities

	What are different strategies and models that we can use to teach missing numbers?	What are different strategies and models that we can use to teach associative property?	What are different strategies and models that we can use to teach the commutative property?	What are different strategies and models that we can use to model true or false statements?
DOK Level 1 (These are questions where students are required to simply recall/reproduce an answer/do a procedure.)	Solve ___ − 5 = 10	$2 + 4 + 2 = 4 + 4$	$2 + 3 = 3 + 2$	Sort the equations into true and false piles.
DOK Level 2 (These are questions where students have to use information, think about concepts, and reason.) This is considered a more challenging problem than a level 1 problem.	Discuss 2 different strategies for solving 5 + ___ = 8	Fill in the missing numbers: $2 + \_ + 2 = 4 + 4$ $2 + 4 + 2 = 4 + \_$ $3 + 4 + 7 = \_ + \_$ Explain your thinking.	Fill in the missing numbers. Explain your thinking. $2 + 3 = 3 + \_$ $3 + \_ = \_ + 3$	Pick 2 equations that are false. Explain why they are false and show how to make them true.
DOK Level 3 (These are questions where students have to reason, plan, explain, justify, and defend their thinking.)	Make your own missing number equation. Solve it. Explain and justify your thinking. ___ − ___ = ___	$5 + 2 + 5 = 10 + 2$ Is this true? Defend your thinking with numbers, words, and pictures.	$2 + 3 = 3 + 2$ Is this true? Defend your thinking with numbers, words, and pictures.	Make 5 equations that are true and 5 equations that are false.

A great resource for asking open questions is Marion Small's *Good Questions: Great Ways to Differentiate Mathematics Instruction in the Standards-Based Classroom* (2017).

Also, Robert Kaplinsky has done a great job in pushing our thinking forward with the Depth of Knowledge Matrices he created. (https://robertkaplinsky.com/depth-knowledge-matrix-elementary-math/). Kentucky Math Department (2007) has these great math matrices as well.

Figure 6.60 Asking Rigorous Questions

DOK 1	DOK 2 At this level, students explain their thinking.	DOK 3 At this level, students have to justify, defend, and prove their thinking with objects, drawings, and diagrams.
What is the answer to . . . ? Can you model the number? Can you model the problem? Is it true or false?	How do you know that the equation is correct? Can you pick the correct answer and explain why it is correct? How can you model that problem? What is another way to model that problem? Can you model that on the . . . ? Give me an example of a . . . type of problem. . . . Which answer is incorrect? Explain your thinking?	Can you prove that your answer is correct? Prove that . . . Explain why that is the answer. . . . Show me how to solve that and explain what you are doing. Defend your answer.

Key Points

◆ Concrete Pictorial Abstract
◆ Commutative Property
◆ Associative Property
◆ Missing Numbers
◆ Equal Sign

Summary

When working on the big ideas of algebra in the primary grades, it is very important that students have a chance to reason about the situations and the numbers. Algebraic thinking must be developed from the beginning of school. In first grade, students are also playing around with the commutative and associative properties. These are fundamental building blocks to later algebraic work. Students must be given multiple opportunities to explore and discuss equations and their meanings with different types of manipulatives and drawings. They also are introduced to the ideas of missing numbers and how to find them using various strategies. Also, in first grade, students are exploring the relationships between addition and subtraction.

In first grade, it is essential that students get to really think about equations and the meaning of the numbers and the equal sign. Students need opportunities to talk in small groups to discuss what is happening, to think about if they understand and agree with what is being said, and also to defend their own thinking and prove their ideas with manipulatives and drawings. So, as this work is being done in small groups, teachers should focus not only on the content but also on the practices.

Reflection Questions

1. How are you currently teaching basic math fact fluency?
2. Are you making sure that you do concrete, pictorial, and abstract activities?
3. How are you currently fostering algebraic thinking with your students?
4. What do your students struggle with the most and what ideas are you taking away from this chapter that might inform your work around those struggles?

References

Common Core State Standards Initiative. (CCSSI). (2010). *Common core state standards for mathematics*. Washington, DC: National Governors Association Center for Best Practices and the Council of Chief State School Officers. Retrieved from www.corestandards.org/wp-content/uploads/Math_Standards.pdf

Greenes, C. (2004). *Algebra: It's elementary*. Retrieved from https://qrc.depaul.edu/algebrainitiative/Articles/Algebra_Elementary_Article_Carole_Greene.pdf

Hoff, D. (2001). Introduction to algebra: It's elementary. *Education Week*. Retrieved September 5, 2019 from www.edweek.org/ew/articles/2001/03/28/28algebra.h20.html

Kentucky Department of Education (2007). Support Materials for Core Content for Assessment Version 4.1 Mathematics. Retrieved from the internet on January 15th, 2017.

National Council of Teachers of Mathematics. (2000). *Principles and standards for school mathematics*. Reston, VA: National Council of Teachers of Mathematics.

Webb, N. L. (2002). *Depth-of-knowledge levels for four content areas*. Madison, WI: Wisconsin Center for Education Research. Retrieved from http://facstaff.wcer.wisc.edu/normw/All%20content%20areas%20%20DOK%20levels%2032802.doc.

7
Small-Group Word Problem Lessons

Word problems are an essential part of first grade. Students are exposed to several types of problems, strategies, and models. We want students to build on their kindergarten foundation. Problem solving should be done every day. We should work with the whole class, in small groups sometimes, and have a workstation that stays up all year long. The important part about teaching word problems is to get students to understand what is happening in the word problem. So they need to think about it, discuss it, explain it, and then work it out in a couple of ways. Remember that we must go beyond answer getting. It is about reasoning, communicating, and modeling the situations. We want students to be able to solve one way and check another way. We want students to be able to look at the answer and decide whether it makes sense. We need students to know how to persevere and keep on working with the problem when they get stuck.

Let's Look at the Research!

- ♦ Students have a tendency to "suspend sense-making" when they are solving problems. They don't stop to reason through the problem (Schoenfeld, 1991; Verschaffel, Greer, & De Corte, 2000). We must find ways to slow the process down so they can think.
- ♦ Students develop a "compulsion to calculate" (Stacey & MacGregor, 1999) that can interfere with the development of the algebraic thinking that is needed to solve word problems (cited in www.cde.state.co.us/comath/word-problems-guide).
- ♦ Research consistently states that we should never use key words. From the beginning, teach students to reason about the context, not to depend on key words. See a great blog post that cites many articles on this: https://gfletchy.com/2015/01/12/teaching-keywords-forget-about-it/

In this chapter, we will look at how to take a deep dive into these discussions with students in small groups. We will look at:

- ♦ Add to Change Unknown
- ♦ Part-Part Whole
- ♦ Take From
- ♦ Compare Difference Unknown
- ♦ 3 Read Problems
- ♦ Picture Prompts

Add to Change Unknown Word Problems

Overview

Figure 7.1 Overview

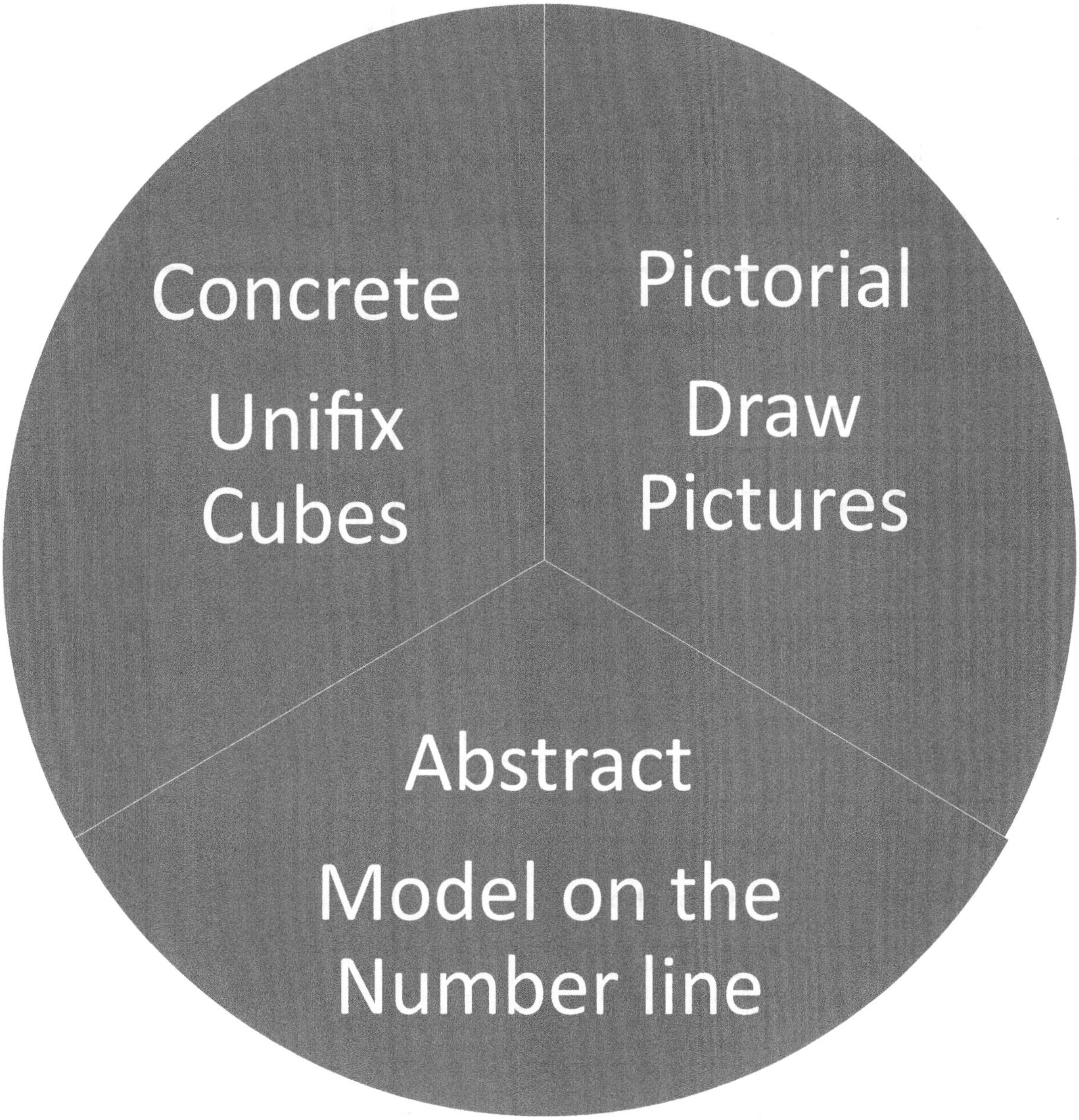

Concrete
Unifix
Cubes

Pictorial
Draw
Pictures

Abstract
Model on the
Number line

Figure 7.2 Planning Template

Add to Change Unknown Word Problems

Big Idea: There are different types of word problems. In this type, we know the start and we know the end and we are looking for the change. **Enduring Understanding:** We can model problems in many ways. **Essential Question:** What are the ways to model this type of problem? **I can statement:** I can model addition word problems where there is a change.	**Materials** ♦ Tools: Cubes ♦ Templates: Ten Frame ♦ Cards ♦ Crayons

Cycle of Engagement **Concrete: Cubes** **Pictorial: Drawing** **Abstract: Model and Solve the Problem** Sue had 5 marbles. She got some more. Now she has 10. How many did she get? Pick a model. Solve. Number Path Grid Paper Drawing Ten Frame Rekenrek	**Vocabulary & Language Frames** ♦ Count Up ♦ Count Back ♦ Addends ♦ Sum ♦ Difference _____ started with _____. _____ got some more. Now there are _____.

Questions 1. What is happening in this problem?	

Figure 7.3 Differentiation

Three Differentiated Lessons	
In this series of lessons, students are working on the concept of *add to change unknown problems*. They are developing this concept through concrete activities, pictorial activities, and abstract activities. Everybody should do the cycle. Some students progress through it more quickly than others. Here are some things to think about as you do these lessons.	

Below Grade Level	On Grade Level	Above Grade Level
Review adding. As you introduce this to students, do a lot of work by acting it out and then doing it with manipulatives. Be sure to have students draw what they acted out and connect it to number models.	The grade-level standard is that students can model it and explain it. So do lots of this work where students are modeling it and explaining it. Students should solve one way and check another.	Once they have the concept, have students work with a larger number range. Also have students work with harder problem types, such as the start unknown one.

 Looking for Misunderstandings and Common Errors

These problems are especially difficult for students because when they see an equation like 4 + ? = 9 they want to add the two numbers. So, often the error pattern is to get 13 as the answer. It is important to challenge these misconceptions by having the students start with 4 and then count up to 9. How many did it take to get there? Doing this with counters and then showing it on a number line can really help students see the math. Oftentimes we want to jump to subtraction to teach this, but it is a more difficult strategy for students to understand. Teach both ways but focus on the addition first because it is more intuitive.

Figure 7.4 Anchor Chart

Solving Add to Change Unknown Problems

Jane has 2 rings. She got some more. Now she has 5. How many did she get?

Ten Frame:

2 + ____ = 5

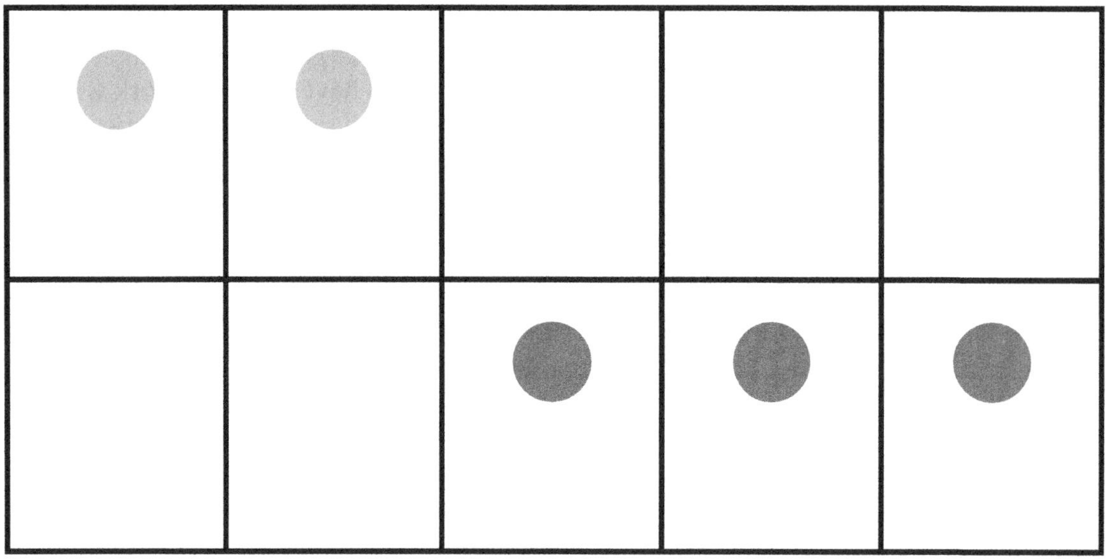

Number Path

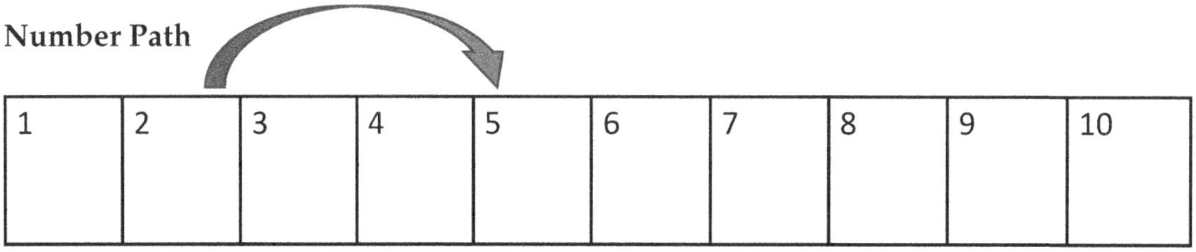

1	2	3	4	5	6	7	8	9	10

Sketch

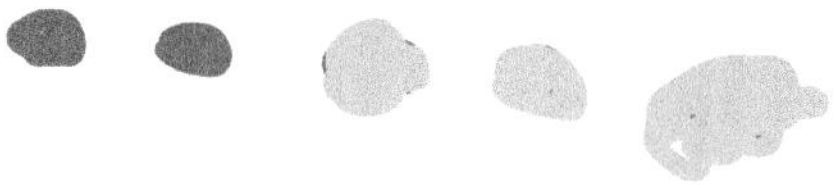

Concrete Lesson

Figure 7.5 Concrete Introduction

	Introduction
Launch	**Teacher:** Today we are going to work on solving word problems where there is a change in the middle. **Vocabulary:** add, change, word problem, count up **Math Talk:** I had _____. I got some more. Now I have _____. How many did I get?
Model	**Teacher:** Listen to the problem. *I had 4 jewels. I got some more. Now I have 5. How many did I get?* Now, who has some ideas how I could model that problem? **Jack:** You can count up. It's just one more. **Teacher:** Excellent! That is a strategy. Now, tell me how you could model that strategy? **Lucy:** We could use the counters. **Teacher:** Show me. **Lucy:** Here are 4 cubes and then 1 more makes 5. **Teacher:** This is great! So we can model it with cubes. What is another way to model that problem? **David:** The rekenrek. . . . See, I had 4 and I moved 1 more over to get 5.
Checking for Understanding	**Teacher:** Ok. I am going to give each one of you your own problem. I want you to read it. Solve it. Be ready to share how you did it. I am going to watch you, and if you need help, look at our anchor charts and of course you can ask me.

Figure 7.6 Student Activity

	Student Activity
Guided Practice/ Checking for Understanding	The teacher passes out the problems. Students pull a card and act out their problems. The students each get a chance to share their problem and explain how they solved it **Maria:** My problem is this: --- **Math Talk:** I had 3. I got some more. Now, I have 7. --- So, I used my rekenrek and I moved over 3. Then, I moved 4 more and I got 7. 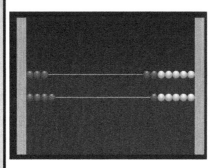 **Teacher:** Why did you move 4 more? **Maria:** Because it said I had 7. So I had to count up to 7. **Teacher:** Who agrees with her? **Hong:** I do. I just know that 3 and 4 are 7. **Teacher:** That is great! You know it automatically. I also need you to show me how you might model it. **Hong:** I could count up on the number line. I could start at 3 and then jump to 7.
Set Up for Independent Practice	**Teacher:** Does everybody see that? That even though we could know the answer because we know our facts, we still need to think about how to model our thinking. Our strategy might be counting up, or using doubles or something else, but our model shows our thinking. We are going to be talking more about that in the upcoming days. Are there any questions? What was interesting today? What was tricky?

Figure 7.7 Lesson Close

Close
◆ What did we do today?
◆ What was the math we were practicing?
◆ Was this easy or tricky?
◆ Turn to a partner and state one thing you learned today.

Figure 7.8 Change Word Problem Cards

The bakery had 2 pies. They made some more. Now they have 10. How many did they make? 2 + ___ = 10	There were 3 monkeys. Some more came. Now there are 7. How many came? 3 + ___ = 7
The bakery had 5 pies. They made some more. Now they have 7. How many did they make? 5 + ___ = 7	There were 4 monkeys. Some more came. Now there are 8. How many came? 4 + ___ = 8
The bakery had 8 pies. They made some more. Now they have 10. How many did they make? 8 + ___ = 10	There were 5 monkeys. Some more came. Now there are 10. How many came? 5 + ___ = 10
The bakery had 5 pies. They made some more. Now they have 9. How many did they make? 5 + ___ = 9	There were 9 monkeys. Some more came. Now there are 10. How many came? 9 + ___ = 10
The bakery had 0 pies. They made some. Now they have 8. How many did they make? 0 + ___ = 8	There was 1 monkey. Some more came. Now there are 7. How many came? 1 + ___ = 7

Pictorial Lesson

Figure 7.9 Pictorial Introduction

<table>
<tr>
<td colspan="2" align="center"><h2>Introduction</h2></td>
</tr>
<tr>
<td>Launch</td>
<td>

Teacher: Today we are going to work on solving word problems where there is a change in the middle.

Vocabulary: add, change, word problem, count up

Math Talk: I had _____. I got some more. Now I have _____. How many did I get?

Listen to the problem. My problem is this:

> There were 4 monkeys. Some more came. Now there are 8. How many came?
>
> $4 + \underline{\hspace{1cm}} = 8$

How could I use this paper to model my thinking?

</td>
</tr>
<tr>
<td>Model</td>
<td>

Taylor: I know the answer is 4. Because 4 plus 4 is 8.

Teacher: Great! How do you know? Remember good mathematicians can model their thinking!

Virginia: Like we do on the whiteboard. You could put 4 on the top and then draw 4 on the bottom. You just have to count how many more you need to have 8.

Teacher: So there were 4 monkeys. I am going to draw that here. And then some more came. So, at the bottom, I am going to draw how many were there at the end. And what do you see . . . ?

Taylor: We need 4. I said 4.

Teacher: Does anybody agree? (*Students say yes.*)

</td>
</tr>
<tr>
<td>Checking for Understanding</td>
<td>

Teacher: Ok. I am going to give each one of you your own problem. I want you to read it. Solve it. Be ready to share how you did it. I am going to watch you and if you need help, look at our anchor charts and of course you can ask me.

</td>
</tr>
</table>

Figure 7.10 Student Activity

	Student Activity
Guided Practice/ Checking for Understanding	The teacher passes out word problem cards. Students pull a card and model their problems. The students each get a chance to share their problem and explain how they solved it.
	Maria: My problem is this:
	There were 2 monkeys. Some more came. Now there are 5. How many came? 2 + _____ = 5
	Maria: 3 monkeys.
	Teacher: How do you know you are correct?
	Maria: Because I counted up 3 more.
	Teacher: Who agrees with her?
	Grace: I do. I counted up 3 too.
	David: 2 and 3 make 5.
	Teacher: That is great! You know it automatically. I am also glad that we can model it.
	Teacher: Does everybody see that? That even though we could know the answer because we know our facts, we still need to think about how to model our thinking. Our strategy might be counting up, or using doubles or something else, but our model shows our thinking.
Set Up for Independent Practice	*The teacher gives everybody a chance to do and discuss a problem. After everyone has shared, the lesson ends.* **Teacher:** We are going to be talking more about that in the upcoming days. Are there any questions? What was interesting today? What was tricky?

Figure 7.11 Lesson Close

Close
♦ What did we do today?   ♦ What was the math we were practicing?   ♦ Was this easy or tricky?   ♦ Turn to a partner and state one thing you learned today.

Figure 7.12 Templates

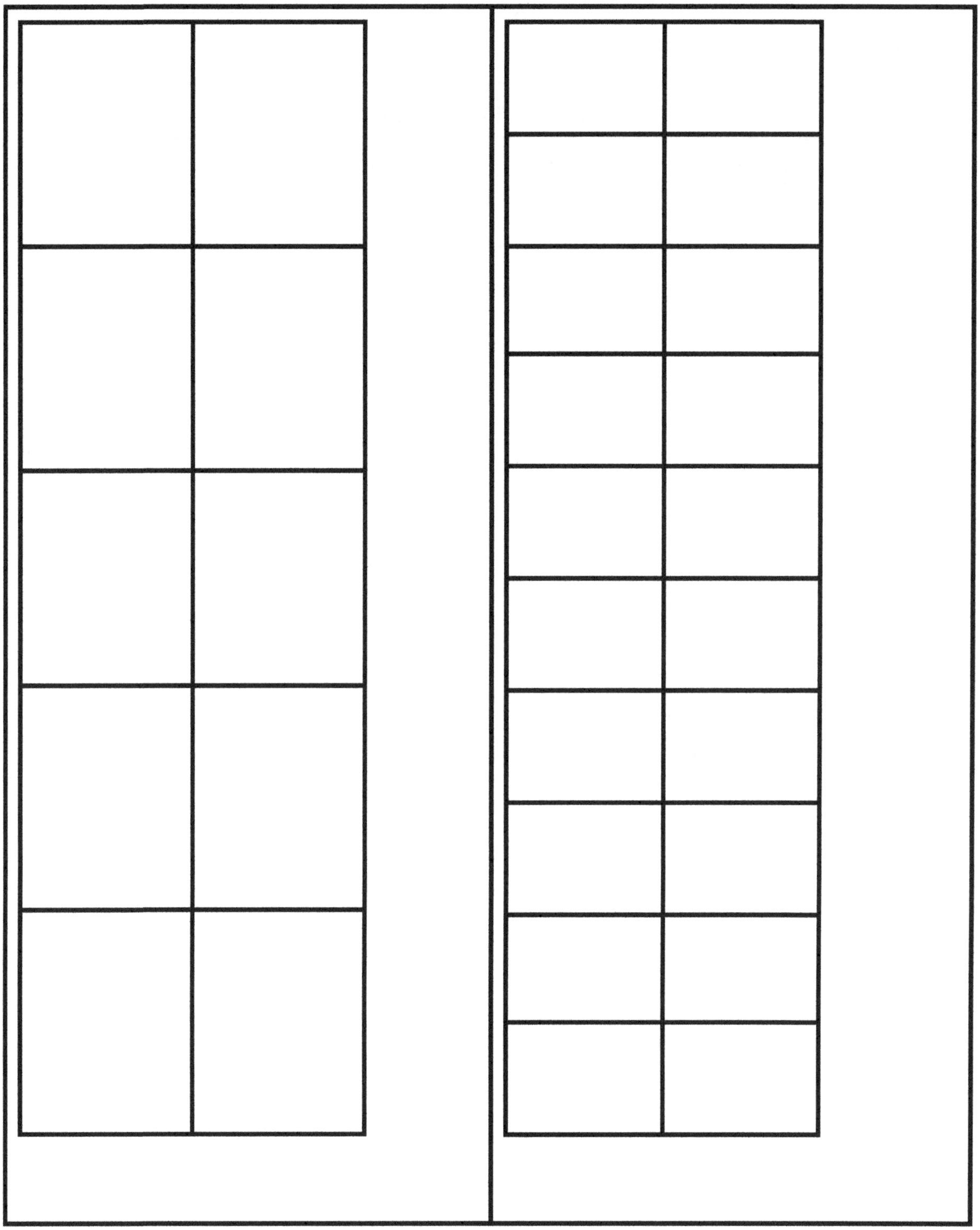

Abstract Lesson

Figure 7.13 Abstract Introduction

	Introduction
Launch	**Teacher:** Today we are going to work on solving word problems where there is a change in the middle. **Vocabulary:** add, change, word problem, count up, number sentence (equation) **Math Talk:** There were _____ _____. Some more came. Now there are ___. How many came? **Teacher:** Today, we are going to read the problem and model it on our part-part whole mats. So, I'll show you and read the problem. You all fill in your part-part whole mats. <table><tr><td colspan="2">7</td></tr><tr><td>5</td><td>?</td></tr></table> Luke had 5 marbles. He got some more. Now he has 7. How many did he get? **Teacher:** Does everybody see this model? Who can explain it?
Model	**Ted:** The 7 on top is the total. The 5 is what he had. The question mark is the missing number. **Teacher:** How do we find the missing number? **Connie:** We could count up to 7 from 5.
Checking for Understanding	**Teacher:** Yes, we could do that. Everybody get their part-part whole mats ready. I am going to read the problem and then you will illustrate it and show it to the group. We will take turns explaining our thinking. Here we go.

Figure 7.14 Student Activity

	Student Activity
Guided Practice/ Checking for Understanding	The teacher reads different problems. The children solve the problems on their part-part whole mats and show them to the group. Each time, a different student explains how they solved the problem. Teacher: There were 5 monkeys. Some more came. Now there are 10. How many came? **Josephine:** I put 10 at the top because that is the total. I put 5 because that is how many were there in the beginning. The question mark is the missing number. **Timmy:** The answer is 5 because 5 and 5 make 10. **Teacher:** Yes.
Set Up for Independent Practice	*Everybody models the problems and shows it on their part-part whole mat. Some students have the numbers in the wrong place and they erase and fix it. The teacher reminds everybody that it is ok to make mistakes because that means you are trying and when you keep trying you will get it.* **Teacher:** We are going to be talking more about that in the upcoming days. Are there any questions? What was interesting today? What was tricky? **Kelly:** I think it is tricky to know where the numbers go. **Teacher:** Yes, it can be tricky. Who can give us some ideas on how to work with the numbers? **Jamal:** You have to look at the total and that goes at the top. The other number is how many there were, so that goes in this box. The missing number always goes here. **Teacher:** Does it always go there or does it depend on the type of problem? **Jamal:** It depends on the type of problem. But in these, it always goes here. **Teacher:** Ok then. Any more comments or questions? If not, you all can go to your next station as soon as I ring the rotation bell.

Figure 7.15 Word Problem Cards Card Match Game

The bakery had 3 pies. They made some more. Now they have 10. How many did they make?	There were 4 monkeys. Some more came. Now there are 7. How many came?
The bakery had 6 pies. They made some more. Now they have 7. How many did they make?	There were 7 monkeys. Some more came. Now there are 10. How many came?
The bakery had 2 pies. They made some more. Now they have 10. How many did they make?	There were 4 monkeys. Some more came. Now there are 8. How many came?
The bakery had 5 pies. They made some more. Now they have 9. How many did they make?	There were 5 monkeys. Some more came. Now there are 10. How many came?
The bakery had 8 pies. They made some. Now they have 9. How many did they make?	There were 9 monkeys. Some more came. Now there are 10. How many came?

Figure 7.16 Lesson Close

Close
◆ What did we do today?
◆ What was the math we were practicing?
◆ Was this easy or tricky?
◆ Turn to a partner and state one thing you learned today.

Section Summary

It is important for students to be able to act out these problems in life-size templates such as five frames, ten frames, twenty frames, part-part whole mats, number bonds, and number lines. We need students to see how they can count up or count back to get to the answer. They should act this out and then do it on smaller tools. They should be explaining what they are doing as they do it.

Part-Part Whole Problems

Overview

Figure 7.17 Overview

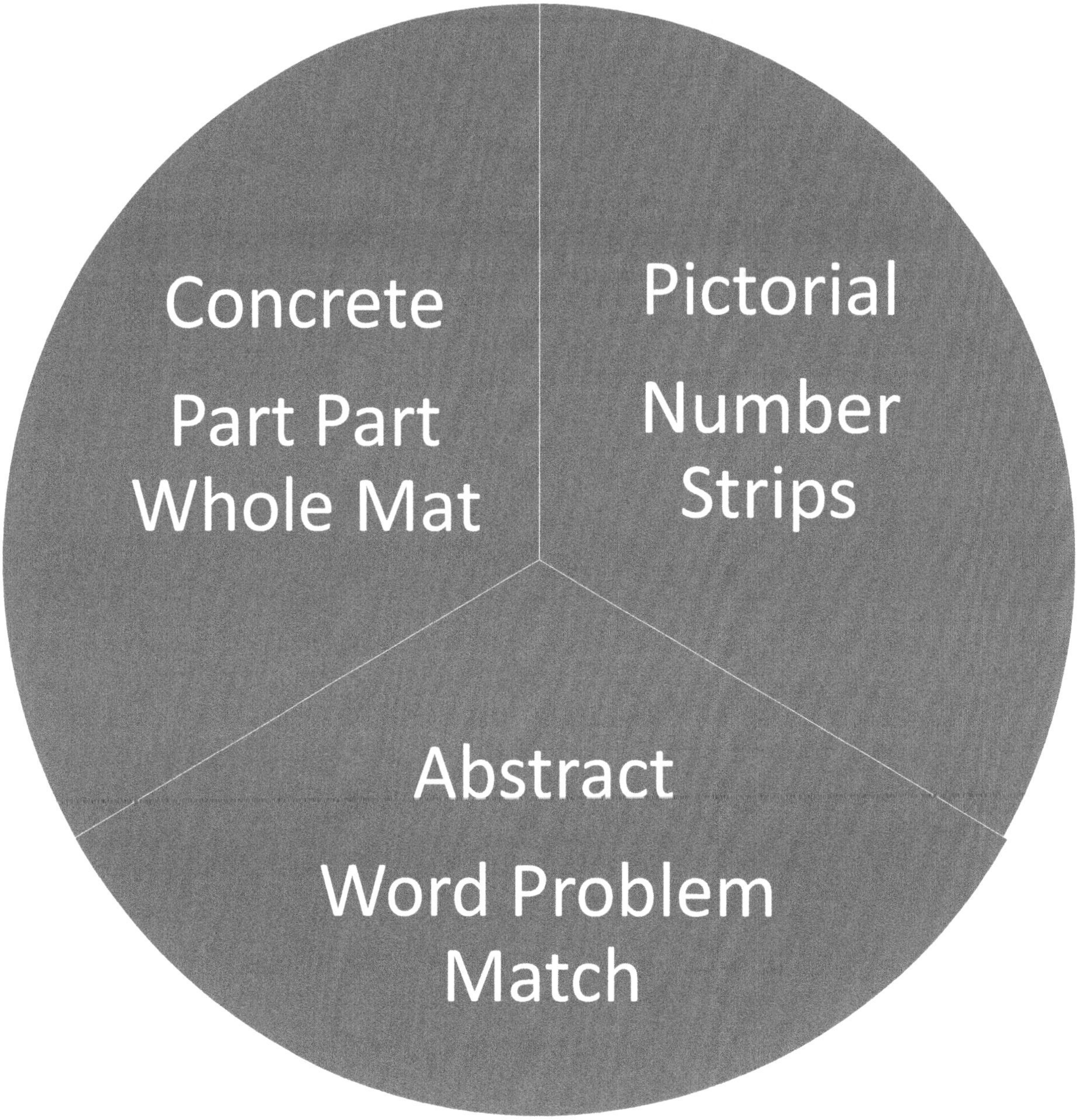

Figure 7.18 Planning Template

Part-Part Whole Problems

Big Idea: There are different types of word problems. In this type, we know one part but we don't know the other. We do know the total though.

Enduring Understanding: We can model problems in many ways.

Essential Question: What are the ways to model this type of problem?

I can statement: I can model part-part whole word problems.

Materials
♦ Tools: Cubes
♦ Templates: Ten Frame
♦ Cards
♦ Crayons

Cycle of Engagement

Concrete:

Whole	
Part	Part

Pictorial: Drawing

Abstract: Match Addends and the Sum

Vocabulary & Language Frames
♦ Count Up
♦ Count Back
♦ Addends
♦ Sum
♦ Difference
___ and ____ make _____.

Figure 7.19 Differentiation

Three Differentiated Lessons	
In this series of lessons, students are working on the concept of *part-part whole problems*. They are developing this concept through concrete activities, pictorial activities, and abstract activities. Everybody should do the cycle. Some students progress through it more quickly than others. Here are some things to think about as you do these lessons.	

Below Grade Level	On Grade Level	Above Grade Level
Review adding. As you introduce this to students, do a lot of work by acting it out and then doing it with manipulatives. Be sure to have students draw what they acted out and connect it to number models.	The grade-level standard is that students can model it and explain it. So do lots of this work where students are modeling it and explaining it. Students should solve one way and check another. They should defend their answer.	There are 15 total single step word problems. 1st graders in most states have to master 11 of them. If students have done that have them work on the other 4.

 Looking for Misunderstandings and Common Errors

Part-part whole problems are usually easy for students. Be sure to use part-part whole mats and templates. Also use number bonds. Use these templates with the manipulatives first, before you go to pictorial and abstract representations.

Figure 7.20 Anchor Chart

Solving Part-Part Whole Problems

Jane has 8 rings. Five rings are square and the rest are circles. How many are circles?

Ten Frame:
$5 + ? = 8$

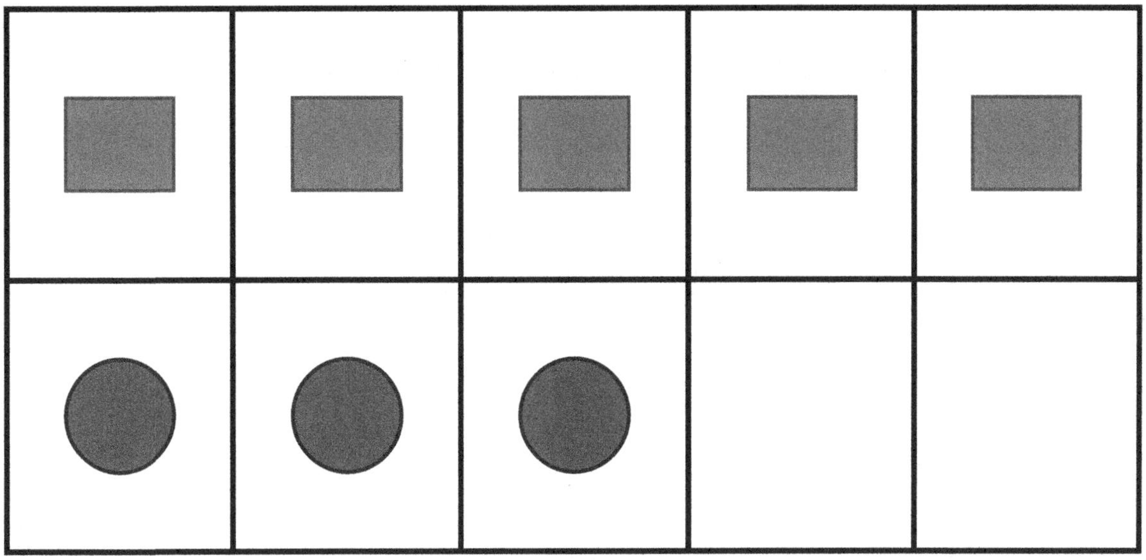

Number Path

1	2	3	4	5	6	7	8	9	10

Sketch

Concrete Lesson

Figure 7.21 Concrete Introduction

<table>
<tr>
<td colspan="2" align="center"><h2>Introduction</h2></td>
</tr>
<tr>
<td>Launch</td>
<td>Teacher: Today we are going to work on word problems. We are word problem detectives. We are going to be looking and thinking about the parts we know and don't know!

Vocabulary: part-part whole, whole, word problem, count up

Math Talk: The whole is _____. One part is _____. The other part is _____.

Listen to the problem. Jamal had 7 marbles. 5 were big and the rest were small. How many small ones does he have?</td>
</tr>
<tr>
<td>Model</td>
<td>Jack: 7

Teacher: Well, he has 7 marbles in all. What are we looking for?

Lucy: The small ones.

Teacher: Let's put our information in our part-part whole mat. (Teacher uses magnetic counters on the mat on the board.)

<table>
<tr><td colspan="2" align="center">Whole
7</td></tr>
<tr><td>Part
5 ●●
● ●
● ●</td><td>Part
?</td></tr>
</table>

Teacher: So what do we see?

David: We see the 5 and we can count 6, 7. We need 2 more.
The teacher reads two more problems that the group discusses.</td>
</tr>
<tr>
<td>Checking for Understanding</td>
<td>Teacher: Ok. I am going to give each one of you your own problem. I want you to read it. Solve it. Be ready to share how you did it. I am going to watch you and if you need help, look at our anchor charts and of course you can ask me.</td>
</tr>
</table>

Figure 7.22 Student Activity

	Student Activity
Guided Practice/ Checking for Understanding	The teacher passes out the problems. Students pull a card and act out their problems. The students each get a chance to share their problem and explain how they solved it. **Timmy:** My problem is this: > **Math Talk:** There were 5 marbles. 2 were red. The rest were yellow. So, I used my part-part whole mat and I saw 2 here and I counted up to 5. 3 were yellow. **Teacher:** Are you sure that is the way to do it? **Timmy:** Yes. See, 3, 4, 5. I counted up to 5 so that is 3 more. And 2 and 3 make 5.
Set Up for Independent Practice	**Teacher:** That is great! Who wants to go next? **Hong:** My problem said, "Jane had 8 marbles. 4 were red and the rest were yellow. How many were yellow?" That's easy because 4 and 4 make 8. *Every child shares out their problem and how they solved it on the part-part whole mat.* **Teacher:** We are going to be talking more about that in the upcoming days. Are there any questions? What was interesting today? What was tricky?

Figure 7.23 Lesson Close

Close
♦ What did we do today? ♦ What was the math we were practicing? ♦ Was this easy or tricky? ♦ Turn to a partner and state one thing you learned today.

Figure 7.24 Part-Part Whole Cards

There are 8 counters. 5 are red and the rest are yellow. How many are yellow?	There are 9 counters. 2 are red and the rest are yellow. How many are yellow?
Whole 8 Part 5 / Part ?	Whole 9 Part 2 / Part ?
There are 7 counters. 5 are red and the rest are yellow. How many are yellow?	There are 10 counters. 5 are red and the rest are yellow. How many are yellow?
Whole 7 Part 5 / Part ?	Whole 10 Part 5 / Part ?

Pictorial Lesson

Figure 7.25 Pictorial Introduction

<table>
<tr>
<td colspan="2" align="center"><h2>Introduction</h2></td>
</tr>
<tr>
<td>Launch</td>
<td>
Teacher: Today we are going to work on solving word problems where we talk about the parts.

Vocabulary: part-part whole, whole, word problem, count up, number sentence (equation), missing number

Math Talk: The whole is _____. One part is _____. The other part is _____.

Math Talk: There were 8 animals. 5 were elephants and the rest were monkeys. How many monkeys were there?
</td>
</tr>
<tr>
<td>Model</td>
<td>
Teacher: Watch me model my thinking on the number strips.

Teacher: Does everybody see this model? Who can explain it?

Ted: It is an 8 strip. We have 5 colored in and 3 not colored in. 5 and 3 make 8.

Teacher: Yes, what does the 5 stand for? What does the 3 stand for? What is our whole?

Marta: I want to try one.

The bakery had 8 cupcakes. 7 were strawberry, the rest were vanilla. How many were vanilla?
</td>
</tr>
<tr>
<td>Checking for Understanding</td>
<td>
Marta: So there were 7 strawberry and 1 vanilla.

This conversation continues with the students using the 8 strips for their stories.
</td>
</tr>
</table>

Figure 7.26 Student Activity

	Student Activity
Guided Practice/ Checking for Understanding	The teacher passes out word problem cards. Students pull a card and model their problems. The students each get a chance to share their problem and explain how they solved it. ┌──┐ │ **There were 9 pies. 4 were lemon and the rest were apple. How many were apple?** │ └──┘ **Maria:** My problem is this: **I got a 9 strip. I colored 4. I see 4 are colored and 5 are not. So 5 were apple. 4 and 5 make 9.** **Teacher:** Does everybody see that? Our model is the counting strip. What is a strategy to add those two numbers? **Carol:** 4 and 4 make 8 and 1 more is 9.
Set Up for Independent Practice	*The teacher gives everybody a chance to do and discuss a problem. After everyone has shared, the lesson ends.* **Teacher:** We are going to be talking more about that in the upcoming days. Are there any questions? What was interesting today? What was tricky?

Figure 7.27 Lesson Close

Close
◆ What did we do today?
◆ What was the math we were practicing?
◆ Was this easy or tricky?
◆ Turn to a partner and state one thing you learned today.

Figure 7.28 Word Problems

There are 6 counters. 5 are red and the rest are yellow. How many are yellow?	There are 9 counters. 3 are red and the rest are yellow. How many are yellow?
There are 7 counters. 4 are red and the rest are yellow. How many are yellow?	There are 10 counters. 5 are red and the rest are yellow. How many are yellow?
There are 8 counters. 7 are red and the rest are yellow. How many are yellow?	There are 8 counters. 4 are red and the rest are yellow. How many are yellow?
There are 7 counters. 5 are red and the rest are yellow. How many are yellow?	There are 6 counters. 3 are red and the rest are yellow. How many are yellow?
There are 7 counters. 5 are red and the rest are yellow. How many are yellow?	There are 6 counters. 3 are red and the rest are yellow. How many are yellow?
There are __ counters. __ are red and the rest are yellow. How many are yellow?	There are 10 counters. ___ are red and the rest are yellow. How many are yellow?

Figure 7.29 Number Strips

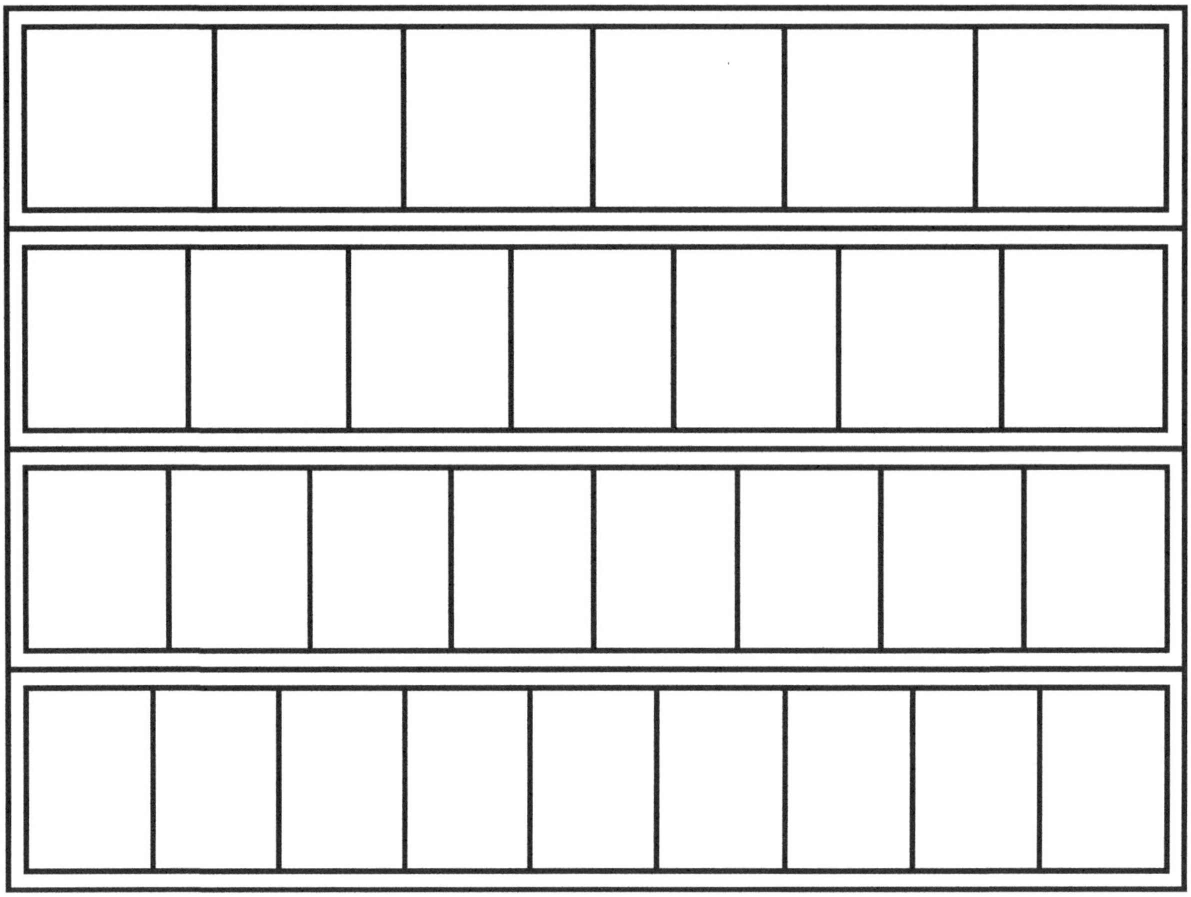

Abstract Lesson

Figure 7.30 Abstract Introduction

	Introduction
Launch	**Teacher:** Today we are going to work on solving word problems where we don't know one of the parts. **Vocabulary:** part-part whole, whole, part, word problem, count up, number sentence (equation) **Math Talk:** The whole is _____. One part is _____. The other part is _____.
Model	**Teacher:** Today we are going to play a match game. We have to find the word problem, the part-part whole diagram and the number sentence that all match. There are three problems that are all mixed up in the bags. I am going to let you work with your partner to talk and discuss the problems and match them up. I am going to listen and ask you questions. Let's do one together. ![diagram: a part-part whole box showing 7 on top, 5 and ? on the bottom; below it the number sentence 5 + ? = 7; to the right a word problem: "Luke had 7 marbles. 5 were red and the rest were yellow. How many were yellow?"] **Teacher:** Does everybody see this model? Who can explain it? **Ted:** The 7 on top is the total. The 5 is what he had. The question mark is the missing number. **Teacher:** How do we find the missing number? **Connie:** We could count up to 7 from 5.
Checking for Understanding	**Teacher:** Yes, we could do that. Are you all ready to work with your partner on your problems? Ok, go!

Figure 7.31 Student Activity

Student Activity	
Guided Practice/ Checking for Understanding	The teacher watches the students as they work together to discuss and match the problems. The teacher watches Leah and Tom. **Teacher:** How do you know this equation goes with the problem? **Leah:** Because it says 4 + what number and in the problem we know there are 7 and we are looking for the 4 plus what number. 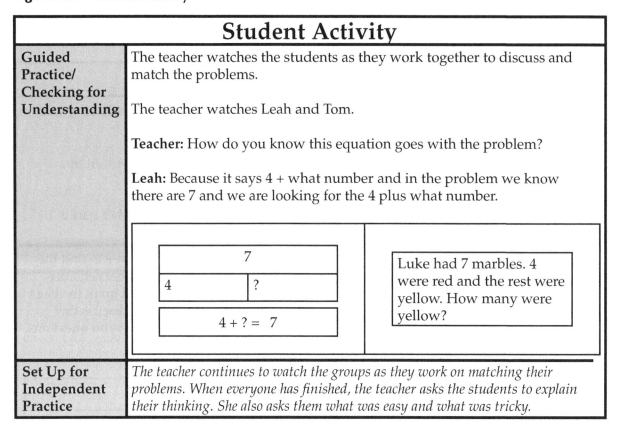
Set Up for Independent Practice	*The teacher continues to watch the groups as they work on matching their problems. When everyone has finished, the teacher asks the students to explain their thinking. She also asks them what was easy and what was tricky.*

Figure 7.32 Lesson Close

Close
◆ What did we do today? ◆ What was the math we were practicing? ◆ Was this easy or tricky? ◆ Turn to a partner and state one thing you learned today.

Figure 7.33 Word Problem Matches

7 3 | ? 3 + ? = 7	Luke had 7 marbles. 3 were red and the rest were yellow. How many were yellow?
7 2 | ? 2 + ? = 7	Lucas had 7 marbles. 2 were red and the rest were yellow. How many were yellow?
8 5 | ? 5 + ? = 8	Lili had 8 marbles. 5 were red and the rest were yellow. How many were yellow?
7 6 | ? 6 + ? = 7	Lulu had 7 marbles. 6 were red and the rest were yellow. How many were yellow?
9 2 | ? 2 + ? = 7	Leticia had 9 marbles. 2 were red and the rest were yellow. How many were yellow?
10 7 | ? 7 + ? = 10	Larry had 10 marbles. 7 were red and the rest were yellow. How many were yellow?
8 4 | ? 4 + ? = 7	Lela had 8 marbles. 4 were red and the rest were yellow. How many were yellow?

Section Summary

Part-part whole problems are rather easy for students. Be sure to use the templates and have the students act them out. Make a life-size part-part whole mat so that students can act out the problems in it. Also make a big number bond that students can stand in. Oftentimes people use hula-hoops to do this. The point is that you need students to see how the parts come together.

Overview

Figure 7.34 Overview

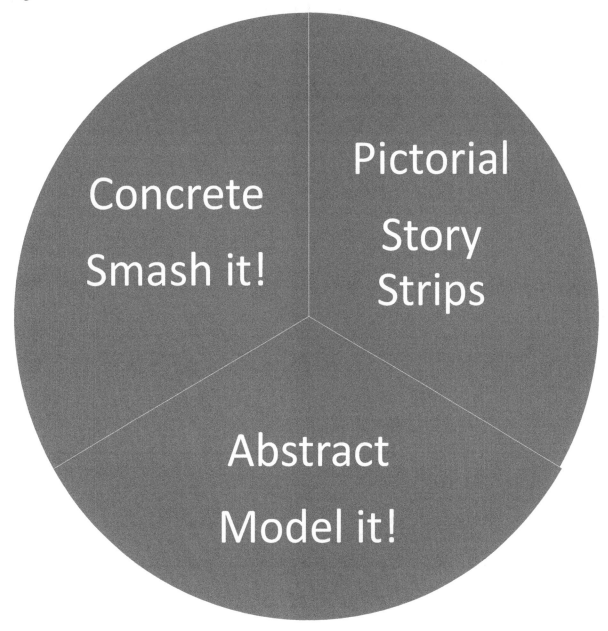

Figure 7.35 Planning Template

Take From Word Problems

Big Idea: There are different types of word problems. In this type, we are taking from. **Enduring Understanding:** We can model problems in many ways. **Essential Question:** What are the ways to model this type of problem? **I can statement:** I can model part-part whole word problems.	**Materials** ♦ Tools: Cubes ♦ Templates: Ten Frame ♦ Cards ♦ Crayons
Cycle of Engagement **Concrete:** 2 – 1 = 1 **Pictorial:** Drawing O ᗞO ∅∅ **Abstract: Mental Number line** | 1 | 2 | 3 | 4 | 5 | 6 | 7 | 8 | 9 | 10 |	**Vocabulary & Language Frames** ♦ Count Up ♦ Count Back ♦ Addends ♦ Difference _____ take away _____ is _____.
Questions: 1. How did you solve that? 2. Are you sure you are correct? 3. Did you double-check your answer? 4. Did you solve one way and check another way?	

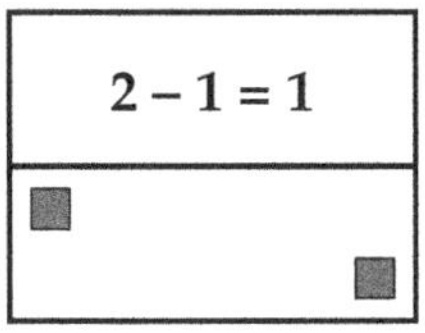

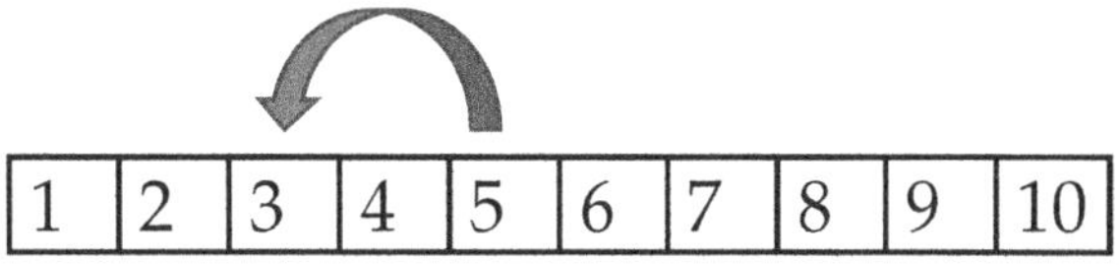

Figure 7.36 Differentiation

Three Differentiated Lessons

In this series of lessons, students are working on the concept of *take away problems*. They are developing this concept through concrete activities, pictorial activities, and abstract activities. Everybody should do the cycle. Some students progress through it more quickly than others. Here are some things to think about as you do these lessons.

Below Grade Level	On Grade Level	Above Grade Level
Review subtraction. As you introduce this to students, do a lot of work by acting it out and then doing it with manipulatives. Be sure to have students draw what they acted out and connect it to number models.	The grade-level standard is that students can model it and explain it. So do lots of this work where students are modeling it and explaining it. Students should solve one way and check another. They should defend their thinking.	There are 15 single-step word problems. In most states students have to work on 11 of them, after they master these work on the other 4. Then go on to two-step problems.

 Looking for Misunderstandings and Common Errors

Subtraction is more difficult than addition. Students should spend a great deal of time acting out the problems. Have the students act the problems out in life-size ten frames. They should also use the subtraction machine that is described in this chapter. This graphic organizer helps students understand the process of taking away.

Figure 7.37 Anchor Chart

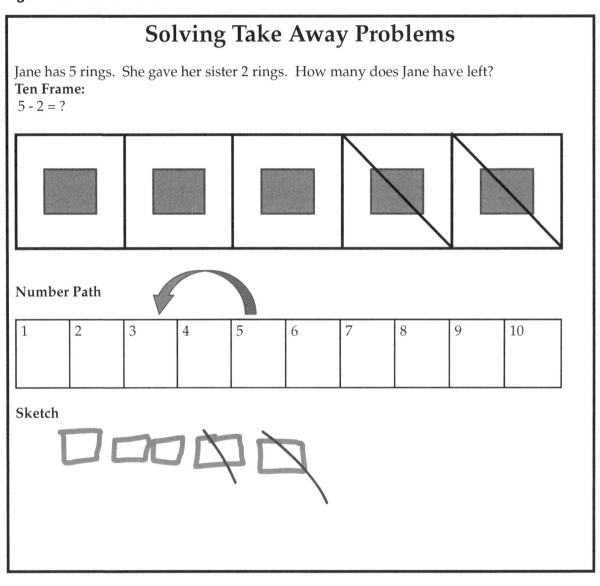

Solving Take Away Problems

Jane has 5 rings. She gave her sister 2 rings. How many does Jane have left?
Ten Frame:
5 - 2 = ?

Number Path

1	2	3	4	5	6	7	8	9	10

Sketch

Concrete Lesson

Figure 7.38 Concrete Introduction

Introduction	
Launch	**Teacher:** Today we are going to work on take away problems. We are going to solve them with our playdough marbles. This game is called "Smash It." **Vocabulary:** take away, subtract, minus sign, difference **Math Talk:** ____ take away ___ is ____.
Model	The teacher gives each student a baggie of 7 playdough balls and then explains the activity. **Teacher:** We are going to tell stories and act them out with the playdough. When I say "smash it," you are going to smash that many "marbles." Listen to this problem. Jamal had 7 marbles. 5 rolled away. Smash it. Ok. How many are left? So 7 take away 5 is 2. The difference is 2. Here's another problem: Michael had 8 marbles. 3 rolled away. Smash it. Ok. Who can explain what happened? You can use the language frame. Be sure to use the vocabulary. <u>8</u> take away <u>3</u> is <u>5</u>. The <u>difference</u> is <u>5</u>. **Timothy:** Michael had 8 marbles. 3 rolled away. **Teacher:** 5 what? **Timothy:** Marbles. **Teacher:** Ok, explain what you did. **Timothy:** I put 8 marbles out and then I smashed 3. There are 5 left. **Teacher:** Who agrees and why? **Yessenia:** I agree. I got 5 too. *The teacher reads two more problems that the group discusses.*
Checking for Understanding	**Teacher:** Ok. I am going to give each one of you your own problem. I want you to read it. Solve it. Be ready to share how you did it. I am going to watch you and if you need help, look at our anchor charts and of course you can ask me.

Figure 7.39 Student Activity

	Student Activity
Guided Practice/ Checking for Understanding	The teacher passes out the problems. Students pull a card and act out their problems. The students each get a chance to share their problem and explain how they solved it. **Timmy:** My problem is this: > Kelly had 5 marbles. 4 rolled away. How many marbles are left? **Kelly:** I put out 5 and I smashed 4. I have 1 left. **Teacher:** Can you describe it in math words? **Kelly:** > 5 take away 4 is 1. The difference is 1
Set Up for Independent Practice	Every child shares out their problem and how they solved it on the part-part whole mat. **Teacher:** We are going to be talking more about that in the upcoming days. Are there any questions? What was interesting today? What was tricky?

Figure 7.40 Lesson Close

Close
♦ What did we do today? ♦ What was the math we were practicing? ♦ Was this easy or tricky? ♦ Turn to a partner and state one thing you learned today.

Figure 7.41 Take From Word Problem Cards

Kelly had 5 rings. She gave away 3. How many does she have left?	Sue had 9 marbles. 1 rolled away. How many does she have now?
Kelly had 10 rings. She gave away 5. How many does she have left?	Sue had 8 marbles. 2 rolled away. How many does she have now?

Kelly had 4 rings. She gave away 2. How many does she have left?	Sue had 6 marbles. 3 rolled away. How many does she have now?
Kelly had 7 rings. She gave away 2. How many does she have left?	Sue had 3 rings. 3 rolled away. How many does she have now?

Pictorial Lesson

Figure 7.42 Pictorial Introduction

	Introduction
Launch	**Teacher:** Today we are going to work on telling take away word problems. I am going to give you a word problem strip. You will look at the strip and tell the take away problem. **Vocabulary:** take away, subtract, minus sign **Math Talk:** _____ take away _____ is _____.
Model	**Teacher:** Look at these story-telling strips. Who can tell a take away story using them? **Marta:** There were 5 birds. 5 flew away. **Teacher:** Excellent story. How many are left? **Raul:** None. **Sharon:** There were 5 birds. 1 flew away. Now there are 4. **Teacher:** Excellent story. 4 what? **Ted:** Birds.
Checking for Understanding	**Teacher:** Who can explain what we are going to do? **George:** We are going to pick a card and tell a subtraction story.

Figure 7.43 Student Activity

	Student Activity
Guided Practice/ Checking for Understanding	**Maria:** My problem is this. There were 7 monkeys and 3 left. Now there are 4 monkeys. **Teacher:** Who can write the number sentence to match that story? **Mary:** I can ... 7 − 3 = 4.
Set Up for Independent Practice	*The teacher gives everybody a chance to do and discuss a problem. After everyone has shared, the lesson ends.* **Teacher:** We are going to be talking more about that in the upcoming days. Are there any questions? What was interesting today? What was tricky?

Figure 7.44 Storytelling Strips

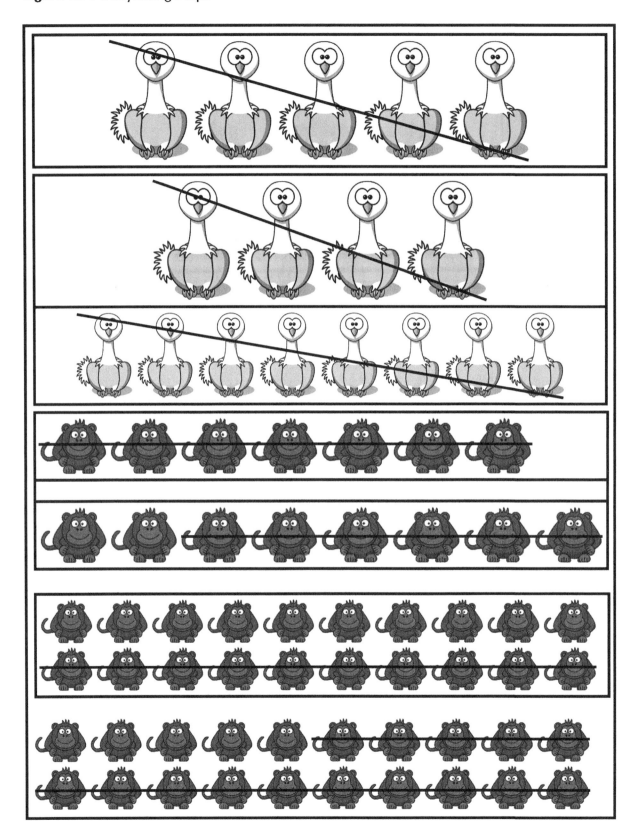

Figure 7.45 Lesson Close

Close
♦ What did we do today?
♦ What was the math we were practicing?
♦ Was this easy or tricky?
♦ Turn to a partner and state one thing you learned today.

Abstract Lesson

Figure 7.46 Abstract Introduction

Introduction	
Launch	**Teacher:** Today we are going to work on solving take away word problems. Here we have word problems on a card. Let's look at our math talk chart: **Vocabulary:** take away, subtract, minus sign **Math Talk:** _____ take away _____ is _____.
Model	**Teacher:** What do you notice about this word problem? Mica had 5 marbles. She gave her sister 2 of them. How many does she have left? | Number Path	Ten Frame	Sketch | | --- | --- | --- | | 1 2 3 4 5 | | | **Todd:** The models are under it.
Checking for Understanding	**Teacher:** Yes. I want you to read your problem and then decide which way you are going to model your problem. Each person is going to get a chance to do one and explain their thinking.

Number Path		Ten Frame			Sketch	

1	2	3	4	5	6	7	8	9	10

Section Summary

Take away problems are difficult. Students have trouble with subtraction, so they often struggle with subtraction problems. Students should do lots of things to act these stories out. They should solve the problems and tell the stories. They should use various tools to model and explain their thinking. They should also discuss their strategies and how they are modeling them. Students should come to understand through explorations that they can add or subtract to find the answer. They should begin to explore the relationship between inverse operations, which will be more deeply explored in second grade.

Compare Word Problems

Overview

Figure 7.50 Overview

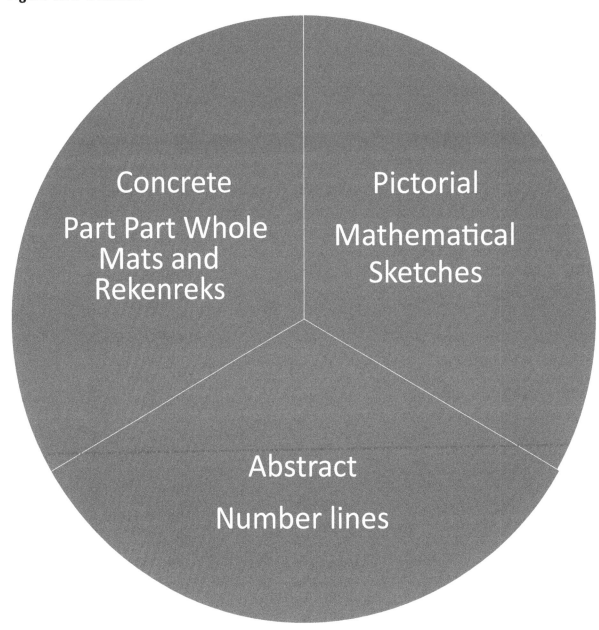

Concrete
Part Part Whole
Mats and
Rekenreks

Pictorial
Mathematical
Sketches

Abstract
Number lines

Figure 7.51 Planning Template

Compare Word Problems

Big Idea: There are different types of word problems. Today we are comparing two things. When we are comparing, it is important to first have students match, then count, and then use their mental number line. **Enduring Understanding:** We can model problems in many ways. **Essential Question:** What are the ways to model this type of problem? **I can statement:** I can model compare word problems.	**Materials** ♦ Tools: Cubes ♦ Templates: Ten Frame ♦ Cards ♦ Crayons

Materials
♦ Tools: Cubes
♦ Templates: Ten Frame
♦ Cards
♦ Crayons

Questions:
♦ How do you know?
♦ Are you sure?
♦ Did you solve more than one way?
♦ Did you check your answer?
♦ Does your answer make sense?

Cycle of Engagement

Concrete:

Pictorial: Drawing

Abstract: Mental Number line

Vocabulary & Language Frames
♦ Count Up
♦ Count Back
♦ Addends
♦ Sum
♦ Difference

_____ is more than _____.

_____ is more than _____.

_____ is equal to _____.

Figure 7.52 Differentiation

Three Differentiated Lessons		
In this series of lessons, students are working on the concept of *compare problems*. They are developing this concept through concrete activities, pictorial activities, and abstract activities. Everybody should do the cycle. Some students progress through it more quickly than others. Here are some things to think about as you do these lessons.		
Below Grade Level	**On Grade Level**	**Above Grade Level**
As you introduce this to students, do a lot of work by acting it out and then doing it with manipulatives. Be sure to have students draw what they acted out and connect it to number models.	The grade-level standard is that students can model it and explain it. So do lots of this work where students are modeling it and explaining it. Students should solve one way and check another. They should defend their answer.	Once they have the concept, increase the number range. Remember there are 6 types of comparison problems. In most states first graders are expected to master 4 of them. Two harder versions are for 2nd grade or more advanced 1st graders.

 Looking for Misunderstandings and Common Errors

Compare problems are the most difficult types of problems. Students should spend a great deal of time acting out the problems. Have the students act the problems out in life-size ten frames. They should compare by matching, then by counting, and eventually by using their mental number line to think through the problems.

Figure 7.53 Anchor Chart

Solving Compare Problems

Jane has 5 rings. Kelly has 3. How many more does Jane have than Kelly?

Ten Frame:
$3 + ? = 5$

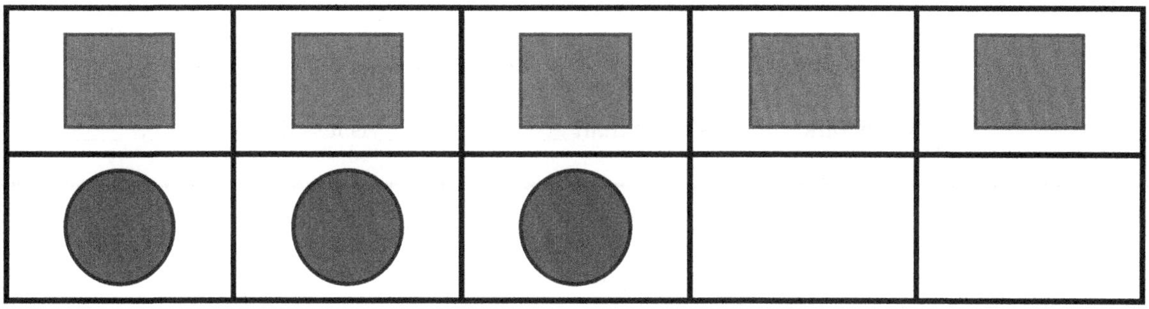

Number Path

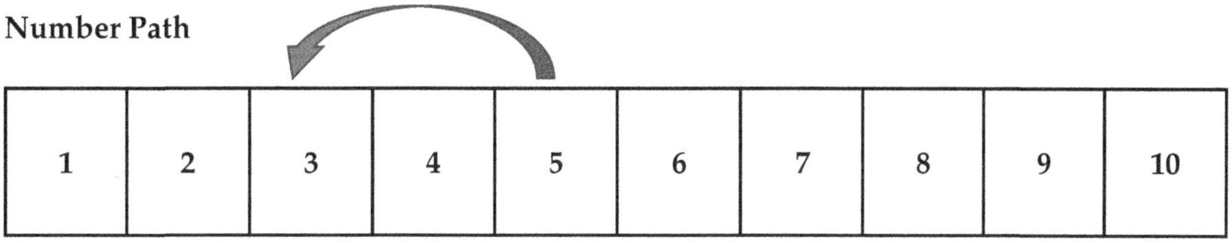

| 1 | 2 | 3 | 4 | 5 | 6 | 7 | 8 | 9 | 10 |

Sketch

Concrete Lesson

Figure 7.54 Concrete Introduction

	Introduction
Launch	**Teacher:** Today we are going to work on compare word problems. We are word problem detectives. We are going to be looking and thinking about problems like, who has more? Who has less? Who has the same? **Vocabulary:** compare, more, less, the same, word problem, count up, count back **Math Talk:** _____ is more than _____. _____ is less than _____. _____ is equal to _____.
Model	Listen to the problem. Jamal had 7 marbles. Luke had 5. How many more did Jamal have than Luke? Let's model it. Let's model it on the rekenrek today. Who wants to explain what they did? **Lucy:** I did it on the rekenrek. I put 7 on the top and 5 on the bottom. He has 2 more. **Teacher:** Ok. Here's another problem: Michael had 8 marbles. Joe had 3. Who had more? How many more? **Timothy:** 5. **Teacher:** 5 what? **Timothy:** marbles. **Teacher:** Ok, explain what you did. **Timothy:** I put 8 on the top and 3 on the bottom. Then I counted. Michael has more. He has 5 more. **Teacher:** Who agrees and why? **Yessenia:** I agree. I got 5 too. See. It's 1, 2, 3, 4, 5 (she says as she points to the beads).
Checking for Understanding	The teacher reads two more problems that the group discusses. **Teacher:** Ok. I am going to give each one of you your own problem. I want you to read it. Solve it. Be ready to share how you did it. I am going to watch you and if you need help, look at our anchor charts and of course you can ask me.

Figure 7.55 Student Activity

	Student Activity
Guided Practice/ Checking for Understanding	The teacher passes out the problems. Students pull a card and act out their problems. The students each get a chance to share their problem and explain how they solved it. **Timmy:** My problem is this: Kelly had 5 rings. Sue had 4. How many more rings does Kelly have than Sue? So, I put 5 on top and 4 on the bottom. There is 1 more on the top. **Teacher:** So who has more? **Timmy:** Kelly. **Teacher:** How many more? **Timmy:** 1 more.
Set Up for Independent Practice	Every child shares out their problem and how they solved it. **Teacher:** We are going to be talking more about that in the upcoming days. Are there any questions? What was interesting today? What was tricky?

Figure 7.56 Lesson Close

Close
♦ What did we do today?
♦ What was the math we were practicing?
♦ Was this easy or tricky?
♦ Turn to a partner and state one thing you learned today.

Figure 7.57 Compare Word Problem Cards

Kelly had 5 rings. Sue had 4. How many more rings does Kelly have than Sue?	Sue had 9 rings. Tami had 8. How many more rings does Kelly have than Tami?
Jane had 7 rings. Sue had 7. How many more rings does Jane have than Sue?	Kelly had 6 rings. Sue had 3. How many more rings does Kelly have than Sue?
Kelly had 4 rings. Sue had 2. How many more rings does Kelly have than Sue?	Sue had 8 rings. Tami had 1. How many more rings does Sue have than Tami?
Jane had 3 rings. Sue had 1. How many more rings does Jane have than Sue?	Kelly had 10 rings. Sue had 5. How many more rings does Kelly have than Sue?

Pictorial Lesson

Figure 7.58 Pictorial Introduction

	Introduction
Launch	**Teacher:** Today we are going to work on solving compare word problems. **Vocabulary:** compare, more than, less than, equal to, same as, whole, word problem, count up, number sentence (equation) **Math Talk:** _____ is more than _____. _____ is less than _____. _____ is equal to _____.
Model	**Teacher:** Watch me model my thinking on the double ten frame. Now I am going to record it on the ten frame paper. Claire had 7 marbles. Marta had 2 more than she did. How many did Marta have? **Teacher:** Does everybody see this model? Who can explain it? **Ted:** You did it on the double ten frame and then you put that on the paper. We did that before. **Teacher:** Yes, we did. We have used the paper a lot. So today we are going to use it to model our word problems. I want you to solve it on the double ten frame and then draw it on the paper. **Marta:** I want to try one. The bakery had 8 cupcakes. 3 were strawberry and 5 vanilla. How many more vanilla ones were there than strawberry? **Marta:** 2. See.
Checking for Understanding	*This conversation continues with the students using the double ten frame and the double ten frame paper for their stories.*

Figure 7.59 Student Activity

Student Activity	
Guided Practice/ Checking for Understanding	The teacher passes out word problem cards. Students pull a card and model their problems. The students each get a chance to share their problem and explain how they solved it. **Maria:** My problem is this: There were 10 pies. 4 were lemon and 6 were apple. How many more apple pies were there than lemon? **Maria:** So I put 4 lemon on top and 6 apples on the bottom. Now I am going to draw it. I got 2 more apple pies than lemon. (double ten frame drawing)
Set Up for Independent Practice	**Teacher:** Does everybody see how she did that? She modeled it on her double ten frame and then she drew it. She can explain what she did. *The teacher gives everybody a chance to do and discuss a problem. After everyone has shared, the lesson ends.* **Teacher:** We are going to be talking more about that in the upcoming days. Are there any questions? What was interesting today? What was tricky?

Figure 7.60 Lesson Close

Close
♦ What did we do today? ♦ What was the math we were practicing? ♦ Was this easy or tricky? ♦ Turn to a partner and state one thing you learned today.

Figure 7.61 Twenty Frames

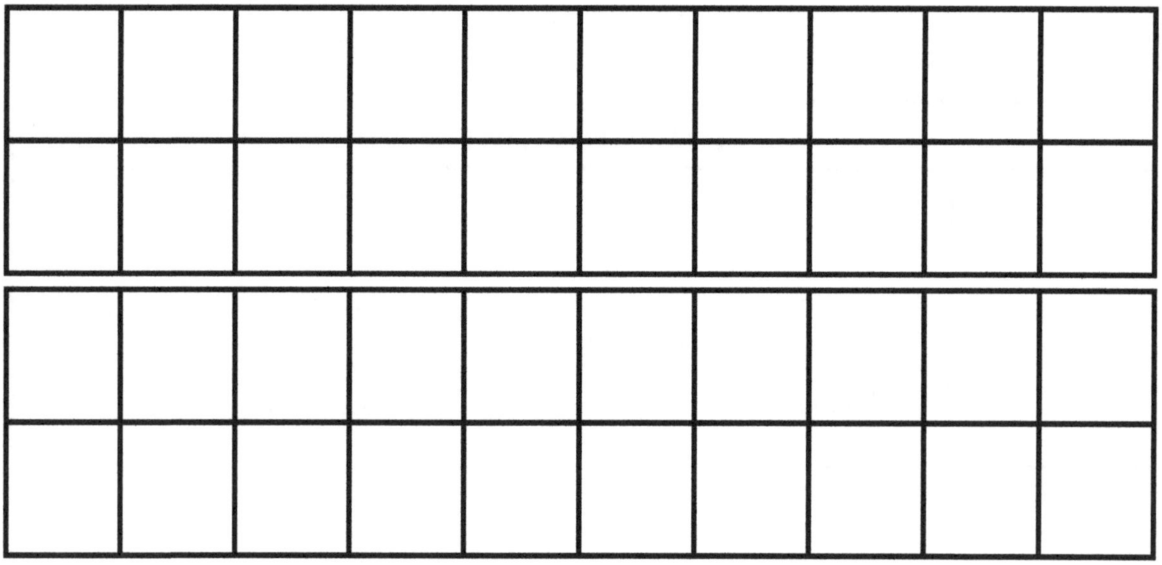

Figure 7.62 Abstract Introduction

	Introduction
Launch	**Teacher:** Today we are going to work on solving word problems where we are comparing numbers. **Vocabulary:** more than, less than, same as, word problem, count up, number sentence (equation) **Math Talk:** ____ is more than _____. ____ is less than _____. ____ is the same as _____.
Model	**Teacher:** Today we are going to solve our word problems, but we are going to compare them on the number line.

<table>
<tr><td>See here is my number line. I can put 1 marker on 7 and 1 marker on 9. Who has more?

Kids: Hong.

Teacher: How many more?

Kids: 2.

Teacher: How do you know?

Katie: Because there are 2 jumps to get to 9.</td><td>Hong had 9 marbles. Luke had 7 marbles. How many more marbles did Hong have than Luke?</td></tr>
</table>

Checking for Understanding	**Teacher:** Tell me more about that. **Katie:** If you start at 7, you have to jump 8 and then 9 so you jump 2 times to get to 9. **Teacher:** Oh, so we can use the number line to compare by counting. Let's try some more.

1	2	3	4	5	6	7	8	9	10

Figure 7.63 Student Activity

Student Activity	
Guided Practice/ Checking for Understanding	The students each have number lines. They take turns solving the word problems using the number lines. **Teacher:** Who can tell me what to do first? **Lisa:** Well, we put the counters on 6 and 3. We count up to see how many more. **Teacher:** Why do we put the counters on the 6 and the 3? **Tom:** Because that is what they had. **Teacher:** Why are we counting up? **Hong:** Because that shows how many more . . . | 1 | 2 | 3 | 4 | 5 | 6 | 7 | 8 | 9 | 10 | Katie had 6 rings and Maya had 3. How many more rings did Maya have than Katie?
Set Up for Independent Practice	*The teacher continues to watch the groups as they work on matching their problems. When everyone has finished, the teacher asks the students to explain their thinking. She also asks them what was easy and what was tricky.*

Figure 7.64 Lesson Close

Close
◆ What did we do today? ◆ What was the math we were practicing? ◆ Was this easy or tricky? ◆ Turn to a partner and state one thing you learned today.

Figure 7.65 Word Problem Cards

The bakery had 8 cupcakes. 3 were strawberry and 5 were vanilla. How many more vanilla ones were there than strawberry?	The bakery had 8 cupcakes. 4 were strawberry, and 4 were vanilla. How many more vanilla ones were there than strawberry?
The bakery had 7 cupcakes. 3 were strawberry 4 were vanilla. How many more vanilla ones were there than strawberry?	The bakery had 7 cupcakes. 2 were strawberry and 5 were vanilla. How many more vanilla ones were there than strawberry?
The bakery had 9 cupcakes. 3 were strawberry 6 were vanilla. How many more vanilla ones were there than strawberry?	The bakery had 9 cupcakes. 5 were strawberry and 4 were vanilla. How many more vanilla ones were there than strawberry?
The bakery had 7 cupcakes. 4 were strawberry and 3 were vanilla. How many more vanilla ones were there than strawberry?	The bakery had 6 cupcakes. 3 were strawberry and 3 were vanilla. How many more vanilla ones were there than strawberry?
The bakery had 5 cupcakes. 3 were strawberry and 2 were vanilla. How many more vanilla ones were there than strawberry?	The bakery had 5 cupcakes. 4 were strawberry and 1 was vanilla. How many more vanilla ones were there than strawberry?
The bakery had 10 cupcakes. 3 were strawberry 7 were vanilla. How many more vanilla ones were there than strawberry?	The bakery had 8 cupcakes. 7 were strawberry and 1 was vanilla. How many more vanilla ones were there than strawberry?
The bakery had ___cupcakes. ___ were strawberry and ___ were vanilla. How many more vanilla ones were there than strawberry?	The bakery had ___ cupcakes. ___were strawberry and ___ were vanilla. How many more vanilla ones were there than strawberry?

Section Summary

Compare word problems are challenging for many students. There are several different types of compare word problems. There is a difference type, for example: Sue has 3 marbles. Mary has 5. Who has more? How many more? There is the bigger part unknown type, for example: Sue has 3 marbles. Mary has 2 more than she does. How many does Mary have? There is the smaller part unknown type, for example: Mary has 5 marbles. Sue has 2 less than she does. How many does Sue have? Then, there are the harder versions of these problems. Spend a great deal of time on these different types of problems and make sure that students can understand them and explain their thinking.

3 Read Problems

Figure 7.66 3 Read Problems

<table>
<tr><td colspan="2" align="center">**3 Read Problems**</td></tr>
<tr>
<td>

Big Idea: We can use different strategies and models to solve word problems.

Enduring Understanding: We can model problems in many ways.

Essential Question: What are the ways to model this type of problem?

I can statement: I can use tools to model my thinking.
</td>
<td>

Materials
- Tools: Cubes
- Templates: Ten Frame
- Cards
- Crayons
</td>
</tr>
<tr>
<td align="center">

Cycle of Engagement

Concrete—Pictorial—Abstract:

In this type of problem, the class chorally reads the problem three times. The first time the class reads the problem, they focus on what is happening in the problem. The second time they focus on what the numbers mean. The third time they focus on asking questions about the problems.
</td>
<td>

Vocabulary & Language Frames
- Strategies
- Models
- Tools
</td>
</tr>
</table>

Figure 7.67 Anchor Chart

---

3 Read Word Problem

We can read a problem three times.

The first time we read it and think about the situation.
What is the story about? Who is in it? What is happening?

The second time we read it and think about the numbers.
What are the numbers? What do they mean? What might we do with those numbers in this situation?

The third time we read it and think about what questions we could ask.
What do we notice in this story? What do we wonder? What do we want to ask about this story?

Jamal had 10 marbles. His brother had 7.

First Read: What is this story about? It is about a guy and his brother and their marbles.
Second Read: What do the numbers mean? Jamal has 10. His brother has 7.
Third Read: What could we ask about this story?

How many do they have altogether?

How many more does Jamal have than his brother?

Figure 7.68 3 Read Word Problems

3 Read Word Problems Lesson	
Launch	**Teacher:** Today we are going to work on word problems. We are going to do a 3 read, like the ones we do in whole group. **Vocabulary:** model, strategy **Math Talk:** How many more...? How many less...? How many altogether?
Model	**Story:** The bakery had 15 cookies. They had 7 chocolate chip, 4 peanut butter, and 5 lemon ones. *First Read: What is this story about?* It is about the bakery. They have 3 different types of cookies. *Second Read: What do the numbers mean?* They have 7 chocolate chip cookies, 4 peanut butter cookies and 5 lemon ones. *Third Read: What could we ask about this story?* How many cookies were there altogether? How many more chocolate chip cookies did they have than peanut butter ones? How many fewer lemon cookies do they have than chocolate chip cookies?
Checking for Understanding	**Teacher:** Ok, pick two questions and answer them. We will come back in a few minutes to discuss them. . . . Who answered question 1? Tell us your strategy and show us a model of your thinking.
Guided Practice/ Checking for Understanding	**Timothy:** I did. How many more chocolate chip did they have than peanut butter? There are 3 more chocolate chip cookies. **Teacher:** Ok, who else did question 2? **Eric:** I did. How many more chocolate chip cookies than peanut butter ones? I drew a picture.
Set Up for Independent Practice	*Students continue to share their thinking with the group. When they are done the teacher facilitates a conversation about what the math was for the day and then what students thought was easy and what they thought was tricky.*

Figure 7.69 Lesson Close

Close
◆ What did we do today?   ◆ What was the math we were practicing?   ◆ Was this easy or tricky?   ◆ Turn to a partner and state one thing you learned today.

Figure 7.70 3 Read Cards

The teacher had 10 pencils. 5 were blue, 4 were green, and 1 was yellow.	Terri biked 1 mile on Wednesday, 2 miles on Thursday, and 3 miles on Friday.
Marta had 3 red marbles, 2 orange marbles, and 2 blue marbles.	The store had 2 red apples, 3 green apples, and 5 yellow apples.
Kelly had 4 blue rings, 2 orange rings, and 1 pink ring.	Grandma made fruit punch. She used 3 apples, 4 oranges, and 2 pineapples.
Grandma made fruit punch. She put 2 apples, 3 peaches, and 4 oranges.	Grandma made some pies. She made 4 apple, 5 lemon, and 6 cherry.
The jewelry store had 5 bracelets, 7 rings, and 2 necklaces.	Sharon had 3 red rings, 4 blue rings, and 7 purple rings.

Picture Prompts

Figure 7.71 Picture Prompt Word Problems

Picture Prompt Word Problems

Big Idea: Word problems are a part of our everyday lives.

Enduring Understanding: We can model problems in many ways. There are many different strategies to solve them.

Essential Question: What are the ways to model problems?

I can statement: I can model problems.

Materials
- Tools: Cubes
- Templates: Ten Frame
- Cards
- Crayons

Questions
- What is your strategy?
- What is your model?
- Why does that work?
- How can you show that?

Cycle of Engagement
Concrete:

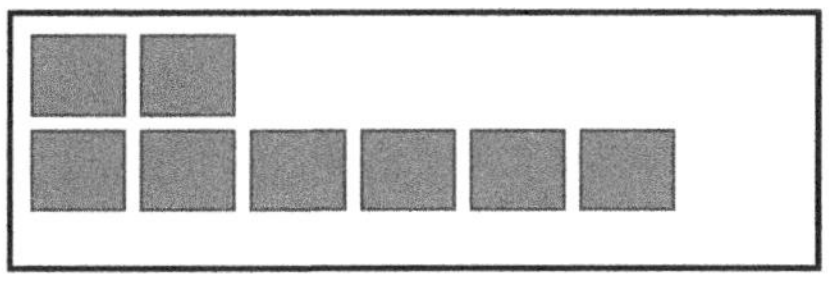

Pictorial: Drawing

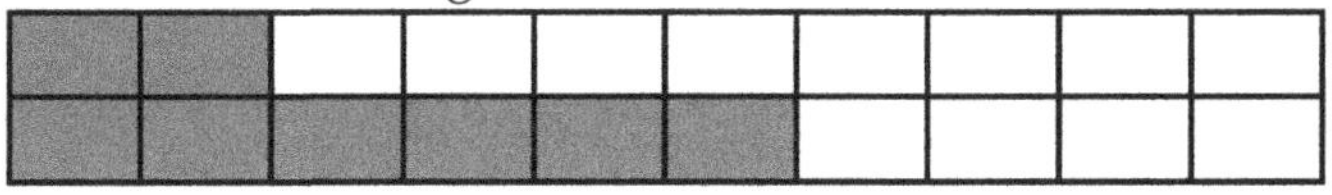

Abstract: Match Addends and the Sum

$2 + 6 = 8$

Vocabulary & Language Frames

My strategy was . . .

My model was . . .

Figure 7.72 Picture Prompt Word Problem

Picture Prompt Word Problems

Teacher: Today we are going to look at pictures and tell word problems. We are working mainly on addition and subtraction stories. Here is a picture. This is my story. There were 12 monsters. Some left. Now there are 6 remaining. How many left?

Luke: That's easy. 6 are left. 6 and 6 make 12.

Teacher: Ok, that works! Who can tell a different story?

Marta: There were 7 monsters. Some left. Now there are 6. How many left?

Kelly: That's easy. 1 because 1 less than 7 is 6. See (*she points to the number line*).

Teacher: Ok. Who's next? (*The teacher goes around the circle and everyone gets a chance to share their stories. They then wrap up and go to workstations.*)

Section Summary

It is important to do open questions with students where they have to contextualize numbers. This is part of the mathematical practices and processes (CCSSM, 2010; NCTM, 2000). We want students to be able to reason about numbers. We want students to be able to tell stories about addition and subtraction. Giving them rich structures to do that is vital.

Depth of Knowledge

Depth of Knowledge is a framework that encourages us to ask questions that require that students think, reason, explain, defend, and justify their thinking (Webb, 2002). Here is snapshot of what that can look like in terms of place value work. It is important to continually reflect on what the level of the lesson is. In working in small groups on problem solving, be sure to ask open questions so that students can think and reason out loud with others.

Figure 7.73 Asking rigorous questions

DOK 1	DOK 2 **At this level, students explain their thinking.**	DOK 3 **At this level, students have to justify, defend and prove their thinking with objects, drawings, and diagrams.**
What is the answer to . . . ? Can you model the problem? Can you identify the answer that matches this equation?	How do you know that the equation is correct? Can you pick the correct answer and explain why it is correct? How can you model that problem in more than one way? What is another way to model that problem? Can you model that on the . . . ? Give me an example of a . . . type of problem. . . . Which answer is incorrect? Explain your thinking.	Can you prove that your answer is correct? Prove that . . . Explain why that is the answer. . . . Show me how to solve that and explain what you are doing.

Resources

A great resource for asking open questions is Marion Small's *Good Questions: Great Ways to Differentiate Mathematics Instruction in the Standards-Based Classroom* (2017).

Also, Robert Kaplinsky has done a great job in pushing our thinking forward with the Depth of Knowledge Matrices he created (https://robertkaplinsky.com/depth-knowledge-matrix-elementary-math/).

Kentucky Math Department (2007) has these great math matrices as well.

Summary

It is important to work with students in small guided math groups focusing on word problems. Word problems have a learning trajectory (Carpenter, Fennema, Franke, Levi, & Empson, 1999/2015). Most states have outlined the word problem types that each grade level is responsible for in their standards. So in a guided math group, the goal is to work with students around the word problem types that they are learning.

Students are usually at different levels when learning word problems. They are scaffolded into a hierarchy that goes from easy to challenging. In most states, first-grade students are responsible for about 11 of the 15 add/subtraction problem types. In some states (like Texas), they are responsible for all the problem types.

The small-group discussion should reference the whole group problem solving work. The focus should be on getting students to think about the context and the numbers, to reason about the problem, and to use visual representations and tools to unpack it. Students should have to write an equation with a symbol for the unknown and solve one way and check another way.

Reflection Questions

1. How are you currently teaching word problems?
2. Are you making sure that you do concrete, pictorial, and abstract activities?
3. What do your students struggle with the most and what ideas are you taking away from this chapter that might inform your work around those struggles?

References

Carpenter, T. P., Fennema, E., Franke, M. L., Levi, L., & Empson, S. B. (2015). *Children's mathematics: Cognitively guided instruction*. Portsmouth, NH: Heinemann.

Kentucky Department of Education (2007). Support Materials for Core Content for Assessment Version 4.1 Mathematics. Retrieved from the internet on January 15th, 2017.

National Council of Teachers of Mathematics (NCTM).(2000). Principles and Standards for School Mathematics. Reston, VA: NCTM.

National Governors Association Center for Best Practices, Council of Chief State School Officers. (2010). *Common core state standards mathematics*. Washington, DC: National Governors Association Center for Best Practices, Council of Chief State School Officers.

Schoenfeld, A. H. (1991). On mathematics as sense-making: An informal attack on the unfortunate divorce of formal and informal mathematics. In J. F. Voss, D. N. Perkins, & J. W. Segal (Eds.), *Informal reasoning and education* (pp. 311–343). Lawrence Erlbaum Associates, Inc.

Stacey, K., & MacGregor, M. (1999). Learning the algebraic method of solving problems. *The Journal of Mathematical Behavior*, *18*(2), 149–167. https://doi.org/10.1016/S0732-3123(99)00026-7

Verschaffel, L., Greer, B., & de Corte, E. (2000). Making sense of word problems. *Educational Studies in Mathematics*, *42*(2), 211–213.

Webb, N. L. (2002). *Depth-of-knowledge levels for four content areas*. Madison, WI: Wisconsin Center for Education Research. Retrieved from http://facstaff.wcer.wisc.edu/normw/All%20content%20areas%20%20DOK%20levels%2032802.doc

8

Place Value

Place value is the linchpin to learning and doing math. Developing an understanding of place value and the base ten number system is considered an essential goal in the primary grades (NCTM, 2000, 2006). In these lessons, we explore how to build an understanding of place value along the learning trajectory so that students understand what it looks like and feels like and how to use it to understand and work with numbers. First graders first encounter place value concepts when they are working with teen numbers in kindergarten. So, at the beginning of the year, it is important to build on this understanding. Make sure that they have a solid understanding of these initial numbers and the concepts of tens and ones. They should build them with unifix cubes and bean sticks, so that they actually practice building tens, before they go to base ten blocks.

When students work with manipulatives where they have to build the ten, the better they understand the idea of unitizing the ten and the ones. Only after they have several experiences building the ten should base ten blocks be introduced, where it is already done for them. The focus of the work in first grade is about getting students to work with tens and ones, such as counting, representing, writing, naming, composing and decomposing, ordering, and comparing them, adding and subtracting tens, and adding ones to them.

Research Note 🔍

♦ A good foundation in place value is essential (National Council of Teachers of Mathematics, 2000; National Research Council, 2009).

♦ Research consistently finds that students struggle with place and have difficulty understanding tens and ones (Hanich, Jordan, Kaplan, & Dick, 2001; Jordan & Hanich, 2000; Kamii, 1985, 1989; Kamii & Joseph, 1988).

♦ National Council of Teachers of Mathematics (NCTM, 2000, in their Number and Operations Standards for Grades Pre-K-2) for students to "use multiple models to develop initial understandings of place value and the base-ten number system."

In this chapter we are going to spotlight:

♦ Grouping Tens and Ones
♦ Adding Tens
♦ Subtracting Tens
♦ Adding Ones to a Two-Digit Number

Overview

Figure 8.1 Overview

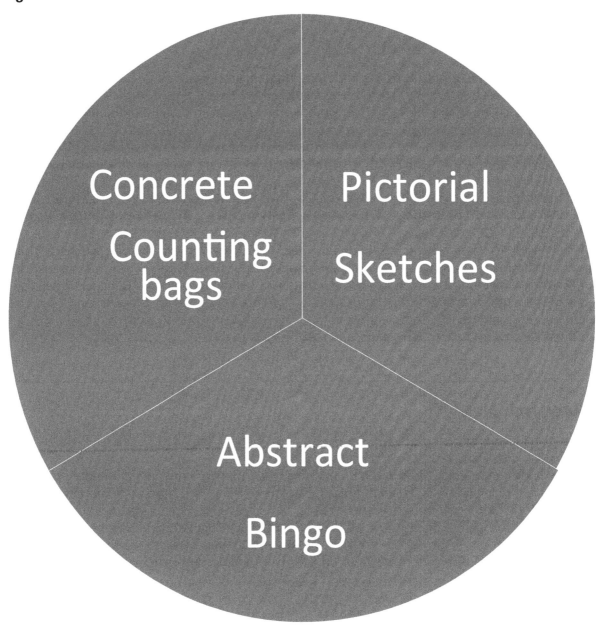

Figure 8.2 Planning Template

Grouping Tens and Ones

Big Idea: We can break up numbers into tens and ones.

Enduring Understanding: Students will understand that our system is based on groups of tens and ones.

Essential Question: What are the ways to model tens and ones?

I can statement: I can break apart a number into tens and ones.

Materials
- Tools: Cubes
- Templates: Ten Frame
- Cards
- Crayons

Cycle of Engagement
Concrete: Base Ten Blocks

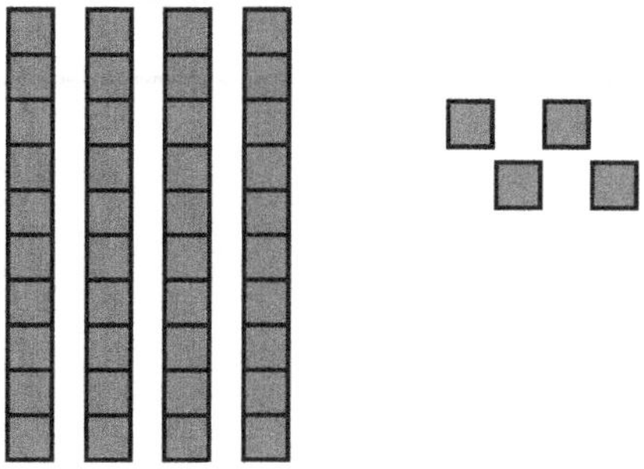

Abstract: Hundred Grid

1	2	3	4	5	6	7	8	9	10
11	12	13	14	15	16	17	18	19	20
21	22	23	24	25	26	27	28	29	30
31	32	33	34	35	36	37	38	39	40
41	42	43	44	45	46	47	48	49	50
51	52	53	54	55	56	57	58	59	60
61	62	63	64	65	66	67	68	69	70
71	72	73	74	75	76	77	78	79	80
81	82	83	84	85	86	87	88	89	90
91	92	93	94	95	96	97	98	99	100

Vocabulary & Language Frames

Vocabulary: add, sum, addend, plus, equals, makes, tens, ones
Math Talk: I have ____ tens and ____ones. I have _____.

Pictorial: Drawing

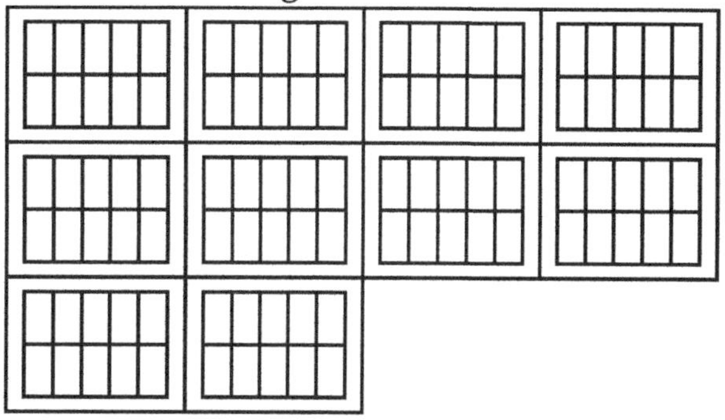

Figure 8.3 Differentiation

Three Differentiated Lessons		
In this series of lessons, students are working on the concept of place value. They are developing this concept through concrete activities, pictorial activities and abstract activities. Here are some things to think about as you do these lessons.		
Emerging	**On Grade Level**	**Above Grade Level**
Do a lot of work with students building the tens and ones on bean sticks, with straws and with unifix cubes.	Do a lot of work on building tens and ones and then transition to place value blocks.	Work with larger numbers.

 Looking for Misunderstandings and Common

Students have a lot of difficulty with understanding tens and ones. It is important to take the time to establish what a ten means so that for example students don't think that 21 has a 2 and a 1 but rather has 2 tens and 1 one. In order to do that students must have the time to build tens and ones before they are introduced to it with place value blocks.

Figure 8.4 Anchor Chart

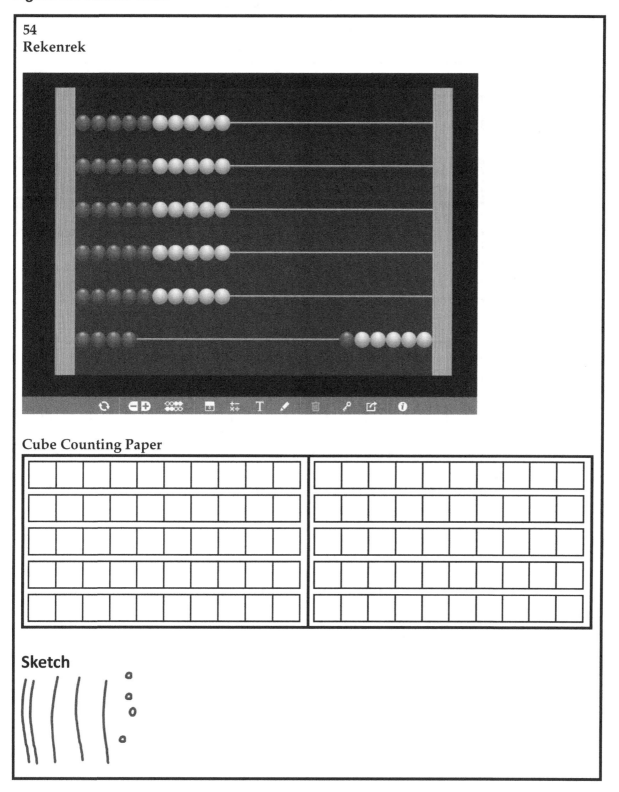

Concrete Lesson

Figure 8.5 Concrete Introduction

Introduction

Launch	**Teacher:** Today we are going to work on counting tens and ones. **Vocabulary:** add, sum, addend, plus, equals, makes, tens, ones **Math Talk:** I have ____ tens and ____ones. I have _____.
Model	**Teacher:** We are working at the fruit factory. We pack fruits in containers of tens and ones. So you pull a bag and count how many containers of fruit you can pack and then how many leftovers (the ones) that you have. I am going to give each one of you a bag. The red ones are apples, the yellow ones are bananas, the blue ones are blueberries, and the orange ones are oranges. You will have this inventory sheet. You have to count and record what you have in your bag. You must remember to group them in tens and then the leftovers. (*The teacher hands out the bags and mats to each of the students.*) Here are counting mats to count out your tens and ones. Put a cube on each square to see how many tens. Each rectangle is a total of 10. **Mike:** I counted 41 oranges. I have 4 tens and 1 extra. **Fruit Inventory:** Bag: 2 **Total:** 41 Tens: 4 Ones: 1
Checking for Understanding	**Teacher:** Ok. I am going to give each one of you your own problem. I want you to read it. Solve it. Be ready to share how you did it. I am going to watch you and if you need help, look at our anchor charts and of course you can ask me.

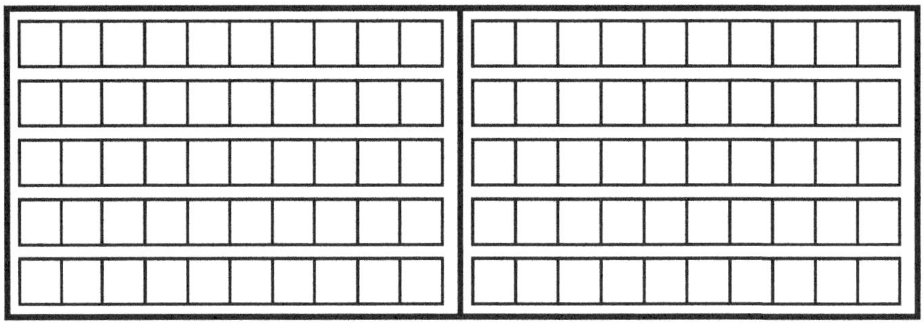

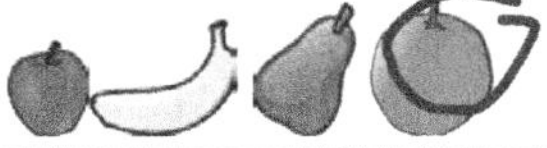

Figure 8.6 Student Activity

Student Activity	
Guided Practice/ Checking for Understanding	The teacher passes out the bags, the mats, and the recording sheets. Students count out their fruit and record their findings. The students each get a chance to share their problem and explain how they solved it. **Carole:** I have 26 bananas. I have 2 tens and 6 ones. <table><tr><td>**Fruit Inventory:** **Bag: 1**</td><td>**Total:** **26**</td></tr><tr><td><table><tr><td>Tens</td><td>Ones</td></tr><tr><td>2</td><td>6</td></tr></table></td><td>**Sketch**</td></tr></table>
Set Up for Independent Practice	*Every child shares out their problem and how they solved it on their beaded number line.* **Teacher:** We are going to be talking more about that in the upcoming days. Are there any questions? What was interesting today? What was tricky?

Figure 8. 7 Lesson Close

Close
◆ What did we do today? ◆ What was the math we were practicing? ◆ Was this easy or tricky? ◆ Turn to a partner and state one thing you learned today.

Figure 8.8 Fruit Inventory

Fruit Inventory: Bag:	Total:

Tens	Ones	Sketch

Pictorial Lesson

Figure 8.9 Pictorial Introduction

	Introduction
Launch	**Teacher:** Today we are going to work on counting tens and ones. **Vocabulary:** add, sum, addend, plus, equals, makes, tens, ones **Math Talk:** I have _____ tens and _____ones. I have _____.
Model	**Teacher:** Today we are going to continue counting tens and ones. We are going to use our white boards. I am going to tell you to sketch out a specific type of number. You have to sketch it, hold it up, and explain it to the group. You can look at the hundred grid to scaffold your thinking: Let's start! Everybody sketch a number that has more than 3 tens and 7 ones. **Clark:** I made 50 because 50 has 5 tens. It is bigger than 3 tens. **Mary:** I made 45 because it has 4 tens. It is bigger than 38.
Checking for Understanding	**Teacher:** I am going to give each one of you a problem. I want you to practice representing it with your ten frames. Then, you will explain what you did. Who wants to go first?

Figure 8.10 Student Activity

	Student Activity
Guided Practice/ Checking for Understanding	The teacher passes out cards. Students pull a card and represent their thinking. The students each get a chance to share their problem and explain how they solved it. **Teacher:** Marta your card said: Sketch out a number that is less than 59 but greater than 39. What did you do? **Marta:** 43 is less than 59 and greater than 39. **Teacher:** Who agrees with Marta? Is she correct? If so, explain why. **Dan:** I agree with Marta because after 39 comes 40 so it is bigger. It is also smaller than 59 because 40 comes before 50.
Set Up for Independent Practice	*The teacher gives everybody a chance to do and discuss a problem. After everyone has shared, the lesson ends.* **Teacher:** We are going to be talking more about that in the upcoming days. Are there any questions? What was interesting today? What was tricky?

Figure 8.11 Lesson Close

Close
◆ What did we do today? ◆ What was the math we were practicing? ◆ Was this easy or tricky? ◆ Turn to a partner and state one thing you learned today.

Figure 8.12 Calling Cards

Sketch out a number that is less than 59 but greater than 39.	Sketch out a number that is less than 40 but greater than 35.
Sketch out a number that is less than 79 but greater than 59.	Sketch out a number that is less than 50 but greater than 40.
Sketch out a number that is in between 59 and 78.	Sketch out a number that is in between 22 and 34.
Sketch out a number that is in between 50 and 60.	Sketch out a number that is less than 90 but greater than 100.
Sketch out a number that is less than 29.	Sketch out a number that is less than 41.
Sketch out a number that is less than greater than 39.	Sketch out a number that is greater than 90.
Sketch out a number that is in between 15 and 25.	Sketch out a number that is less than 50 but greater than 85.
Sketch out a number that is less than 52.	Sketch out a number that is less than 29.

Abstract Lesson

Figure 8.13 Abstract Introduction

	Introduction
Launch	**Teacher:** Today we are going to play bingo. I am going to call out a number by tens and ones and if you have it, you will cover that number. For example: ┊ 4 tens and 5 ones ┊ 7 ones and 2 tens ┊ 3 tens and 3 ones ┊ On your board, if you have 45 you could cover it. If you have 27 you could cover it. If you have 33 you could cover it. You have to listen carefully to how many tens and how many ones though. It can be tricky. Ready? Any questions?
Model	**Teacher:** Here is a board. You win if you get 4 in a row, horizontally, vertically or diagonally or all 4 corners. <table><tr><td>25</td><td>33</td><td>44</td><td>59</td></tr><tr><td>61</td><td>77</td><td>89</td><td>99</td></tr><tr><td>14</td><td>70</td><td>55</td><td>72</td></tr><tr><td>81</td><td>93</td><td>35</td><td>27</td></tr></table>
Checking for Understanding	**Teacher:** Ok, who can tell me how to play? **Yoli:** You have to match the number to the number that you call on the card. You look for the tens and the ones. **Mark:** You have to get 4 in a row to win. **Teacher:** Ok, let's start.

Figure 8.14 Student Activity

Student Activity	
Guided Practice/ Checking for Understanding	**Teacher:** Ok. Here is a card for each of you. You can win up and down, all the way across, or 4 corners.

25	33	44	59
61	77	89	99
14	70	55	72
81	93	35	27

12	25	16	77
52	30	45	57
31	42	99	62
88	26	55	44

33	27	18	22
53	31	44	56
99	79	81	22
11	36	65	55

99	23	19	17
54	32	49	50
31	25	43	54
77	46	75	80

The teacher calls out various numbers by tens and ones. Students listen and cover. |
| **Set Up for Independent Practice** | **Teacher:** What was the math that we were doing today?

Tami: Working on tens and ones.

Keith: We had to cover the number. For example, if you say it has 2 tens and 2 ones, then the number is 22.
Teacher: Any questions? Ok, we will be playing this game in the workstations. |

Figure 8.15 Lesson Close

Close
♦ What did we do today? ♦ What was the math we were practicing? ♦ Was this easy or tricky? ♦ Turn to a partner and state one thing you learned today.

Figure 8.16 Bingo Playing Cards

25	33	44	59
61	77	89	99
14	70	55	72
81	93	35	27

35	43	54	79
41	57	99	19
12	78	59	73
19	90	27	30

50	33	57	40
65	72	80	99
19	70	55	72
80	93	35	27

22	33	44	54
62	77	88	92
11	40	50	74
80	90	99	21

Figure 8.17 Bingo Calling Cards

2 tens and 5 ones	3 tens and 3 ones	4 ones and 4 tens
9 ones and 5 tens	6 tens and 1 one	7 tens and 7 ones
8 tens and 9 ones	9 tens and 9 ones	1 ten and 4 one
7 tens	5 tens and 5 ones	7 tens and 2 ones
8 tens and 1 one	9 tens and 3 ones	3 tens and 5 ones
2 tens and 7 ones	4 tens and 3 ones	5 tens and 4 ones
7 tens and 9 ones	4 tens and 1 one	5 tens and 7 ones
1 ten and 9 one	1 ten and 2 ones	7 tens and 8 ones
5 tens and 9 ones	7 tens and 3 ones	1 ten and 9 ones
9 tens	2 tens and 7 ones	3 tens
5 tens	3 tens and 3 ones	5 tens and 7 ones
4 tens	6 tens and 5 ones	9 tens and 3 ones
8 tens	7 tens and 2 ones	3 tens and 5 ones
2 tens and 2 ones	4 tens and 4 ones	5 tens and 4 ones
6 tens and 2 ones	7 tens and 7 ones	8 tens and 8 ones
9 tens and 2 ones	1 ten and 1 one	7 tens and 4 ones

Section Summary

When working with tens and ones, it is important to have students build it, draw it, and then match it. It is also really important to have students name a number in many different ways. So for example, they should name 78 as 7 tens and 8 ones but also 6 tens and 18 ones or 5 tens and 28 ones, etc. You want to build flexibility around number. They should do number mats where they write a number and build and sketch it many different ways. Also, in the beginning have the students build bean sticks for tens and ones, so they get the idea of a ten. Have them play "race to 100" games where they have to keep making exchanges of ones to tens to get to 100. The point is to provide many opportunities for students to work with tens and ones throughout the year, not only in the place value unit.

Overview

Figure 8.18 Overview

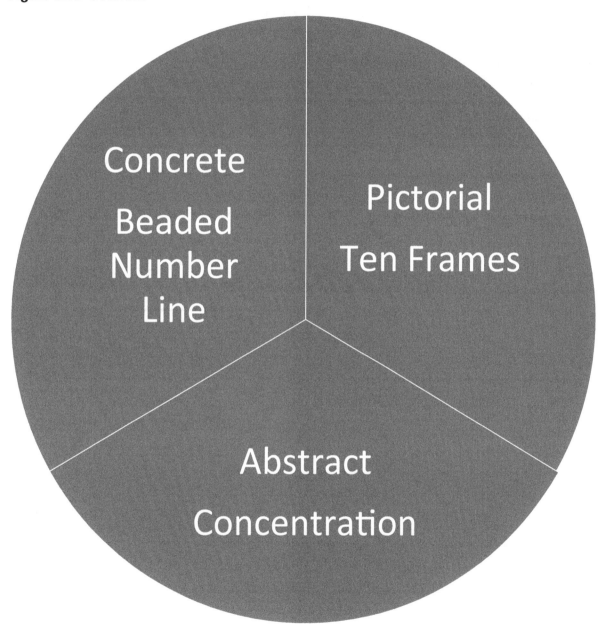

Figure 8.19 Planning Template

ADDING TEN TO A NUMBER

Big Idea: Using place value you can add 10 to a multiple of 10. **Enduring Understanding:** We can model problems in many ways. **Essential Question:** What are the ways to model this type of problem? **I can statement:** I can model adding 10 to a number in many different ways.	**Materials** ♦ Tools: Beaded Number Line ♦ Templates: Ten Frame ♦ Cards ♦ Crayons

Cycle of Engagement.

Concrete:

30 + 10

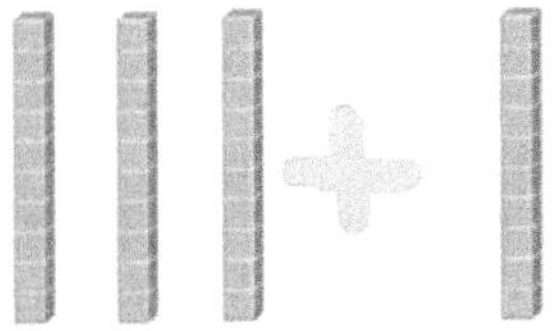

Pictorial: Drawing

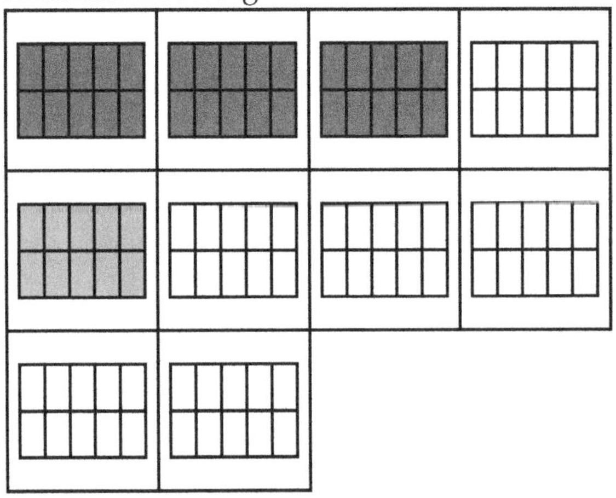

Vocabulary & Language Frames

♦ Count Up
♦ Addends

_____ plus 10 makes ____.

Abstract: Mental Number Line

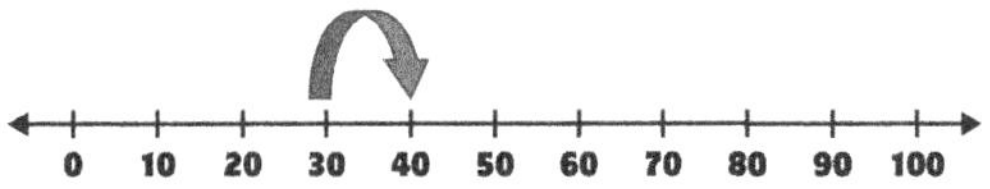

Figure 8.20 Differentiation

<table>
<tr><td colspan="3">Three Differentiated Lessons
In this series of lessons, students are working on the concept of adding ten to a number. They are developing this concept through concrete activities, pictorial activities, and abstract activities. Here are some things to think about as you do these lessons.</td></tr>
<tr><td>Emerging</td><td>On Grade Level</td><td>Above Grade Level</td></tr>
<tr><td>Do a lot of concrete activities.</td><td>The standard is that eventually students can do this mentally.</td><td>Use larger numbers.</td></tr>
<tr><td colspan="3"> Looking for Misunderstandings and Common Errors</td></tr>
<tr><td colspan="3">Oftentimes teachers teach this from the hundred grid. It is important to start with manipulatives so that students can see and count the amount.</td></tr>
</table>

Figure 8.21 Anchor Chart

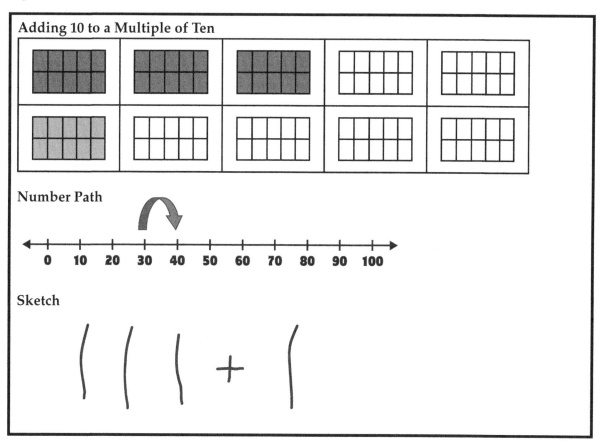

Concrete Lesson

Figure 8.22 Concrete Introduction

<table>
<tr>
<td colspan="2" align="center"><h2>Introduction</h2></td>
</tr>
<tr>
<td>Launch</td>
<td>Teacher: Today we are going to work adding 10 to a number.

Vocabulary: add, ten, sum, addend, plus, equals, makes

Math Talk: ____ plus 10 is _____.</td>
</tr>
<tr>
<td>Model</td>
<td>Teacher: What if I had 20 marbles and I got 10 more? Who thinks they can model that?

Marcus: I can. See you count 20 and then 10 more you grab these. Now you have 10, 20, 30.

Teacher: Ok. What about if Kiyana had 40 marbles and she got 10 more?

Mike: You would count out –40. . . 10,20,30,40 and then 10 more would be 50.

Teacher: How would we write and read that equation?

Tom: 40 + 10 = 50.
Teacher: Yes and I just have a question . . . what does that word "equals" mean?

Katie: Equals means the same as, so 40 plus 10 is the same as 50.</td>
</tr>
<tr>
<td>Checking for Understanding</td>
<td>The teacher reads two more problems that the group discusses.

Teacher: Ok. I am going to give each one of you your own problem. I want you to read it. Solve it. Be ready to share how you did it. I am going to watch you and if you need help, look at our anchor charts and of course you can ask me.</td>
</tr>
</table>

Figure 8.23 Student Activity

	Student Activity
Guided Practice/ Checking for Understanding	The teacher passes out the problems. Students pull a card and act out their problems. The students each get a chance to share their problem and explain how they solved it. **Timmy:** Woooahh! My problem is this: $$80 + 10$$ **Timmy:** So I count out 80. . . 10,20, 30, 40,50,60,70,80 and then add 10 more . . . 90! **Teacher:** Ok, what is the number sentence? **Timmy:** 80 + 10 is the same 90.
Set Up for Independent Practice	*Every child shares out their problem and how they solved it on the part-part whole mat.* **Teacher:** We are going to be talking more about that in the upcoming days. Are there any questions? What was interesting today? What was tricky?

Figure 8.24 Lesson Close

Close
♦ What did we do today? ♦ What was the math we were practicing? ♦ Was this easy or tricky? ♦ Turn to a partner and state one thing you learned today.

Figure 8.25 Add Ten Cards

80 + 10	90 + 10
30 + 10	40+ 10
20 + 10	10 + 10
50 + 10	60 + 10
70 + 10	Make up your own problem!

Figure 8.26 Challenge version

10 + __ = 20	10 + __ = 30
30 + 10= ___	___ + 10 = 50
__ + 10 = 60	10 + __ = 40
___ + 10 = 80	___+ 10 = 90
___ + 10 = 70	___+ 10 = ___

Pictorial Lesson

Figure 8.27 Pictorial Introduction

	Introduction
Launch	**Teacher:** Today we are going to continue working on adding 10 to a number. We will be looking at how we can do that pictorially. **Vocabulary:** add, ten, sum, addend, plus, equals, makes **Math Talk:** ____ plus 10 is _____.
Model	**Teacher:** Notice what I have here. This is our hundred mat that we have worked with before. Today we are going to do shading to add tens. Look at my example. See I shaded in 30 and then I shaded in 10 more. I have represented 30 + 10 to get a total of 40. I can say 30 plus 10 makes 40.
Checking for Understanding	**Teacher:** I am going to give each one of you an equation. I want you to practice representing it with your ten frames. Then, you will explain what you did and what the equation is. Who wants to go first?

Figure 8.28 Student Activity

Student Activity

Guided Practice/ Checking for Understanding	The teacher passes out cards with equations. Students pull a card and represent their thinking. The students each get a chance to share their problem and explain how they solved it. I got $\boxed{40 + 10}$ 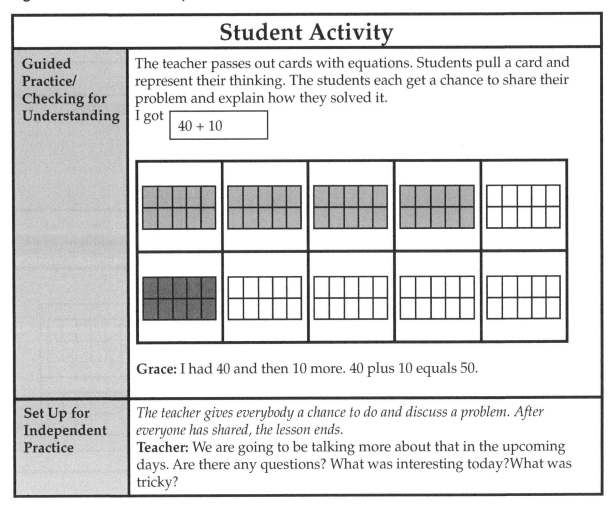 **Grace:** I had 40 and then 10 more. 40 plus 10 equals 50.
Set Up for Independent Practice	*The teacher gives everybody a chance to do and discuss a problem. After everyone has shared, the lesson ends.* **Teacher:** We are going to be talking more about that in the upcoming days. Are there any questions? What was interesting today? What was tricky?

Figure 8.29 Lesson Close

Close

♦ What did we do today?
♦ What was the math we were practicing?
♦ Was this easy or tricky?
♦ Turn to a partner and state one thing you learned today.

Figure 8.30 Ten Cards

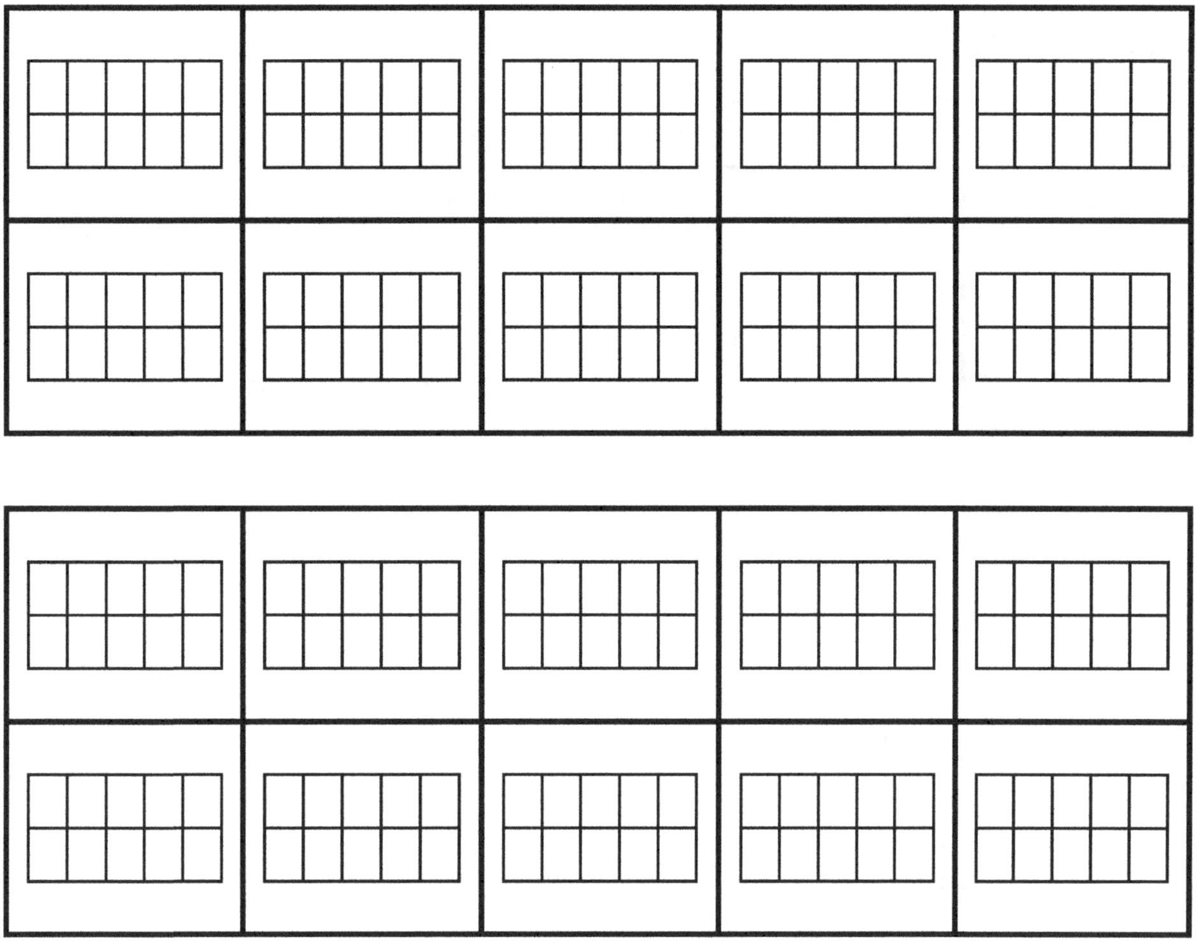

Abstract Lesson

Figure 8.31 Abstract Introduction

	Introduction
Launch	**Teacher:** Today we are going to continue to work on adding 10 to a number. I am going to teach you how to play an add 10 concentration. This is a concentration game—you all know how to play concentration. But today you are going to be matching the "expression" with the "sum." Let me show you what that looks like. 	40 + 10	50	40	10 + 30	
Model	So you will take turns trying to match the cards. Who can tell me how these cards should match up? **Ann:** 40 + 10 makes 50. **Chung:** 10 + 30 equals 40. **Teacher:** Yes, you got it. This is exactly what you are going to do. I am going to give you and your partner a set of cards and you will take turns looking for the matches. When all the cards are gone, whoever has the most pairs wins the game. When you are done, just mix them up and play again. If you get stuck you can use your number lines: 0 10 20 30 40 50 60 70 80 90 100
Checking for Understanding	**Teacher:** Who can explain what we are going to do and what is the math? **Yasmin:** We are practicing adding 10. **Raul:** It's a match game.

Figure 8.32 Student Activity

	Student Activity
Guided Practice/ Checking for Understanding	The teacher continues to watch the groups as they work on matching their problems. When everyone has finished, the teacher asks the students to explain their thinking. She also asks them what was easy and what was tricky.

Ted and Ann play the game. Each time they find a pair they have to state the equation.
Ted: Oh, that's not a match.

	50		20 + 10

Ann: Yay! I got a match. 10 plus 30 equals 40.

10 + 30		40	

The students continue to play the game until they are done.

Set Up for Independent Practice	*The teacher watches how the students are doing to see who knows the answer right away and who gets stuck. Also, the teacher checks to see who has to use their tools and who just knows it by heart.*

Ted he is having some trouble . . . he uses the number line a lot	Ann she knows it
Chung he knows it	Lisa she is skip counting to figure it out

Figure 8.33 Lesson Close

Close
♦ What did we do today? ♦ What was the math we were practicing? ♦ Was this easy or tricky? ♦ Turn to a partner and state one thing you learned today.

Figure 8.34 Add Ten Cards

$10 + 10$	$20 + 10$
$30 + 10$	$40 + 10$
$50 + 10$	$60 + 10$
$70 + 10$	$80 + 10$
$10 + 30$	$0 + 10$
$50 + 10$	$90 + 10$

Figure 8.35 Add Ten Cards Answers

20	30
40	50
60	70
80	90
40	10
60	100

Section Summary

Adding ten to a number is easier for some students than others. All students should start with the concept concretely and then sketch it out and connect it to the equation. Too often we jump to abstract practice, only having students solve these with equations, so students stay shaky all year long. Which brings us to the next big idea, that this skill should be done as energizers and routines and workstations throughout the year.

Overview

Figure 8.36 Overview

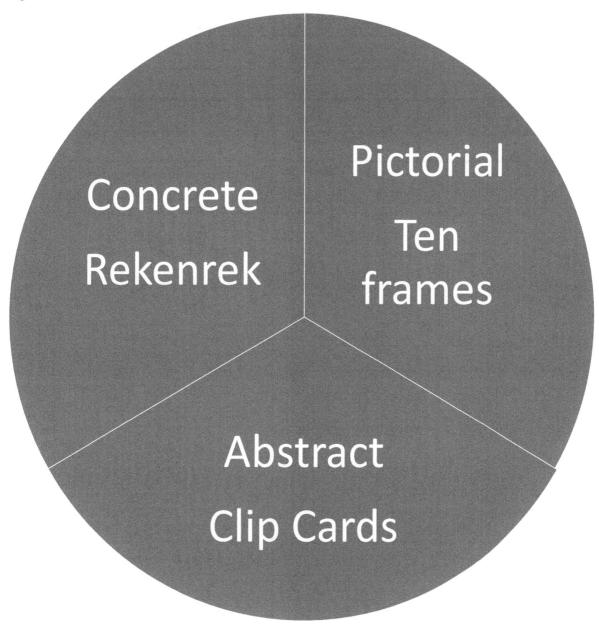

Concrete
Rekenrek

Pictorial
Ten
frames

Abstract
Clip Cards

Figure 8.37 Planning Template

Subtracting Multiples of 10 From Multiples of 10

Big Idea: Using place value you can subtract multiples of 10 from multiples of 10.

Enduring Understanding: We can model problems in many ways.

Essential Question: What are the ways to model this type of problem?

I can statement: I can model subtracting multiples of 10 from multiples of 10 in different ways.

Materials
♦ Tools: Rekenrek
♦ Templates: Ten Frames
♦ Cards
♦ Crayons

Cycle of Engagement

Concrete: Base Ten Blocks

Pictorial: Drawing
$60 - 30 = 30$

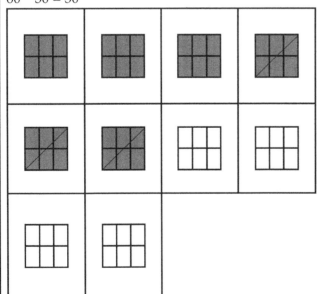

Vocabulary & Language Frames

♦ Count back
♦ Difference

_____ minus _____ makes ____.

Abstract: Mental Number Line

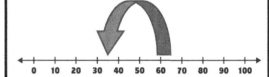

Figure 8.38 Differentiation

Three Differentiated Lessons

In this series of lessons, students are working on the concept of subtracting multiples of ten from multiples of ten. They are developing this concept through concrete activities, pictorial activities, and abstract activities. Here are some things to think about as you do these lessons.

Emerging	On Grade Level	Above Grade Level
Spend a lot of time with physical manipulatives.	The standard is that students can do this easily.	Work with larger number range.

 Looking for Misunderstandings and Common Errors

Students need to actually do this in ways other than the hundred grid. They should do this with base ten blocks, the rekenrek, ten frames, and sketches so that they can represent and understand the math.

Figure 8.39 Anchor Chart

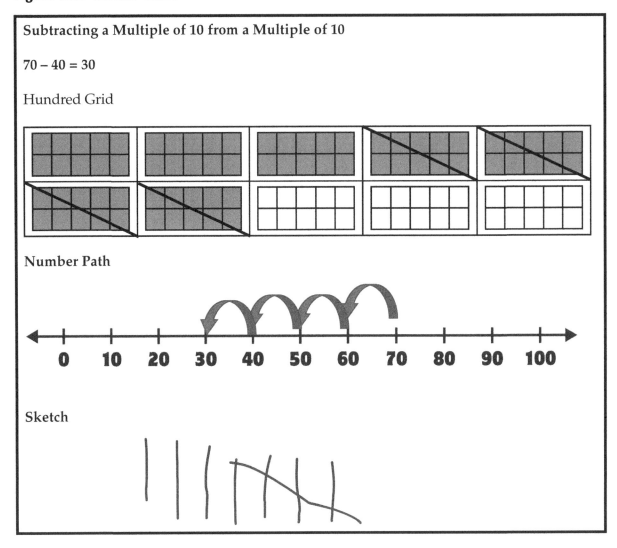

Subtracting a Multiple of 10 from a Multiple of 10

70 − 40 = 30

Hundred Grid

Number Path

Sketch

Concrete Lesson

Figure 8.40 Concrete Introduction

	Introduction
Launch	**Teacher:** Today we are going to work on subtracting tens from tens using our place value blocks. **Vocabulary:** subtract, tens, minus, equals, makes **Math Talk:** ____ minus ____ equals _____.
Model	**Teacher:** What if I had 30 marbles and I gave away 10? Who thinks they can model that with the place value blocks? **Jason:** I can. See you count 30 and then you take away 10. Now you have 20 left. 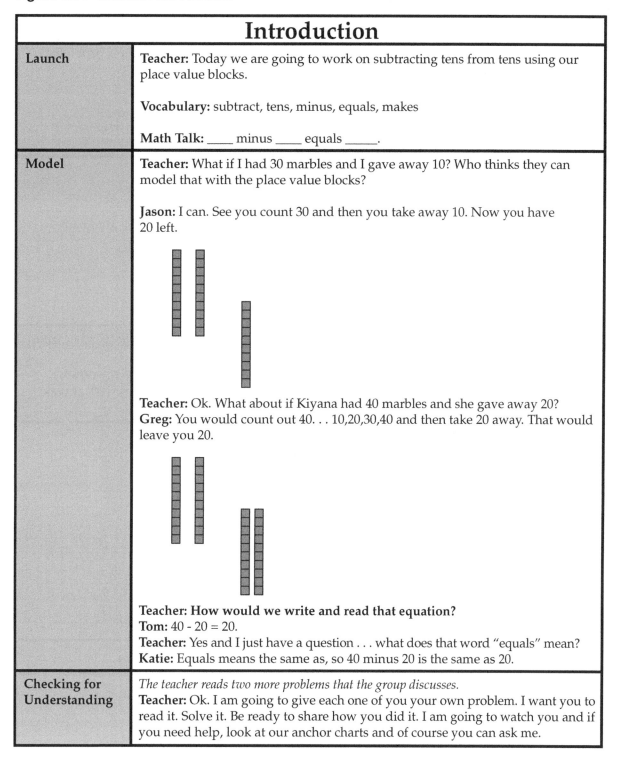 **Teacher:** Ok. What about if Kiyana had 40 marbles and she gave away 20? **Greg:** You would count out 40. . . 10,20,30,40 and then take 20 away. That would leave you 20. **Teacher: How would we write and read that equation?** **Tom:** 40 - 20 = 20. **Teacher:** Yes and I just have a question . . . what does that word "equals" mean? **Katie:** Equals means the same as, so 40 minus 20 is the same as 20.
Checking for Understanding	*The teacher reads two more problems that the group discusses.* **Teacher:** Ok. I am going to give each one of you your own problem. I want you to read it. Solve it. Be ready to share how you did it. I am going to watch you and if you need help, look at our anchor charts and of course you can ask me.

Figure 8.41 Student Activity

	Student Activity
Guided Practice/ Checking for Understanding	The teacher passes out the problems. Students pull a card and act out their problems. The students each get a chance to share their problem and explain how they solved it. **Timmy:** Woooahh! My problem is this: $$50 - 40$$ **Timmy:** So I count out 50. . . 10,20, 30, 40,50, and then take away 40! **Teacher:** Ok, what is the number sentence? **Timmy:** 50 − 40 is the same 10.
Set Up for Independent Practice	*Every child shares out their problem and how they solved it with the place value blocks.* **Teacher:** We are going to be talking more about this in the upcoming days. Are there any questions? What was interesting today? What was tricky?

Figure 8.42 Lesson Close

Close
◆ What did we do today? ◆ What was the math we were practicing? ◆ Was this easy or tricky? ◆ Turn to a partner and state one thing you learned today.

Figure 8.43 Subtracting Multiples of Ten Cards

80 – 20	90 – 30
30 – 30	40 – 20
20 – 10	10 – 10
50 – 20	60 – 40
70 – 50	Make up your own problem!

Figure 8.44 Challenge Version

80 – __ = 60	20 – __ = 10
_ – 20 = 50	__ – 30 = 50
_ – 20 = 40	50 – __ = 40
__ – 40 = 20	60 – __ = 30
__ – 50 = 30	70 – __ = 20
__ – 60 = 10	100 – __ = 70
__ – 20 = 70	20 – __ = 10
__ – 30 = 50	80 – __ = 40

Pictorial Lesson

Figure 8.45 Pictorial Introduction

	Introduction
Launch	**Teacher:** Today we are going to work on subtracting tens from tens using our place value blocks. **Vocabulary:** subtract, tens, minus, equals, makes **Math Talk:** ____ minus ____ equals ____.
Model	**Teacher:** Today we are going to continue working on subtracting tens from tens. We will be looking at how we can do that pictorially with our ten frame mat. **Teacher:** Notice what I have here. This is our ten frame hundred mat that we have worked with before. Today we are going to do shading to subtract tens from tens. Look at my example. See, I shaded in 80 and then I subtracted 50. I have represented 80 – 50 to get a total of 30. I cans say 80 minus 50 equals 30.
Checking for Understanding	**Teacher:** I am going to give each one of you an equation. I want you to practice representing it with your ten frames. Then, you will explain what you did and what the equation is. Who wants to go first?

Figure 8.46 Student Activity

	## Student Activity
Guided Practice/ Checking for Understanding	The teacher passes out cards with equations. Students pull a card and represent their thinking. The students each get a chance to share their problem and explain how they solved it. I got 40 − 20 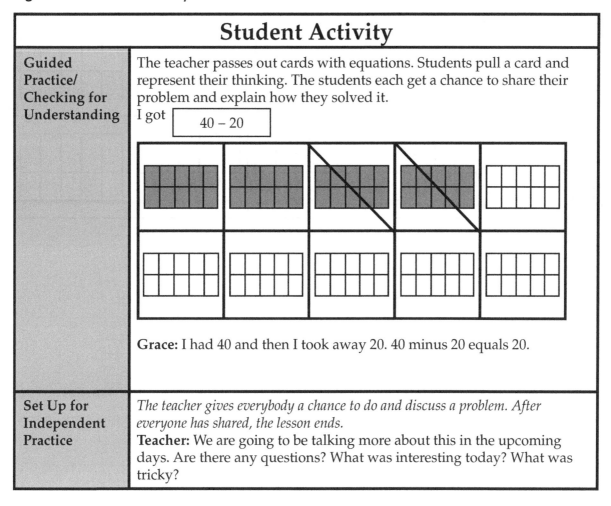 **Grace:** I had 40 and then I took away 20. 40 minus 20 equals 20.
Set Up for Independent Practice	*The teacher gives everybody a chance to do and discuss a problem. After everyone has shared, the lesson ends.* **Teacher:** We are going to be talking more about this in the upcoming days. Are there any questions? What was interesting today? What was tricky?

Figure 8.47 Lesson Close

Close
◆ What did we do today?   ◆ What was the math we were practicing?   ◆ Was this easy or tricky?   ◆ Turn to a partner and state one thing you learned today.

Figure 8.48 Ten Frames

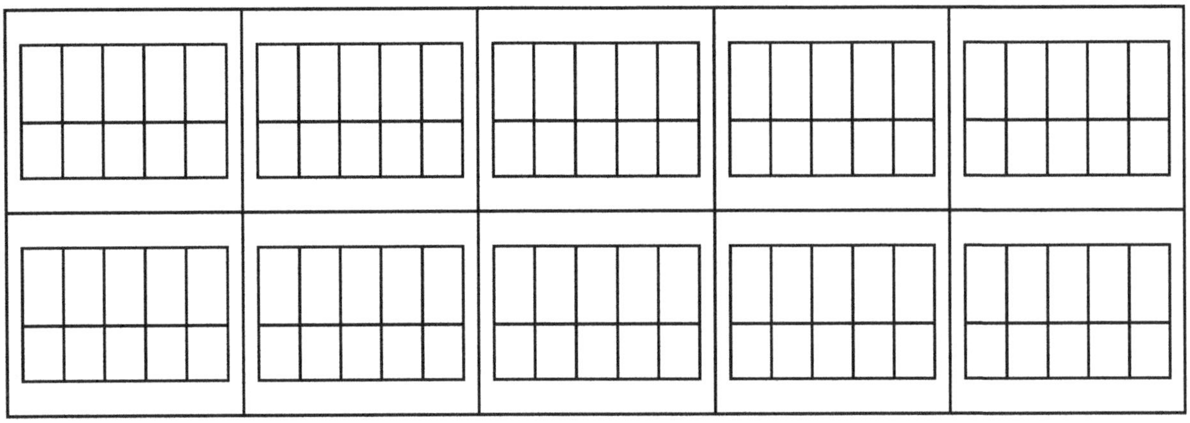

Abstract Lesson

Figure 8.49 Abstract Introduction

	Introduction
Launch	**Teacher:** Today we are going to work on subtracting tens from tens using our place value blocks. **Vocabulary:** subtract, tens, minus, equals, makes **Math Talk:** ____ minus ____ equals ____.
Model	**Teacher:** Today we are going to continue to work on subtracting tens from tens. We are going to do it with our clip cards. Here is an example. You have to read the problem and then clip the correct answer. Then, when you are done, you check it by turning it over and seeing if the dot is where you clipped it. You just keep playing until you have done the whole pack. As you are doing it, sort them into piles of the ones you got right and the ones you got wrong. When you are finished, try the ones you got wrong over again. <table><tr><td colspan="3">80 – 20</td></tr><tr><td>50</td><td>60</td><td>10</td></tr></table> **Ann:** 80 – 20 equals 60. (She then flips it to check her answer.)
Checking for Understanding	**Teacher:** Yes, you got it. This is exactly what you are going to do. I am going to give each of you your own set of cards. Also, here is a number line if you want to use it to scaffold your thinking. 0 10 20 30 40 50 60 70 80 90 100

Figure 8.50 Student Activity

Student Activity	
Guided Practice/ Checking for Understanding	The teacher continues to watch the groups as they work on matching their problems. When everyone has finished, the teacher asks the students to explain their thinking. She also asks them what was easy and what was tricky. **Katie:** | 70 – 20		
---	---	---
50	40	10	 It is 50. Let's see . . . I'm correct.
Set Up for Independent Practice	The students continue to play the game until they are done. The teacher watches how the students are doing, who knows the answer right away and who gets stuck. She notices who has to use their tools and who just knows it by heart. 	Ted he can do it	Katie she can do it
Chung he is counting back by tens	Lisa she knows it automatically	

Figure 8.51 Lesson Close

Close
♦ What did we do today? ♦ What was the math we were practicing? ♦ Was this easy or tricky? ♦ Turn to a partner and state one thing you learned today.

Figure 8.52 Cards

80 – 20		
50	60	10

80 – 20		
50	60	10

90 – 30		
50	60	10

20 – 10		
50	60	10

40 – 20		
20	30	10

50 – 30		
30	20	30

60 – 10		
50	60	10

70 – 40		
50	60	30

30 – 20		
50	60	10

Section Summary

Students should do a lot of work at the concrete level when subtracting tens. They should build it and draw it as well as work it out on the hundred grid. Play subtract from 100, where they roll or pull tens and subtract from 100 until they get to zero. Also, have them do workstations, where they subtract it concretely enough so that the concept becomes internalized, and then have them show it on a number line and then eventually do it from their mental number line. Use a plethora of models for students to actually own this concept.

Adding a Single-Digit and a Double-Digit Number

Overview

Figure 8.53 Overview

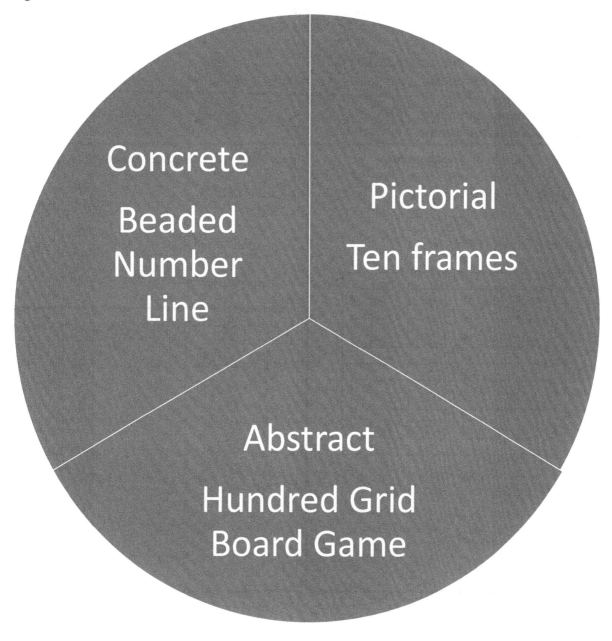

Figure 8.54 Planning Template

Adding a Single Digit to a Double-Digit Number

Big Idea: Using place value, you can add a single digit to a double-digit number. **Enduring Understanding:** We can model problems in many ways. **Essential Question:** What are the ways to model this type of problem? **I can statement:** I can model adding a single digit to a double-digit number.	**Materials** ♦ Tools: Beaded Number Line ♦ Templates: Ten Frame ♦ Cards ♦ Crayons

Cycle of Engagement	Vocabulary & Language Frames
Concrete: 33 + 4 = 37 **Pictorial:** Drawing 25 + 7 = 32 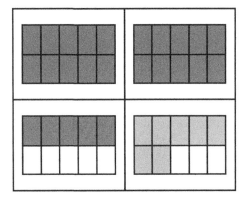	♦ Count Up ♦ Addends _____ plus 10 makes _____.

Abstract: Hundred Grid

1	2	3	4	5	6	7	8	9	10
11	12	13	14	15	16	17	18	19	20
21	22	23	24	25	26	27	28	29	30
31	32	33	34	35	36	37	38	39	40
41	42	43	44	45	46	47	48	49	50
51	52	53	54	55	56	57	58	59	60
61	62	63	64	65	66	67	68	69	70
71	72	73	74	75	76	77	78	79	80
81	82	83	84	85	86	87	88	89	90
91	92	93	94	95	96	97	98	99	100

Figure 8.55 Differentiation

Three Differentiated Lessons		
In this series of lessons, students are working on the concept of *adding a single digit to a double-digit number*. They are developing this concept through concrete activities, pictorial activities, and abstract activities. Here are some things to think about as you do these lessons.		
Emerging	**On Grade Level**	**Above Grade Level**
Review composing and decomposing numbers.	Grade-level standard is that students can make tens as they add across them.	Extend number range.

 Looking for Misunderstandings and Common Errors

Students get confused adding 29 + 3. Sometimes they will add the 2 tens and the 3 ones and get 59. So you should present the problems in both vertical and horizontal forms and stress the conversation on the place and value of the numbers. I like to actually teach this using a beaded number line, because the students can physically locate the number and then also count up. They can see how to get to the nearest ten and then jump on. So in this example, they can see how to go from 29 to 30 and then add 2 more.

Figure 8.56 Anchor Chart

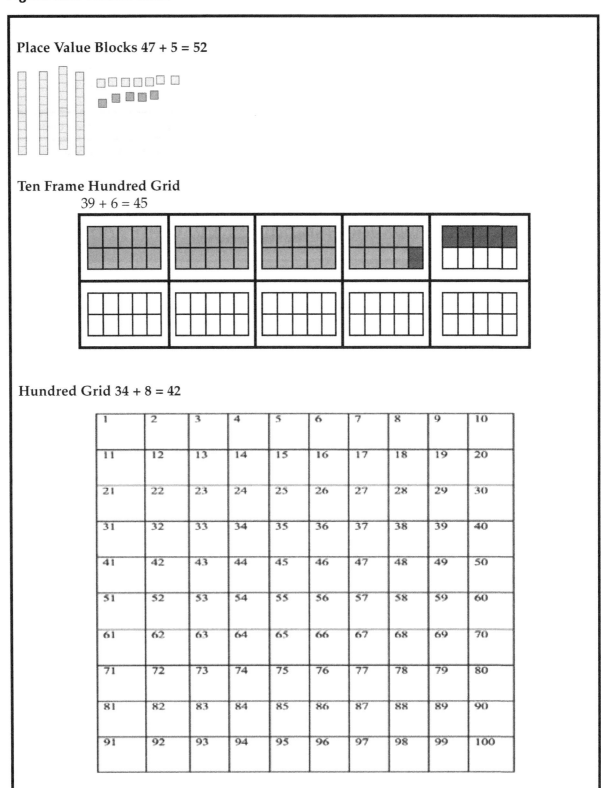

Concrete Lesson

Figure 8.57 Concrete Introduction

<table>
<tr>
<th colspan="2" style="text-align:center"><h2>Introduction</h2></th>
</tr>
<tr>
<td>Launch</td>
<td>Teacher: Today we are going to work on adding a double-digit and a single-digit number the place value blocks. We were doing this on the rug with the whole class and the place value blocks. Who can tell me something important when adding a two-digit number and a one-digit number?

Vocabulary: add, sum, addend, plus, equals, makes

Math Talk: ____ plus ____ equals ____.</td>
</tr>
<tr>
<td>Model</td>
<td>Carole: Get to a 10 because it is our friend! It makes it easy.

Teacher: What if I had 28 and I got 5 more? Who thinks they can model that with the place value blocks?

Marcus: I can. See you count 28 and then 2 more makes 30 and 3 more makes 33.

Teacher: Ok. What about if Kiyana had 47 marbles and she got 4 more?

Mike: You would count out 47 and then 48, 49, 50 and then 51.

Teacher: How would we write and read that equation?

Tom: $47 + 4 = 51$.

Teacher: Yes, and I just have a question . . . what does that word "equals" mean?

Katie: Equals means the same as, so 47 plus 4 is the same as 51.

The teacher reads two more problems that the group discusses.</td>
</tr>
<tr>
<td>Checking for Understanding</td>
<td>Teacher: Ok. I am going to give each one of you your own problem. I want you to read it. Solve it. Be ready to share how you did it. I am going to watch you and if you need help, look at our anchor charts and of course you can ask me.</td>
</tr>
</table>

Figure 8.58 Student Activity

Student Activity	
Guided Practice/ Checking for Understanding	The teacher passes out the problems. Students pull a card and act out their problems. The students each get a chance to share their problem and explain how they solved it. **Timmy:** Woooahh! My problem is this: $$88 + 7$$ **Timmy:** So I count out 88. . . Then 89, 90 then 5 more. **Teacher:** Ok, tell me why you stopped at 90.
Set Up for Independent Practice	**Timmy:** Because it is like when we were doing it on the floor with the big beaded number line. We need to get to 90 because it is a 10 and it is easy to count from a 10. *Every child shares out their problem and how they solved it with their place value blocks.* **Teacher:** We are going to be talking more about this in the upcoming days. Are there any questions? What was interesting today? What was tricky?

Figure 8.59 Lesson Close

Close
◆ What did we do today? ◆ What was the math we were practicing? ◆ Was this easy or tricky? ◆ Turn to a partner and state one thing you learned today.

Figure 8.60 Cards for Adding a Single-Digit and a Double-Digit Number

87 + 4	78 + 7
38+ 3	47+ 5
25 + 6	83 + 9
59 + 2	65 + 8
77 + 7	Make up your own problem!

Pictorial Lesson

Figure 8.61 Pictorial Introduction

<table>
<tr><td colspan="2" align="center"><h2>Introduction</h2></td></tr>
<tr>
<td>Launch</td>
<td>

Teacher: Today we are going to continue working on adding a double-digit and a single-digit number. We will be looking at how we can do that pictorially. What should we be thinking about when we are adding a double-digit and a single-digit number?

Hong: Getting to a 10 because it makes it easier to add.

Vocabulary: add, sum, addend, plus, equals, makes
Math Talk: ____ plus 10 is _____.

</td>
</tr>
<tr>
<td>Model</td>
<td>

Teacher: Notice what I have here. This is our hundred mat that we have worked with before. Today we are going to do shading to add double-digit numbers and single-digit numbers. Remember we are thinking about how tens can help us. Look at my example. See, I shaded in 36 and then I shaded in 5 more. Do you see how that 36 becomes a 40 and then 1 more. I can say that 36 + 5 is the same as 41.

</td>
</tr>
<tr>
<td>Checking for Understanding</td>
<td>

Teacher: I am going to give each one of you an equation. I want you to practice representing it with your ten frames. Then, you will explain what you did and what the equation is. Who wants to go first?

</td>
</tr>
</table>

Figure 8.62 Student Activity

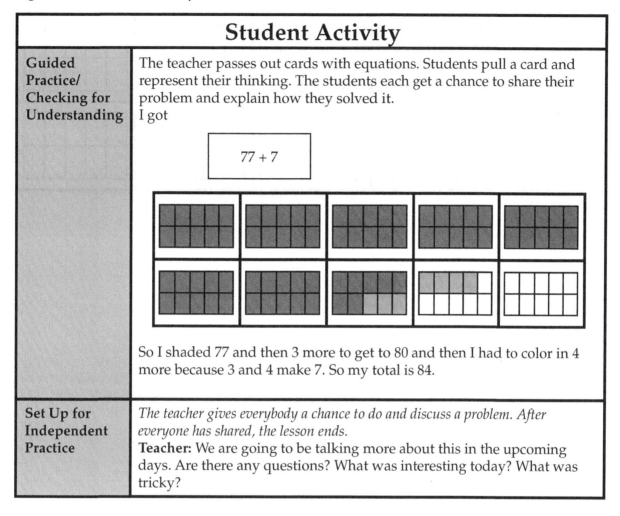

Guided Practice/ Checking for Understanding	The teacher passes out cards with equations. Students pull a card and represent their thinking. The students each get a chance to share their problem and explain how they solved it. I got 77 + 7 So I shaded 77 and then 3 more to get to 80 and then I had to color in 4 more because 3 and 4 make 7. So my total is 84.
Set Up for Independent Practice	*The teacher gives everybody a chance to do and discuss a problem. After everyone has shared, the lesson ends.* **Teacher:** We are going to be talking more about this in the upcoming days. Are there any questions? What was interesting today? What was tricky?

Figure 8.63 Lesson Close

Close

♦ What did we do today?
♦ What was the math we were practicing?
♦ Was this easy or tricky?
♦ Turn to a partner and state one thing you learned today.

Figure 8.64 Template

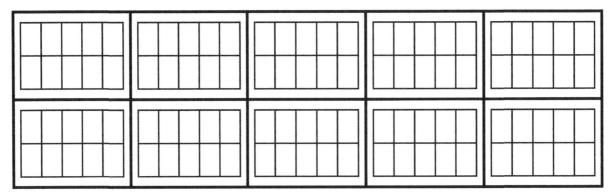

Abstract Lesson

Figure 8.65 Abstract Introduction

	Introduction
Launch	**Teacher:** Today we are going to continue working on adding a double-digit and a single-digit number. We will be looking at how we can do that pictorially. What should we be thinking about when we are adding a double-digit and a single-digit number? **Hong:** Getting to a 10 because it makes it easier to add. **Vocabulary:** add, sum, addend, plus, equals, makes **Math Talk:** _____ plus 10 is _____.
Model	**Teacher:** Today we are going to continue to work on adding a single-digit and a double-digit number. We are going to play a board game where you have to pick up the card, add, and then if you are correct you can move. Whoever reaches the finish line first wins! You can add them up using your best strategy. I put the hundred grid on the card to scaffold your thinking. Remember we had been practicing using this tool in the whole group. Who wants to model using the cards? Start Finish **Tami:** I got 38 plus 5. I am going to hop up 2 to get to 40 and then 3 more make 43. **Teacher:** Why did she get to 40 first? **Todd:** Because 40 is a ten. Tens are like a bridge. They help us to cross over. So we know 2 and 3 make 5. She hopped 2 so she had 3 more. 40 and 3 make 43.
Checking for Understanding	**Teacher:** You will play this game in pairs with your partner. You will roll to see who goes first. Pull a card. Solve. If you get it correct, move however many spaces the card says. If you are incorrect, stay where you are. Any questions?

Figure 8.66 Student Activity

Student Activity

Guided Practice/ Checking for Understanding	**Teacher:** Today we are going to continue to work on adding a single-digit and a double-digit number. We are going to play a board game where you have to pick up the card, add and then if you are correct you can move. Whoever reaches the finish line first wins! You can add them up using your best strategy. I put the hundred grid on the card to scaffold your thinking. Remember we had been practicing using this tool in the whole group. Who wants to model using the cards?

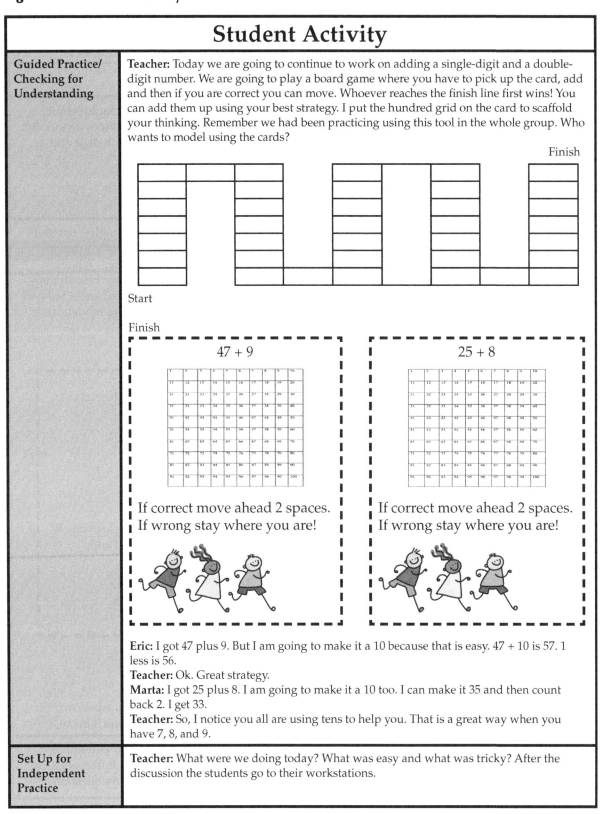

Eric: I got 47 plus 9. But I am going to make it a 10 because that is easy. 47 + 10 is 57. 1 less is 56.
Teacher: Ok. Great strategy.
Marta: I got 25 plus 8. I am going to make it a 10 too. I can make it 35 and then count back 2. I get 33.
Teacher: So, I notice you all are using tens to help you. That is a great way when you have 7, 8, and 9.

Set Up for Independent Practice	**Teacher:** What were we doing today? What was easy and what was tricky? After the discussion the students go to their workstations.

Figure 8.67 Lesson Close

Close
◆ What did we do today? ◆ What was the math we were practicing? ◆ Was this easy or tricky? ◆ Turn to a partner and state one thing you learned today.

Figure 8.68 Playing Cards

87 + 5

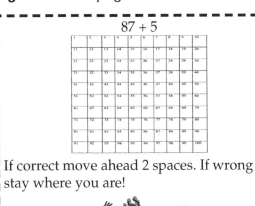

If correct move ahead 2 spaces. If wrong stay where you are!

28 + 3

If correct move ahead 2 spaces. If wrong stay where you are!

57 + 4

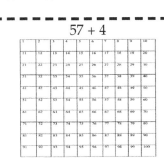

If correct move ahead 2 spaces. If wrong stay where you are!

25 + 7

If correct move ahead 2 spaces. If wrong stay where you are!

37 + 4

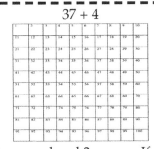

If correct move ahead 2 spaces. If wrong stay where you are!

49 + 2

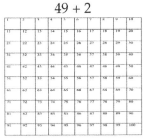

If correct move ahead 2 spaces. If wrong stay where you are!

Figure 8.68 (Continued)

65 + 5

If correct move ahead 2 spaces. If wrong stay where you are!

75 + 6

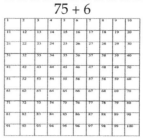

If correct move ahead 2 spaces. If wrong stay where you are!

_____ + _____

If correct move ahead 2 spaces. If wrong stay where you are!

_____ + _____

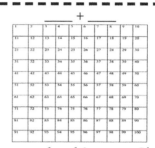

If correct move ahead 2 spaces. If wrong stay where you are!

_____ + _____

If correct move ahead 2 spaces. If wrong stay where you are!

_____ + _____

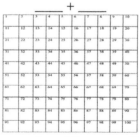

If correct move ahead 2 spaces. If wrong stay where you are!

Section Summary

Adding a one digit to a two-digit number is an important skill. This is where all the composing and decomposing are put to use. We want students to know that when they see 45 + 7 they are going to break apart the 7 into 5 and 2 to do 45 plus 5 to get to 50 and then add 2 more. However, when they see 49 plus 7 they are going to break 7 into 6 and 1 and add 49 plus 1 to get 50 and then 6 more. This idea of getting to a 10 is a crucial part of doing mental math and hopping flexibly up and down the number line. We need to introduce this with the beaded number line, and then do a great deal of work with this and also with base ten blocks. We should then connect these ideas to the marked number line so that by the end the students are very comfortable doing this.

Levels of Rigor

Depth of Knowledge (Figure 8.69) is a framework that encourages us to ask questions that require that students think, reason, explain, defend, and justify their thinking (Webb, 2002). Figure 8.70 is another snapshot of what that can look like in terms of place value work.

Figure 8.69 DOK Activities

	What are different strategies and models that we can use to teach place and value?	What are different strategies and models that we can use to compare two numbers?	What are different strategies and models that we can use to model subtracting tens from multiples of tens?
DOK Level 1 (These are questions where students are required to simply recall/reproduce an answer/do a procedure.)	How many tens and how many ones are in 31?	What number is greater, 35 or 78?	What is 50 – 30?
DOK Level 2 (These are questions where students have to use information, think about concepts, and reason.) This is considered a more challenging problem than a level 1 problem.	Can you model the number 31 in two different ways?	Name a number that is greater than 27 and less than 44. Explain why your number is correct.	Can you model 50 – 30 in two different ways?
DOK Level 3 (These are questions where students have to reason, plan, explain, justify, and defend their thinking.)	Write a number that has more than 3 tens and less than 9 ones. Explain how you know your number is correct.	Name a number that is greater than 55 and less than 61. Prove that your number is correct with numbers, words, and pictures.	Make up your own problem. Subtract multiples of tens from multiples of tens. Solve it. Defend your answer.

Figure 8.70 DOK Examples

	Order numbers	What are different strategies and models that we can use to add 10 to a number?	What are different strategies and models that we can use to teach students to add a single-digit and a double-digit number?
DOK Level 1 (these are questions where students are required to simply recall/reproduce an answer/do a procedure)	Fill in the missing numbers . . . 31, ___, 33 ___, ___, 35	What is 20 + 10?	What is 29 + 5?
DOK Level 2 (These are questions where students have to use information, think about concepts, and reason.) This is considered a more challenging problem than a level 1 problem.	Order these numbers from least to greatest. Explain how you know that you are correct. 33, 12, 45, 19, 75	Can you model 20 + 10 in two different ways?	Can you model 29 + 5 in two different ways? Explain your thinking.
DOK Level 3 (These are questions where students have to reason, plan, explain, justify, and defend their thinking.)	Pick the number line that is not correct. Defend your thinking. ⟷ 1 2 3 4 5 6 7 8 9 ⟷ 2 3 4 6 8 9 10 11 ⟷ 11 12 13 14 15 16	Can you pick a number and add 10 and explain and prove how you know your answer is correct?	Pick and add a 2-digit number and a 1-digit number. Model your thinking. Defend your answer.

Adapted from Kaplinsky (https://robertkaplinsky.com/depth-knowledge-matrix-elementary-math/). *A great resource for asking open questions is Marion Small's* Good Questions: Great ways to differentiate mathematics instruction in the standards-based classroom *(2017).* Also Robert Kaplinsky has done a great job in pushing our thinking forward with the Depth of knowledge matrices he created. Kentucky Math Department (2007) has these great math matrices as well.

Figure 8.71 DOK

Asking rigorous questions:

DOK 1	DOK 2 At this level, students explain their thinking.	DOK 3 At this level, students have to justify, defend, and prove their thinking with objects, drawings, and diagrams.
What is the answer to . . . ? Can you model the number? Can you model the problem? Can you identify the answer that matches this equation? How many tens and how many ones are in the number?	How do you know that the equation is correct? Can you pick the correct answer and explain why it is correct? How can you model that problem? What is another way to model that problem? Can you model that on the . . . ? Give me an example of a . . . type of problem. . . . Which answer is incorrect? Explain your thinking.	Can you prove that your answer is correct? Prove that . . . Explain why that is the answer. . . . Show me how to solve that and explain what you are doing. Defend your thinking.

Key Points

♦ Concrete/Pictorial/Abstract
♦ Grouping Tens and Ones
♦ Adding Ten
♦ Subtracting Tens
♦ Adding Ones to a Two-Digit Number

Summary

It is important to spend time developing place value throughout the year. At the beginning of the year be sure to spend a bit of time reviewing the place value standards from the year before through energizers and routines. During the first week of school, set up workstations to review the priority place value standards from the year before. Keep those workstations up all year and add the new ones as they are taught. Also be sure to make sure that parents understand what the place value standards are and ways that they can help to develop it.

Reflection Questions

1. How are you currently teaching place value lessons?
2. Are you making sure that you do concrete, pictorial, and abstract activities?
3. What do your students struggle with the most and what ideas are you taking away from this chapter that might inform your work around those struggles?

References

Hanich, L. B., Jordan, N. C., Kaplan, D., & Dick, J. (2001, September). Performance across different levels of mathematical cognition in children with learning difficulties. *Journal of Educational Psychology, 93*(3), 615–626.

Jordan, N. C., & Hanich, L. B. (2000, November–December). Mathematical thinking in second-grade children with different forms of LD. *Journal of Learning Disabilities, 33*(6), 567–578.

Kamii, C. (1985). *Young children reinvent arithmetic: Implications of Piaget's theory.* New York: Teachers College Press.

Kamii, C. (1989). *Young children continue to reinvent arithmetic, 2nd grade: Implications of Piaget's theory.* New York: Teachers College Press.

Kamii, C., & Joseph, L. (1988). Teaching place value and double-column addition. *Arithmetic Teacher, 35*(6), 48–52.

Kentucky Department of Education (2007). Support Materials for Core Content for Assessment Version 4.1 Mathematics. Retrieved from the internet on January 15th, 2017.

National Council of Teachers of Mathematics (NCTM). (2000). *Principles and standards for school mathematics.* Reston, VA: NCTM.

National Council of Teachers of Mathematics (NCTM). (2006). *Curriculum focal points for prekindergarten through grade 8 mathematics: A quest for coherence.* Reston, VA: NCTM.

National Research Council. (2009). Mathematics learning in early childhood: Paths toward excellence and equity. In C. T. Cross, T. A. Woods, & H. Schweingruber (Eds.), *Committee on early childhood mathematics, center for education: Division of behavioral and social sciences in education.* Washington, DC: The National Academies Press.

Webb, N. L. (2002). *Depth-of-knowledge levels for four content areas.* Madison, WI: Wisconsin Center for Education Research. Retrieved from http://facstaff.wcer.wisc.edu/normw/All%20content%20areas%20%20DOK%20levels%2032802.doc

9
Action Planning and FAQs

Well, to get started, you must get started. So, pick where you want to start and just begin. Begin small. Here is an Action Checklist (see Figure 9.1):

Figure 9.1 Action Checklist

Before the Lesson	
Decide on the topic that you want to do.	
Why are you doing this topic?	
Is this emerging, on grade level, or advanced?	
Map out a three-cycle connected lesson plan.	
What are you going to do concretely?	
What are you going to do pictorially?	
What are you going to do abstractly?	
What misconceptions and error patterns do you anticipate?	
During the Lesson	
What are your questions?	
How are the students doing?	
What do you notice?	
What do you hear?	
What do you see?	
After the Lessons	
What went well?	
What will you tweak?	
What will you do the same?	

What will you do differently?	
What made you say "Wow!"	
What made you think "Uh-oh. . . ."	
What did you notice?	
What did you wonder?	
Other Comments	

Frequently Asked Questions

1. **What is a guided math group?**
   Guided math is when you pull a temporary small group of students for instruction around a specific topic. Sometimes the groups are heterogeneous and sometimes they are homogeneous. It depends what you are teaching. If you are teaching a specific skill, like adding within 10, and you have some students who know it and others who are struggling, then you would pull the students who need to learn it, sometimes in a small homogenous group altogether to work on the concept. Other times you might pull them in a heterogenous group to all work on it together, with those who need it using scaffolds. Othertimes, you are working on general concepts, like solving word problem with models. You can pull a heterogeneous group to teach this.

2. **Why do guided math?**
   You do guided math for a variety of reasons. Lillian Katz (n.d.) said it best:

   > When a teacher tries to teach something to the entire class at the same time, chances are, one-third of the kids already know it; one-third will get it; and the remaining third won't. So two-thirds of the children are wasting their time.

   You do guided math so that everyone gets to learn. You can pull students for remedial work, on grade-level work, and enrichment. You do guided math so that students understand the math they are doing. You work with students in small groups so that they can talk, understand, reason, and do math!

3. **What are the types of lessons?**
   There are five different types of guided math lessons: conceptual, procedural, reasoning, strategy, and disposition. Disposition lessons are mostly integrated throughout the other lessons, but sometimes you just pull students and talk about their journey. That could look like, "what is tricky about what we are learning?" And, "what is easy?"

4. **Do you always use manipulatives in a guided math group?**
   No. It depends where you are in the cycle of developing the concepts and student understanding. You certainly should use manipulatives in the beginning when you are developing concepts, but eventually, when students are practicing at the abstract level, they probably won't be working directly with manipulatives. Although, sometimes they still use them to check their answers or even solve problems if they need to.

5. **What about doing worksheets in guided math groups?**
   Never. It's simple. Guided math is students doing math, not doing a worksheet. Sometimes, you do pull students to work on some specific problems on a journal page but that is not the norm or the regular structure of a guided math group.

Reference

Katz, L. Retrieved April 15, 2019, from www.azquotes.com/author/39264-Lilian_Katz

For Product Safety Concerns and Information please contact our EU
representative GPSR@taylorandfrancis.com Taylor & Francis Verlag GmbH,
Kaufingerstraße 24, 80331 München, Germany

Printed and bound by CPI Group (UK) Ltd, Croydon, CR0 4YY
11/04/2025
01843980-0003